PENGUIN CLASSICS

REVELATIONS OF DIVINE LOVE

JULIAN OF NORWICH (*c.* 1342–after 1416) is the first writer in English who can be certainly identified as a woman. Nothing is known of her background, not even her real name. On 8 May 1373, when seriously ill and apparently dying, she received an extraordinary series of 'showings' or revelations from God, beginning when her parish priest held up a crucifix before her and she saw blood trickling down Christ's face. After her recovery, she spent many years pondering the significance of the showings, which she believed to be messages to all Christians. They taught, among other things, that God is our mother as well as our father, that he cannot be angry with us and that no Christian will be damned – doctrines which Julian had great difficulty in reconciling with the Church's teachings. She wrote two accounts of the showings: an earlier, shorter version of *Revelations of Divine Love* and a later, longer version, in which we can recognize her development from a visionary into the most remarkable English theologian of her time. In later life she lived as an anchoress at St Julian's Church, Norwich (from which she adopted the name by which she is known), and became famous as a spiritual adviser. This volume includes both version of the *Revelations*. They are major works of religious devotion, of theology and of English literature; their beauty and originality have won them many modern admirers (including T. S. Eliot), and in recent years they have attracted special attention for their female authorship and their attribution of feminine characteristics to God.

ELIZABETH SPEARING holds a D.Phil. from the University of York. Her previous publications include an edition of *The Life and Death of Mal Cutpurse* and articles on the *Amadis* cycle and on Aphra Behn.

A. C. SPEARING is William R. Kenan Professor of English at the University of Virginia and a Fellow of Queens' College, Cambridge. He has published numerous books and articles on medieval literature, including books on dream-poetry, on the *Gawain*-poet, and *The Medieval Poet as Voyeur*.

Elizabeth Spearing and A. C. Spearing have collaborated previously on editions of Chaucer's *Reeve's Tale*, Shakespeare's *The Tempest* and an anthology *Poetry of the Age of Chaucer*. They live near Norwich.

JULIAN OF NORWICH

Revelations of Divine Love

(SHORT TEXT AND LONG TEXT)

Translated by ELIZABETH SPEARING
With an Introduction and Notes by A. C. SPEARING

PENGUIN BOOKS

PENGUIN BOOKS

Published by the Penguin Group
Penguin Books Ltd, 80 Strand, London WC2R 0RL, England
Penguin Putnam Inc., 375 Hudson Street, New York, New York 10014, USA
Penguin Books Australia Ltd, 250 Camberwell Road, Camberwell, Victoria 3124, Australia
Penguin Books Canada Ltd, 10 Alcorn Avenue, Toronto, Ontario, Canada M4V 3B2
Penguin Books India (P) Ltd, 11 Community Centre, Panchsheel Park, New Delhi – 110 017, India
Penguin Books (NZ) Ltd, Cnr Rosedale and Airborne Roads, Albany, Auckland, New Zealand
Penguin Books (South Africa) (Pty) Ltd, 24 Sturdee Avenue, Rosebank 2196, South Africa

Penguin Books Ltd, Registered Offices: 80 Strand, London WC2R 0RL, England

www.penguin.com

This translation published in Penguin Classics 1998
17

Translation copyright © Elizabeth Spearing, 1998
Introduction and Notes © A. C. Spearing, 1998
All rights reserved

The moral rights of the editors have been asserted

Set in 10/12.5 pt Monotype Bembo
Typeset by Rowland Phototypesetting Ltd, Bury St Edmunds, Suffolk
Printed in England by Clays Ltd, St Ives plc

ISBN-13: 978-0-140-44673-9

CONTENTS

Revelations of Divine Love

INTRODUCTION

Julian of Norwich and her Book

Julian of Norwich is the first writer in English who can be identified with certainty as a woman. Before her, a few works survive written by women in other languages used in England – notable among them are the short romances and fables in French by the great twelfth-century poet Marie de France – and, since a large proportion of writing in medieval English is anonymous, some of it may have been by women of whom nothing is now known. But most medieval Englishwomen were not educated or even literate, and those who were would not generally have been encouraged to write works intended to outlive some immediate purpose. Julian's period, the late fourteenth and early fifteenth centuries, is now recognized as one of the great ages of English literature – the age of William Langland, John Gower, the *Gawain*-poet, Geoffrey Chaucer and his first major disciple Thomas Hoccleve in verse, and of Walter Hilton, Nicholas Love, the Wycliffite translators of the Bible and the anonymous writer of *The Cloud of Unknowing* in prose. These were all men, and it took some very unusual stimulus to impel a woman to write, and especially to write a work designed to teach others. What this stimulus was for Julian is revealed by the texts translated here – the two versions of her *Revelations of Divine Love*,[1] her only known writings, an earlier short version (ST) and a later long version (LT).

Julian states in LT that 'These revelations were shown to a simple, uneducated creature in the year of our Lord 1373, on the eighth day of May' (chapter 2).[2] She adds that she was then 'thirty and a half years old' (chapter 3) – about the age of Chaucer. Apparently at the point of death from a severe illness, for which she had earlier prayed as a means to be 'purged by the mercy of God and afterwards to live more to God's glory' (chapter 2), she received a series of 'showings' (we retain the word she normally uses for each separate religious experience). These were extraordinary experiences conveyed in three modes: in sensory and especially visual imagery, in words perceived directly by the mind, and in the form of insight so far transcending the sensory and the verbal that 'I neither can nor may show the spiritual vision as openly or as fully as I would like to' (chapter 9). On 8 May she experienced fifteen showings: the first 'began early in the morning, at about four o'clock' and the series continued 'until it was well past the middle of the day' (chapter 65). A sixteenth came 'on the following night', sandwiched between two dreamlike experiences of diabolic temptation, and was 'conclusion and confirmation' to the entire sequence (chapter 66). The showings were so compelling and so rich in meaning that Julian understood them to come directly from God and to be messages not just to herself but to all Christians. This led her to put them in writing and to convey her sense of their significance, as it was revealed in the course of many years of meditation, renewed by 'flashes of illumination and touches, I hope, of the same spirit which was shown in them all' (chapter 65). One supplementary showing came 'fifteen years and more later' – that is, about 1388 – and this she recounts in the final chapter of LT: it was that God's meaning in the whole series of experiences from 1373 was no more nor less than love. Julian wrote for private readers; they rather than listeners would have needed the list of contents in chapter 1 of LT and the summaries heading the other chapters (if these are authorial). Her target audience was initially 'all men and women who wish to lead the contemplative life' (ST chapter 4), but in LT she drops this limitation and seems to envisage a broader public of devout laypeople – a public that was on the increase in her lifetime. Since her work was adapted into modern English in 1901, her readership has expanded to far greater numbers than could have known it in earlier times.[3]

What Julian meant by describing herself as uneducated (*that cowde no letter*) has been much discussed. Some have argued that it indicates that she was illiterate, so that her writings must have been penned on her behalf by someone else, presumably a man. The concept of literacy is not a simple one: in late medieval England the language of learning was Latin, known only to a few, nearly all of them men and those mostly clerics, but the ability to read and write in English was becoming more widespread. Many who knew no Latin had access to Latin culture with the assistance of clerics, and many who could not write or even read English could similarly enjoy some of the fruits of literacy with the help of those who could. (An example of the latter is Julian's younger contemporary, Margery Kempe, of whom more below.) English culture was strongly patriarchal, and the ability to write even in the mother tongue was thought unsuited to women; on the other hand, by Julian's time women were becoming increasingly interested in personal forms of religious devotion, and this encouraged 'a textuality of the spoken as well as the written word', originating in books, perhaps read aloud, but then 'transmitted among the women by word of mouth'.[4] Julian is manifestly a woman of exceptional intelligence, and she shows not just an understanding of theology, the province of learned male clerics, but a capacity for powerful new theological thought; moreover, her prose, while owing much to speech, is distinctive and distinguished. If she emphasizes her ignorance, describing herself as 'a woman, ignorant, weak and frail' (ST chapter 6), this is likely to have been both out of genuine humility and so as to avoid her contemporaries' unease with female learning, especially in theological matters. She may have had little or no Latin (to know 'no letter' could well mean that) and nothing is known for certain of her reading, but there seems no reason to deny her authorship, in the fullest sense, of the work attributed to her.

Julian reveals little of her life, beyond certain details that authenticate her religious experiences. This reticence was evidently a matter of principle, and in LT she omits even some of the few personal items mentioned in ST. She urges her readers to concentrate on the revelation itself and 'stop paying attention to the poor being to whom [it] was shown' (chapter 8), and later explains that, when she desired to know whether a certain friend would 'continue to lead a good life', she learned that it was not to God's glory to be concerned about 'any particular thing' (chapter 35; cf. ST chapter 16) – hence the omission of nearly all such particulars from her writing. External documents place her in Norwich in her later years; we cannot be sure that she was there in May 1373 (what can be discerned of her dialect in the scribal copies of her work suggests that she came from further north), but there is no reason to think otherwise. Norwich was among the largest and most prosperous English cities in the later Middle Ages, and East Anglia, the region where it is situated, was 'one of the great centres of artistic creation in late medieval England'.[5] Commercial wealth and religion were closely connected in the later Middle Ages, and, though Julian's way of life indicates her wish to separate herself from the city's bustling commerce, even the religious language she adopted was shaped by ideas of buying and selling, profit and loss. Religion was the focus of most cultural activity, and in East Anglia generous patronage supported enterprises ranging from the composition of elaborate poems, often by members of religious orders such as the Benedictine monk John Lydgate and the Augustinian canon Osbern Bokenham, to the building and decoration of magnificent churches. Norwich had over fifty churches, most of which still survive. East Anglia's many ports (including Norwich itself, linked to the coast by the rivers Wensum and Yare) enabled close connections across the North Sea with continental Europe; the chief exports were wool and cloth, and imports included works of art and the latest forms of religious devotion. Julian's account of the gifts she desired from God in early life (chapter 2) implies an exceptionally devout young woman with the leisure to devote herself to religious experience, thus presumably one from a background of material comfort. Some have thought she may have been a nun,[6] but the details in ST of her circumstances in 1373 indicate a secular domestic setting: when she seemed about to die, her parish priest was sent for, he was accompanied by a boy, and later 'My mother, who was standing with others watching me, lifted her hand up to my face to close my eyes, for she thought I was already dead' (ST chapter 10). Probably then Julian was at this time either an unmarried daughter living at home or a widow. The centrality of motherhood in her religious thought might suggest that she had been a mother herself. Later, presumably influenced by the showings, she adopted a fully religious mode of life, becoming not a nun but an anchorite.

An anchorite was a person who had entered into an enclosed solitary life in a fixed place, in order to achieve greater spiritual perfection. (The thirteenth-century _Ancrene Wisse_ is an important English text offering guidance for such a way of life.[7]) Options of this kind, allowing for individual forms of devotion, became increasingly popular in late medieval England, and more anchorites and hermits are recorded in Norwich than in any other medieval English town.[8] It has been suggested that such options, offering a 'medieval version of Virginia Woolf's "room of one's own" ', might have been especially appealing to women, 'because there a woman could find privacy, autonomy, and a chance for intellectual development unavailable even in a convent'.[9] Many anchorites lived in cells attached to churches, and Julian can be identified as the anchoress who occupied a cell at St Julian's church in Norwich, within earshot of the busy quayside; her name was presumably adopted from the church. The cell, with an opening into the church from which to see the tabernacle containing the sacrament, did not survive the Reformation; the church was largely destroyed by German bombing in 1942, but has been rebuilt.

The manuscript of ST has a rubric describing Julian as 'recluse at Norwyche' and as still alive in 1413. She is similarly mentioned in wills dating from 1394 to 1416, but the most striking reference to her as an anchorite occurs in _The Book of Margery Kempe_. This, the first autobiography in English, dictated by a woman of passionate and eccentric religious devotion from the nearby port of Lynn, describes how in 1415 she visited 'an anchoress . . . who was called Dame Julian' and received what sounds like wise and tactful advice.[10] (Though they lived in solitude, anchorites were expected to give spiritual counsel to others.[11]) The date of Julian's death is unknown; she may have lived into the 1420s.

ST and LT form two distinct versions of Julian's work.[12] ST consists mainly of an account of the 1373 showings and Julian's initial interpretation of their meaning, but it omits the parable of the lord and the servant recounted in chapter 51 of LT. Though this was part of the 1373 experience, Julian initially found it too baffling to set down alongside the other showings, 'for a full understanding of this marvellous parable was not given to me at that time' (chapter 51). As mentioned above, ST also omits the further experience of about 1388 recounted in LT chapter 86. All scholars agree that ST was composed earlier than LT, which incorporates most of ST's material but with more about some of the showings and far fuller interpretation of what Julian originally saw (especially in the thirteenth and fourteenth showings): she 'reads' her memories of these showings over and over again, as if they formed a treasured book. Introducing the parable of the lord and the servant, she explains that the initial showing, the 'inner learning' she has subsequently gained, and the light thrown on it by the entire sequence of revelations 'which our Lord God in his goodness often shows freely to the eyes of my mind', are by now 'so united in my mind that I neither can nor may separate them' (chapter 51). Experience, memory and meaning could never be fully separable. Like her contemporary William Langland, author of at least three successive versions of his great religious poem *Piers Plowman*, Julian seems to have devoted her life to thinking and rethinking the meaning of her visionary insights. She was never satisfied that she had plumbed their depths, for the final chapter of LT opens, 'This book was begun by God's gift and his grace, but it seems to me that it is not yet completed.' Like *Piers Plowman*, Julian's work owes much of its difficult fascination to its status as a text of repeated new beginnings, lacking the final conclusion that for both writers would be possible only at the end of the world.

Most scholars have assumed that ST dates from shortly after the 1373 experiences and LT from 1393, in accordance with Julian's explanation that understanding of the lord and servant showing was granted to her 'twenty years after the time of the showing, all but three months' (chapter 51). These assumptions have been questioned, however, in an important study by Nicholas Watson.[13] Considering the likely historical context for Julian's work, he suggests that ST would most naturally belong not to 1373–4 but to some years later, when the visionary writings of continental female mystics such as Catherine of Siena and Bridget of Sweden had begun to circulate in East Anglia, and that Julian's repeated insistence on her submission to 'the teaching of Holy Church' (ST chapter 13), especially in regard to 'paintings of crucifixes . . . in the likeness of Christ's Passion' (ST chapter 1), seems appropriate to the 1380s or later, when the critique of images by Wyclif's followers, the Lollards, had gained notoriety and been condemned. It could then have been the 1388 experience that stimulated the writing of ST, and Watson further proposes that LT may date from the early fifteenth century, perhaps after 1413 (the date mentioned in the ST manuscript) – for why would the ST copyist have disregarded the later, fuller version if it existed then? The question of dating cannot be regarded as settled, but Watson's hypothesis is persuasive.

Medieval Religious Devotion

In both texts, Julian begins by telling of her desire for three gifts from God: imaginative identification with Christ's sufferings on the cross, bodily sickness in youth to the verge of death and three 'wounds' of contrition, compassion and longing for God. Six centuries later, in an age when Christianity has come to be centred in moral conduct and social concern, many readers, believers or not, may find an almost perverse egocentricity and masochism in such desires. Although current interest in Julian's writing shows that she can speak directly to many modern readers, it may be helpful to sketch the tradition of religious devotion in which her desires could seem normal and praiseworthy.

Through most of the first thousand years of western Christianity, Christ was widely seen as a remote, awesome judge and hero, who had fought and conquered the devil to gain the possibility of salvation for the human souls seized as a consequence of Adam's sin. In this struggle, human beings were little more than spectators. A famous English expression of this view occurs in the eighth-century *Dream of the Rood*, where the cross appears to the poet in a vision and tells how 'the young warrior who was God almighty stripped himself, stalwart and resolute; he stepped on to the high gallows, bold in the sight of many, when he determined to liberate mankind'.[14] That conception of Christ as divine warrior did not disappear in later centuries (it is present in *Piers Plowman*), but alongside it there grew up a different emphasis on Christ as suffering man, arousing compassion in his fellow human beings. In this new theology, developed in the eleventh and twelfth centuries by learned Latin writers such as Saint Anselm, Peter Abelard and Saint Bernard of Clairvaux, God's Incarnation as man was seen not primarily as a device for defeating the Devil but as a means of drawing human love towards God as an object for identification and imitation. Bernard remarked:

I think this is the principal reason why the invisible God willed to be seen in the flesh, and to converse with men as a man. He wanted to recapture the affections of carnal men who were unable to love in any other way, by first drawing them to the salutary love of his own humanity, and then gradually to raise them to a spiritual love.[15]

Bernard was preaching to Cistercian monks, but this focus on Christ's fleshly existence and its appeal to fleshly love became the central feature of the less communal, more personal kinds of religious devotion that flourished from the twelfth century onwards. As the Church became more centralized and its teachings pervaded western society more effectively, this devotion attracted the laity as well as those committed to a religious life; the kind of meditations originally recommended for monks began to be practised by devout laypeople. The new devotion was more *Christocentric* and more *affective* than that of earlier Christianity: that is, it centred in God's human nature and in the powerful feelings of love and pity aroused in men and women by his bodily sufferings. There was a longing to share imaginatively in the life of the Holy Family but above all in the experience of Jesus in his Passion. For the desired feelings to be continually renewed, Christ's torments had to be evoked in ever-intensifying detail, to an extent that modern readers of Julian and other devotional writers may find repellent and even nauseating. Meditation on the Passion, often imagined with a gruesome hallucinatory realism, with the aid of details borrowed from apocryphal sources such as the Gospel of Nicodemus, was the central theme of later medieval devotion. This was where Julian's showings began, with blood seeming to trickle down Christ's face as she gazed at the crucifix.

From one point of view, the process just described might be called a feminization of devotion. The predominant ideology of the Middle Ages connected men with rationality and the spirit, women with emotion and the flesh. The change began with men like Saint Bernard, eliciting in themselves and their fellows the tender and passionate feelings traditionally attributed to women; but it went on to appeal to women also, and was subsequently associated with an increasing part played by women as readers and patrons, and ultimately as writers, of devotional works. From the thirteenth century on an increasing proportion of saints are female; and in Julian's time the rood-screens of East Anglian churches displayed images of holy women old and new. In the late fourteenth century the writings of passionately devout continental women began to be read in England and were greatly admired. Whether or not Julian knew them, her milieu must have been dominated by this emotional and bodily piety of the later Middle Ages. For this piety, as Caroline Bynum puts it, 'bodiliness provides access to the sacred',[16] and bodily sensations such as pain, heat and sweetness, and bodily fluxes such as blood and tears, were seen as signs of God's presence and means to union with him. In this context, the three gifts that Julian desired would not seem abnormal; indeed what is striking is the way that her religious aspirations, without ever abandoning the bodily and the emotional,[17] go beyond the gifts she initially desired to achieve penetrating and difficult intellectual insights – a process that has been described as 'Julian's transformation . . . from a visionary into a theologian'.[18]

A brief introduction cannot offer a comprehensive analysis of these insights and the means by which she expresses them. What follows concentrates chiefly on LT and considers two aspects of Julian's work that have particularly interested modern readers: the ways in which her writing was affected by the fact that she was a woman, and the ideas about salvation that are focused in the longest chapter of LT, containing the parable of the lord and the servant. As will be seen, these two aspects are closely connected.

Julian as Woman Writer

Julian must have continued working on her *Revelations* over many years (especially if the later dates for the two versions are correct), choosing the exact words to record her showings and to convey their meaning as it gradually emerged. Her determination to represent and understand her experiences with scrupulous accuracy, indicated by repeated use of phrases such as 'as I see it' and 'as I understand it', makes for an exploratory style, in which even the most definite statement remains provisional. English, much used for devotional writing, was an unaccustomed medium for theology, and in her quiet struggles with her mother tongue Julian persuades it to release richnesses of meaning that careless readers might dismiss as imprecision or ambiguity. In L T especially, her prose can be memorably figured and patterned; but that may also be true of speech, and her writing resembles speech more closely than it resembles medieval Latin prose or even the learned English prose into which Chaucer had translated Boethius' Latin. As Felicity Riddy puts it, 'Julian's text has the fluidity of talk, now brief, now expansive, moving in and out of autobiography.'[19] This 'fluid' style is often seen as distinctively feminine, and with some justification: not because it constitutes an *écriture féminine*, a form of writing that expresses some transhistorical essence of femaleness, but for specific historical reasons. Some of these are expounded by Bynum in a general discussion of religious writing by medieval women:

... part of the reason for the more open, experiential style of women's writings is the fact that women usually wrote not in the formal scholastic Latin taught in universities, but in the vernaculars – that is, in the languages they grew up speaking. The major literary genres available in these languages were various kinds of love poetry and romantic stories: the vocabulary provided by such genres was therefore a vocabulary of feelings ... Furthermore, women's works, especially their accounts of visions, were often dictated (that is, spoken) rather than penned – a fact that is clearly one of the explanations for women's more discursive, conversational, aggregative, tentative, empathetic and self-reflective style. As Elizabeth Petroff has recently pointed out, the prose of a female writer such as Julian of Norwich, which tends to circle around its point, evoking a state of being, displays exactly those traits Walter Ong has seen as characteristic of oral thought and expression.[20]

Not just the style of Julian's prose is at issue here but the style of her thought. The formal education received by male writers, based in Latin and practised in disputation, emphasized opposition, combativeness, triumph or defeat in argument, and tended to shape men's thought accordingly; it was an intellectual counterpart to the martial training that produced medieval knights. In a disputation, you can uphold one view only by opposing its contrary, unhorsing your opponent as if in a joust. Far from being carried away by emotion, Julian is always careful to analyse what she sees, feels and understands as exactly as she can, often in the form of numbered lists; but this disputative, adversarial quality is quite lacking in her writing. In that sense, while doubtless more learned than most women, she does write as a woman, and gains a real advantage by doing so.

Medieval culture offered strong resistance to writing and teaching by women, a resistance justified by statements of Saint Paul such as 'Let women keep silence in the churches; for it is not permitted them to speak, but to be subject' (1 Corinthians 14:34) and 'Nor I suffer not a woman to teach, nor to use authority over the man; but to be in silence' (1 Timothy 2:12).[21] In Julian's time Jean Gerson, chancellor of the University of Paris, wrote as follows, possibly with Catherine of Siena in mind:

... the female sex is forbidden on apostolic authority to teach in public ... All women's teaching, particularly formal teaching by word and by writing, is to be held suspect unless it has been diligently examined, and much more fully than men's. The reason is clear: common law – and not any kind of common law, but that which comes from on high – forbids them. And why? Because they are easily seduced, and determined seducers; and because it is not proved that they are witnesses to divine grace.[22]

This attitude was probably even more unquestioned in England than on the continent, where there was already a tradition of female visionaries claiming an authority alternative to that of male clerics. In

England there was no such tradition; religious devotion was generally
moderate and cautious, and there is little evidence of female visionaries
before Julian herself. From the 1380s, on the anticlericalism of Wyclif's
followers gave some encouragement to female teaching, but that
meant that any woman who seemed to be offering to teach was likely
to be suspected of heresy – which was what happened to Margery
Kempe. Any work discussing theological issues in the vernacular was
suspect, for 'at the same time that literacy and the tendency toward
private devotion were beginning to increase, an official distrust of
both was also on the rise',[23] but this was especially so when any
connection was found between *women* and books. Hence Julian's need
for the careful, modest self-presentation found in ST chapter 6:

But God forbid that you should say or assume that I am a teacher, for that is
not what I mean, nor did I ever mean it; for I am a woman, ignorant, weak
and frail. But I know well that I have received what I say from him who is
the supreme teacher . . . Just because I am a woman, must I therefore believe
that I must not tell you about the goodness of God, when I saw at the same
time both his goodness and his wish that it should be known?

This passage is lacking from LT, perhaps because Julian later came to
feel more confidence in herself as female visionary writer and in her
ability to balance her revelations against the Church's teaching. Yet
even here in ST Julian's very modesty casts her as a spokeswoman
for God himself; and more generally the role she adopts, of the mere
woman who accepts and proclaims her incapacity to teach, is not
necessarily disadvantageous to her. She seems to have thoroughly
internalized her culture's downgrading of her sex,[24] but from it,
consciously or unconsciously, she fashions a textual self that serves
her purpose admirably. She avoids the outward trappings of learning
– the use of Latin, of technical terminology, of citations of authority
– in order to share her own meekness with her readers and with a God
whose power is exercised through womanly meekness and motherly
forgiveness. Within this shared space, Julian's acknowledged womanli-
ness, far from separating her from the male God of Christianity, could
have the effect of identifying her more closely with Christ in his
humanity. To quote Bynum again,

Medieval men and women did not take the equation of woman with body merely as the basis for misogyny. They also extrapolated from it to an association of woman with the body or the humanity of Christ. Indeed, they often went so far as to treat Christ's flesh as female, at least in certain of its salvific functions, especially its bleeding and nurturing.[25]

In another way too, Julian turns to the advantage of her writing a disadvantage culturally imposed on her sex. In the Middle Ages most women had no public role; their sphere was private rather than public, and their religious self-expression was likely to be in private devotion. The female realm was the home – the place of direct and intimate relations among human beings, the place where children were born, fed and taught the mother tongue, the place of nourishment and sleep, where bodies met bodies for comfort, affection, procreation. Medieval laypeople were accustomed to think of their favourite saints as sharing this intimate space; thus Julian writes of Saint John of Beverley, 'our Lord showed him very clearly to encourage us by his familiarity [*homlyhed*], and he reminded me that he is a very near neighbour and we know him well' (chapter 38). But Julian goes further; as she sees it, even God accommodates himself to the domestic sphere, the home in which he visited her in 1373. In the earlier chapters of LT she repeatedly stresses God's 'homeliness' with us, *homely* retaining the full emotional resonance of *home* itself, including friendliness, familiarity, intimacy, without the pejorative associations it has in American English. God is a great lord, 'holy and awe-inspiring' (chapter 4), infinitely superior to his creatures, but he possesses the lordly quality of courtesy, and shows his courtesy to human beings precisely in his *homelyhede* towards them (see especially LT chapter 7). As Julian perceives him, he is 'everything that we find good and comforting' (chapter 5), so familiar and accessible that we must be reminded not to forget the respect that medieval courtesy demanded from inferior to superior: 'But be careful not to take this friendliness [*homelyhede*] too casually, so that we neglect courtesy; for our Lord himself is supreme friendliness, and he is as courteous as he is friendly; for he is truly courteous' (chapter 77).

The images Julian uses to describe the supernatural phenomena of her showings often belong to the same sphere of the domestic and familiar, appropriate to her as a woman and to the God who accommodates himself to that sphere. When she sees Christ's blood dripping from beneath his crown of thorns, she compares the drops to pills, to herring scales and to raindrops falling from the eaves of a house (chapter 7). (Herring from the North Sea would have been available in Norwich market-place, and any housewife would have found their scales clinging to her kitchen.) As Christ dies on the cross, his skin resembles 'a sagging cloth', and then in the cold wind that she imagines accompanying the crucifixion (a familiar feature, this, of the dry, chilly East Anglian climate) she sees it as 'hung in the air, as a cloth is hung to dry', until eventually it is 'like a dry board when it has been scorched' (chapter 17). Similarly, the 'little thing' that she is told 'is all that is made' is described as 'the size of a hazel-nut in the palm of my hand' (chapter 5). The Devil too is perceived in domestic similes; when Julian first sees his face, 'The colour was red like newly fired tiles, with black spots on it like black freckles, fouler than the tiles themselves' and 'His hair was as red as rust' (chapter 66). But the homeliness of Julian's revelations is not a matter of cosiness, reducing the divine and the diabolic to what can be easily understood and controlled. The medieval home was the place of birth and death, and the scene of an unending struggle against squalor and confusion;[26] women's tasks of feeding, cleansing and comforting demanded incessant labour and courage, demands from which men were shielded by the supposedly larger responsibilities of the public world. If God relinquished his transcendence to take on human flesh, it was not to step boldly on to the cross as a liberating warrior but to become a cloth hung up to dry, to undergo the 'feminine' squalor of blood and water, herring scales and rain; and one effect of Julian's writing is to confront the hidden but inescapable horrors of the body and the home. They are epitomized in her vision – a housewife's nightmare – of an immovable ugliness stinking and swelling uncontrollably: 'I saw a body lying on the earth, a body which looked dismal and ugly, without shape or form as if it were a swollen and heaving mass of stinking mire' (chapter 64).

Christ as Mother

The element in Julian's work that now seems most strikingly feminine
is her insistence that God is not only our father but our mother. In
family roles as conceived in medieval culture, the father is associated
with authority, punishment and fear, the mother with kindness,
gentleness, mercy, protectiveness, and with nourishing and clothing.[27]
'It is fitting that God's lordship and fatherhood should be feared',
Julian writes, and from that fear we take refuge 'like a child upon its
mother's bosom' (chapter 74). Medieval people felt less difficulty than
we may in associating God with stern punishment; but in the later
Middle Ages an increasing wish to find an element of motherly love
in a religion dominated by maleness was one factor responsible for
the rise of devotion to the Blessed Virgin. Julian places Mary in this
role in a way entirely normal in her time – 'our Lady is our mother
in whom we are all enclosed and we are born from her in Christ; for
she who is mother of our Saviour is mother of all who will be saved
in our Saviour' – but she adds, more unusually, 'And our Saviour is
our true mother in whom we are eternally born and by whom we
shall always be enclosed' (chapter 57).

The idea that God is our mother, absent from ST, is first mentioned
briefly at the beginning of LT chapter 52. It returns in chapter 57 in
the words just quoted, seeming to come as a resolution to theological
complexities in which Julian has become hopelessly entangled. It is
developed most fully in the following six chapters. Julian begins by
associating God's motherhood especially with Christ, the second
person of the Trinity, identified with divine wisdom, which was
traditionally personified as female (*Sapientia*): 'God all wisdom is our
mother by nature' and 'the great power of the Trinity is our father,
and the deep wisdom of the Trinity is our mother, and the great love
of the Trinity is our lord' (chapter 58). She then focuses on two less
abstract aspects of motherhood, creation and nourishment. God gave
birth to humanity, but he also became human himself, 'And so Jesus
is our true mother by nature, at our first creation, and he is our true
mother in grace by taking on our created nature' (chapter 59). But

the agony of the crucifixion was also an act of giving birth, by which human beings, born of their human mothers to pain and death, were reborn through Christ's 'pangs and . . . sufferings' (chapter 60) to the possibility of heavenly bliss. And the body that died in its birth-pangs on the cross remains a source of generous maternal nourishment for humanity: 'So next he had to feed us, for a mother's dear love has made him our debtor. The mother can give her child her milk to suck, but our dear mother Jesus can feed us with himself, and he does so most generously and most tenderly with the holy sacrament which is the precious food of life itself.' The consecrated host, truly God's body in Catholic doctrine, is imagined as life-giving food; and the parallel between mother's milk and Christ's blood is no literary conceit but a reflection of medieval scientific understanding that milk is reprocessed blood.[28] The embodiment that associates God-become-man with femaleness makes Christ homely and motherly in the most literal way, transforming violation into nourishment, the wound into a breast: 'The mother can lay the child tenderly to her breast, but our tender mother Jesus, he can familiarly [homley] lead us into his blessed breast through his sweet open side' (chapter 60). And God's dealings with humanity in its daily sinfulness are no less motherly, calling up intensely homely images of a child frightened, dirty and ashamed, turning to mother for comfort:

But often when our falling and our wretched sin is shown to us, we are so terrified and so very ashamed that we hardly know where to put ourselves. But then our kind Mother does not want us to run from him, there is nothing he wants less. But he wants us to behave like a child; for when it is hurt or frightened it runs to its mother for help as fast as it can; and he wants us to do the same, like a humble child, saying, 'My kind Mother, my gracious Mother, my dearest Mother, take pity on me. I have made myself dirty and unlike you and I neither may nor can remedy this without your special help and grace.' (chapter 61)

Julian's teachings on the motherhood of God reflect the experience of a woman for whom 'mother' was a 'fair, lovely word' (chapter 60). Her own mother was present at her sick-bed in ST; omitted from LT, she is replaced by Christ as mother. But these teachings, strongly

felt and intricately developed, to an extent unexpected in a medieval
writer, were not original with Julian; they have precedents in writings
by men. As early as Isaiah, God was presented as mother of his chosen
people, asking, 'Can a woman forget her infant, so as not to have pity
on the son of her womb? And if she should forget, yet will not I forget
thee' (49:15). And in the New Testament Jesus rebukes Jerusalem for
its callousness by contrast with his own motherly concern: 'How often
would I have gathered together thy children, as the hen doth gather
her chickens under her wings, and thou wouldest not?' (Matthew
23:37). In these texts that Julian would have known, God is mother
only by analogy; there are also medieval writers who wrote directly
of God's motherhood, and whose work she might or might not have
encountered. One of the originators of the theology underpinning
the affective, Christocentric devotion of the later Middle Ages was
Saint Anselm of Canterbury. He wrote prayers as well as theology,
and in a *Prayer to Saint Paul*, sent to Countess Mathilda of Tuscany in
the late eleventh century, he begins from the image in Matthew of
Jesus as a hen protecting her young:

> And you, Jesus, are you not also a mother?
> Are you not the mother who, like a hen,
> gathers her chickens under her wings?
> Truly, Lord, you are a mother;
> for both they who are in labour
> and they who are brought forth are accepted by you.
> You have died more than they, that they may labour to bear.
> It is by your death that they have been born,
> for if you had not been in labour,
> you could not have borne death;
> and if you had not died, you would not have brought forth.[29]

This is only one instance among various medieval treatments of God
as mother noted by modern scholars.

Julian then was not eccentric or unorthodox in exploring this
theme; what is remarkable is the intensity of her treatment, and the
theological implications developed from it. It must be stressed that,
though she did not write in Latin or employ the logical and analytic

methods of scholasticism, Julian *was* a theologian; her work has been described as 'the most remarkable theological achievement of the English late Middle Ages'.[30] Vernacular devotional writers were rarely original theologians – the works of the most widely read of all such writers in English, Richard Rolle, have little doctrinal content of their own[31] – and that a medieval woman should mature 'from a visionary into a theologian' is truly extraordinary. What specially drove Julian towards theology seems to have been her difficulty in seeing the 'fatherly' side of God, in the medieval sense of anger and punishment. Belief in hell and purgatory, the manifestations of divine punitiveness, was required by Catholicism, and she insists that she 'firmly believed that hell and purgatory have the purpose taught by Holy Church'. She wished for 'a complete vision of hell and purgatory', yet found that what her showings revealed was 'of goodness, and there was little mention of evil'. Her vision of the Passion itself was affected by this absence of evil, for she saw Christ's pain and his friends' sorrow, but nothing of those who caused his pain. The 'Jews who did him to death' (chapter 33), usually prominent in medieval pictures and plays of the Passion, are conspicuously absent from Julian's showing. If Christ is our mother and his pains those of a woman in childbed, they are in a sense natural and even healthy, and emphasis on the cruelty and wickedness of those who caused them is unnecessary and even misleading. Similarly, if the Passion involves a spiritual feeding of humanity from Christ's own body, we need think only of 'his sweet open side' and not of any human malice that tore it open.

In God's showings to Julian of his own nature, fatherly anger played no part; this she repeatedly stresses. According to the Church's teaching she must acknowledge herself a sinner and must recognize 'that sinners deserve blame and anger one day; and I could see no blame and anger in God' (chapter 45). Not only is she unable to see blame and anger in God, she sees that 'God is the goodness that cannot be angry, for he is nothing but goodness' (chapter 46). Moreover, our very existence proves that God cannot be angry: 'it seems to me that if God could be even slightly angry we could never have any life or place or being'. Anger exists, but only on man's part; God forgives us, but in regard to himself he cannot forgive, for he cannot be angry – 'it would be an impossibility' (chapter 49). The implications of this impossibility are far-reaching, leading Julian to an apparent impasse: 'My good Lord, I see that you are truth itself and I know for certain that we sin grievously every day and deserve to be bitterly blamed; and I can neither give up the knowledge of this truth, nor can I see that you show us any kind of blame. How can this be?' (chapter 50). The path is blocked, and Julian can only trust to God's assurance that 'you shall see for yourself that all manner of things shall be well' (chapter 31). She interprets this promise as entailing that, at the Day of Judgement, beyond present human understanding, God will perform a 'great deed' to reconcile his motherly love with the unquestionable fact of human sin:

... there is a deed which the Holy Trinity shall do on the last day, and when that deed shall be done and how it shall be done is unknown to all creatures under Christ, and shall be until it has been done ... This is the great deed ordained by our Lord God from eternity, treasured up and hidden in his blessed breast, only known to himself, and by this deed he shall make all things well; for just as the Holy Trinity made all things from nothing, so the Holy Trinity shall make all well that is not well. (chapter 32)

Just as God made everything at the beginning of the world, like a mother giving birth to a child, so that deed will be matched by another equally motherly deed at the end of the world: we do not know what it will be, but it will 'make all well that is not well'. It is for that comfort, that making well or making better, that children have historically turned to their mothers rather than their fathers.

Julian repeatedly affirms her acceptance of the Church's teachings, and by leaving the nature of the great deed mysterious she avoids head-on conflict with orthodoxy. Nevertheless, a God who cannot be angry without self-contradiction, and who will ultimately make all well, surely leaves no place for damnation; Julian is troubled by this, yet remains unshaken in her conviction of what God has directly revealed to her. She acknowledges the Church's teaching that 'many shall be damned', including the fallen angels, the heathen and Christians who die as unrepentant sinners.

Holy Church teaches me to believe that all these shall be condemned everlastingly to hell. And given all this, I thought it impossible that all manner of things should be well, as our Lord revealed at this time. And I received no other answer in showing from our Lord God but this: 'What is impossible to you is not impossible to me. I shall keep my word in all things and I shall make all things well.' (chapter 32)

Despite the statement in 1 Timothy 2:4 that God 'will have all men to be saved', belief that all would be saved at the Last Judgement was a heresy, known as universalism; but Julian clearly entertains it as a possibility. In this she was not alone in her time. Earlier, it had been held that most Christians and certainly all non-Christians would be damned, but by the fourteenth century opinion was shifting. There was discussion of the possibility that virtuous pagans might be saved, and many felt, with the fourteenth-century devotional writer Walter Hilton, that the salvific power of Christ's sacrifice must match its greatness: 'It had been a little purchase to Him to have come from so far to so near, and from so high to so low, for so few souls. Nay, His mercy is spread larger than so.'[32] In *Piers Plowman*, too, when Langland sees Jesus harrowing Hell, he hears him promise mercy to his human brothers despite the orthodox teaching that 'no evil shall go unpunished', and he identifies that promise with Saint Paul's 'secret words which it is not given to man to utter'.[33] Langland's vision throughout his poem is strongly and often harshly masculine, with no suggestion of God's motherhood, but he and Julian are at one in their vision of a divine mercy that will encompass all humanity.

It has been said of writing by medieval women that 'There is, more often than in men's writing, a lack of apriorism, of predetermined postures: again and again we encounter attempts to cope with human problems in their singularity – not imposing rules or categories from without, but seeking solutions that are apt and true existentially.'[34] To return to our earlier point: if such a generalization holds good, it is less as a consequence of unchanging truths about the sexes than because it reflects the roles and powers allotted them in actual historical societies. Men on the whole have been in a position to impose 'rules or categories from without', and women have not; but women's powerlessness could enable them to recognize what was omitted or obscured by the systematic official teachings of their time. Even a woman's silence can be eloquent; and, as final aspects of Julian as a woman writer, we note her complete silence about Eve's alleged responsibility for Adam's sin (there is no figure corresponding to Eve in the parable of the lord and servant in LT chapter 51), and her equally complete silence about chastity and celibacy,[35] the distorting obsessions of so many of the Church's male teachers from Saint Paul and Saint Augustine onwards.

The Parable of the Lord and the Servant

Julian's vision of a God whose mercy is universal is supported by her conception of the human soul as having two aspects, which she calls *substance* and *sensualyté*, here generally translated as 'essential being' and 'sensory being' or as higher nature and lower nature. As she explains in chapter 37, '. . . in every soul that shall be saved there is a godly will which never consented to sin and never shall; just as there is an animal will in our lower nature which can have no good impulses, there is a godly will in our higher nature which is so good that it can never will evil but only good . . .' She begins chapter 45 by distinguishing between two kinds of judgement corresponding to these aspects of the soul: human beings judge in terms of the *sensualyté*, and thus judge severely, but 'God judges us in terms of our natural essence, which is always preserved unchanged in him, whole and safe for ever' (chapter 45). God's judgement expresses justice, but (contrary to normal medieval assumptions) is not harsher but less harsh than men's judgements, because human beings see only the 'animal will' corrupted by the Fall, while God sees the 'godly will' that reflects his own purity and remains uncorrupt. True, that 'godly will' exists only 'in every soul that shall be saved'; but Julian cannot help suspecting that this may mean all souls.

Her most penetrating insight into this mystery of salvation comes in the parable of the lord and the servant, expounded in LT chapter 51, by far the longest chapter she wrote and 'the heart of the entire work'.[36] Just as the idea of God's motherhood emerges in chapter 57 as the solution to theological difficulties that seemed insoluble through logical argument, so earlier this parable had emerged to resolve the fundamental discrepancy between human judgement as conveyed by the Church's teachings and divine judgement as revealed in her showings: 'So this was what I longed for: that through him I might see how what is taught in this matter by the judgement of Holy Church is true in the sight of God, and how it befits me to know it truly; so that both judgements might be preserved to the glory of God and in the right way for me. And the only answer I had to this was a wonderful parable of a lord and a servant . . .' (chapter 45). This parable (*example*, or exemplary story) is a showing of a different kind from the others. First Julian recounts it as it was originally shown her, 'spiritually in bodily likeness' (chapter 51), but already accompanied by some degree of understanding beyond what could be represented in bodily form. A lord is sitting peacefully and a servant stands by, ready to do his commands. The lord, whose looks convey his love for the servant, sends him on an errand, and the servant sets off in haste to do the lord's will; but in his very eagerness he falls into a slough, is injured and laments that he cannot help himself or look towards the lord, even though still near him. Absorbed though the servant is in his misery, the lord does not blame him, 'for his good will and his great longing were the only cause of his fall'; indeed he promises to reward him for his sufferings, beyond what he would have received if he had not fallen. There 'the showing of the parable vanished', and Julian is left to ponder its meaning.

At first she does not see the story's point, but God encourages her to 'read' it closely as an allegory about sin, redemption and salvation. It resembles a New Testament parable, but one originally delivered in pictures rather than words; and Julian comes to see that it deserves and rewards minute decoding of the kind applied to Scriptural parables by medieval scholars. Like Jesus' parables of the Kingdom, it offers a glimpse of God's view of reality, translated into human terms, but terms that initially seem utterly strange to human readers, and that challenge all their interpretative powers. It then turns out to convey a mysterious truth, compatible perhaps with theological orthodoxy, but lying beyond the scope of normal theological discourse.

Reflection on the story leads to problems. Accustomed like most medieval people to symbolic narratives of the kind found in sermons and fables, Julian recognizes that the servant who falls is likely to stand for Adam; yet in him she sees 'many different properties which could in no way be attributed just to Adam'. The only solution is to interpret more closely, 'to pay attention', as God later instructed her, 'to all the properties and conditions of what you were shown in the parable, though they may seem mysterious and insignificant in your eyes'. The pictorial detail exists not just to provide verisimilitude or incite emotional response, but to carry meaning that will yield itself up only to persistent rumination. So the interpretation begins, as Julian retells the story bit by bit, now summoning up every detail to see what she can make of it. The lord must be God, and the servant Adam, yet Adam not as an individual but as a representative human being, 'for in the sight of God, all men are one'. The fuller realization of the lord's and servant's appearance and clothing, and of the setting in which she sees them, is often reminiscent of late-medieval manuscript illumination, or of panel painting of the kind that decorated many East Anglian churches. Yet some details go beyond the bounds of pictorial representation, as when Julian sees within the lord 'a great refuge, long and wide and all full of endless heavens'.

As in other late-medieval religious art,[37] elements contributing to realism are also rich in symbolic meaning, and this Julian proceeds to expound as it has come to her over the years. She explains that, though God the Father is not really a man, 'he shows himself in a familiar way [homley], like a man', and is so represented in her vision. God might be expected to appear in heavenly bliss or in the human soul that he created as his dwelling, so the setting on barren earth also has further meaning:

. . . he made man's soul to be his own city and his dwelling-place, the most pleasing to him of all his works; and once man had fallen into sorrow and pain he was not fit to serve that noble purpose, and therefore our kind Father would prepare no other place for himself but sit upon the earth waiting for mankind, who is mixed with earth, until the time when, through his grace, his beloved Son had bought back his city and restored its noble beauty with his hard labour.

Now the servant is more exactly described. Outwardly he resembles a labourer prepared for work, wearing a garment which is white but scanty, sweat-stained and ragged. As often, a parallel from *Piers Plowman* suggests itself: the figure of Haukyn in B XIII–XIV, the representative of the active life of work in the world, with his coat soiled with all the sins. (Haukyn is a kind of degraded version of Piers, and Piers, the ideal labourer, is ultimately identified with Christ's Humanity.) But here too Julian finds contradiction, for outwardly the servant seems to have been 'a labourer continuously for a long time', yet her 'inward sight' tells her that he is 'newly beginning to labour, a servant who had never been sent out before'. More narrative detail emerges: the servant has been sent to find a treasure in the earth. Perhaps we should recall Matthew 13:44 – 'The kingdom of heaven is like unto a treasure hidden in a field' – but this treasure is food, 'sweet and pleasing to the lord'. The servant labours as a gardener (and Julian conveys a keen sense of the hard bodily labour involved in gardening), so as to get food for his lord, which he alone can provide. Meanings flicker into life and accumulate in bewildering profusion, not hierarchically layered as in orthodox Scriptural exegesis but coexisting regardless of logic: if the servant is a gardener, we cannot help thinking of Adam both in the garden before the Fall and in the life of labour to which he was condemned afterwards. And now, in the most startling insight of the whole vision, Julian grasps that the servant is Christ as well as Adam, and that this double identity underlies the narrative contradictions. The idea that Christ was the second Adam, sent to make good the sin inherited from the first, was familiar in medieval thought, but this vision of complete identity goes beyond such parallelism. A further, crucial stage of interpretation follows: in a passage of exceptional beauty, Julian sees that the Fall of Adam and the Incarnation of Christ *are the same event*.

When Adam fell, God's son fell; because of the true union made in heaven, God's son could not leave Adam, for by Adam I understand all men. Adam fell from life to death into the valley of this wretched world, and after that into Hell. God's son fell with Adam into the valley of the Virgin's womb (and she was the fairest daughter of Adam), in order to free Adam from guilt in heaven and in earth; and with his great power he fetched him out of hell.

This insight abolishes temporal extension and historical difference, and in doing so offers a glimpse of what Julian has desired – to see reality as God sees it. The orthodox solution to the problem of predestination and free will was that for God, who exists in eternity, past and future coexist in an eternal present to which the 'present of this brief and fleeting moment' is the nearest human equivalent.[38] In the parable Julian apprehends this divine vision of reality not as theory but as experience. It ends with the lord and the servant reigning together in heaven as Father and Son, the Son crowned with mankind; God's triumph is also, through Jesus, the triumph of humanity. At the very centre of Julian's vision is a God inseparable from man and woman: transcendent in some sense, yes, but unable to set aside the bodily kinship he has chosen with his creatures.

NOTES

1 Julian's work, like many medieval English writings, lacks a title; this title has been given to it by modern editors and translators, and we retain it for its familiarity.

2 Unless prefaced by 'ST', references in the Introduction are to LT.

3 The adaptation was that of Grace Warrack. Julian's most famous reader has perhaps been T. S. Eliot, who quotes her in 'Little Gidding' (1942); he had read her in a seventeenth-century adaptation by Serenus de Cressy. (See Helen Gardner, *The Composition of Four Quartets*, London, 1978, p. 71, n. 84.)

4 Felicity Riddy, ' "Women talking about the things of God": a late medieval sub-culture', in *Women and Literature in Britain, 1150–1500*, ed. Carol M. Meale (Cambridge, 1993), pp. 104–27; quotations from p. 111.

5 *Medieval Art in East Anglia 1300–1520*, ed. P. Lasko and N. J. Morgan (Norwich, 1973), p. 6.

6 E.g. Denise N. Baker, *Julian of Norwich's Showings: From Vision to Book* (Princeton, 1994), p. 34; the opposing case is persuasively made by Sr Benedicta

(Ward), 'Julian the Solitary', in *Julian Reconsidered*, ed. Kenneth Leech and Sr Benedicta (Oxford, 1988), pp. 10–31.

7 See *Ancrene Wisse: Guide for Anchoresses*, trans. Hugh White (London, 1993).

8 Norman P. Tanner, *The Church in Late Medieval Norwich 1370–1532* (Toronto, 1984), p. 58.

9 Elizabeth Robertson, *Early English Devotional Prose and the Female Audience* (Knoxville, 1990), p. 23.

10 *The Book of Margery Kempe*, trans. B. A. Windeatt (Harmondsworth, 1985), p. 77. For the complete passage, see Appendix III.

11 As one scholar puts it, 'The ministry of an anchoress could be compared in some respects with that of a modern psychotherapist or professional counsellor' (Grace M. Jantzen, *Julian of Norwich: Mystic and Theologian*, London, 1987, p. 47).

12 For further details see the 'Translator's Note'.

13 Nicholas Watson, 'The composition of Julian of Norwich's *Revelation of Love*', *Speculum*, 68 (1993), 637–83.

14 Lines 39–41 (my translation).

15 *Sermons on the Song of Songs* 20, in *The Works of Bernard of Clairvaux*, vol. 2, trans. Kilian Walsh (Spencer, Mass., 1971), p. 152.

16 Caroline Walker Bynum, *Fragmentation and Redemption: Essays on Gender and the Human Body in Medieval Religion* (New York, 1992), p. 186.

17 Thus when she is gazing at Christ's suffering body and her reason urges her, 'Look up to his Father in heaven', she rejects the temptation of transcendence and tells Christ, 'No, I cannot, for you are my heaven' (LT chapter 19; cf. ST chapter 10).

18 Baker, *Julian of Norwich's Showings*, p. 12.

19 Riddy, ' "Women talking" ', p. 114.

20 Bynum, *Fragmentation and Redemption*, p. 196, referring to Elizabeth Petroff, *Medieval Women's Visionary Literature* (Oxford, 1986), pp. 28–32, and Walter J. Ong, *Orality and Literacy: The Technologizing of the Word* (London, 1982).

21 Throughout this volume, the Bible is quoted in the Douai version, translated from the Latin Vulgate read in the Middle Ages. The titles of some books and the numbering of the Psalms differ from those in Protestant Bibles.

22 Quoted in Edmund Colledge and James Walsh, eds., *A Book of Showings to the Anchoress Julian of Norwich* (Toronto, 1978), 2 vols., p. 151.

23 Lynn Staley Johnson, 'The trope of the scribe and the question of literary authority in the works of Julian of Norwich and Margery Kempe', *Speculum*, 66 (1991), 820–38; quotation from p. 828.

24 Cf. Nicholas Watson, ' "Yf wommen be double naturelly": remaking "woman" in Julian of Norwich's Revelation of Love', *Exemplaria*, 8 (1996), 1–34.

25 Bynum, *Fragmentation and Redemption*, p. 204.

26 Emphasized in earlier devotional writings such as the anonymous *Holy Maidenhood*, which describes how a wife 'hears her child screaming, sees the cat at the flitch and the dog at the hide, her loaf burning on the hearth and her calf sucking, the pot boiling over into the fire – *and* her husband is complaining' (in *Medieval English Prose for Women*, ed. Bella Millett and Jocelyn Wogan-Browne, Oxford, 1990, p. 35).

27 Cf. Julian's statement that God is 'our clothing, wrapping us for love, embracing and enclosing us for tender love' (chapter 5).

28 See Caroline Walker Bynum, *Jesus as Mother: Studies in the Spirituality of the High Middle Ages* (Berkeley, 1982), p. 132.

29 *Prayers and Meditations of Saint Anselm*, trans. Benedicta Ward (Harmondsworth, 1973), p. 153.

30 Eamon Duffy, *The Stripping of the Altars: Traditional Religion in England c. 1400–c. 1580* (New Haven, 1992), p. 314.

31 See Nicholas Watson, *Richard Rolle and the Invention of Authority* (Cambridge, 1991), pp. 54–5.

32 *The Scale of Perfection*, ed. Evelyn Underhill (London, 1923), II:10, p. 256. In the next sentence, however, Hilton goes on to warn against the view that 'there shall no soul be damned'.

33 *The Vision of Piers Plowman*, ed. A. V. C. Schmidt (London, 1978), B-text, XVIII 390–6, quoting 2 Corinthians 12:4.

34 Peter Dronke, *Women Writers of the Middle Ages* (Cambridge, 1984), p. x.

35 Cf. Jantzen, *Julian of Norwich*, p. 157.

36 Watson, 'The composition of Julian of Norwich's *Revelation of Love*', p. 638.

37 See Erwin Panofsky, *Early Netherlandish Painting: Its Origins and Character* (Cambridge, Mass., 1953), vol. 1, ch. 5.

38 So put by Boethius, in Book V, prose 6, of his *Consolation of Philosophy*, trans. S. J. Tester, Loeb Classical Library (London, 1918), p. 425. See also Augustine, *De diversis quaestionibus* II, qu. 2, n. 2.

FURTHER READING

Baker, Denise N., *Julian of Norwich's Showings: From Vision to Book* (Princeton, 1994)

Barker, Paula S. Datsko, 'The Motherhood of God in Julian of Norwich's Theology', *Downside Review*, 100 (1982), 290–304

Beer, Frances, *Women and Mystical Experience in the Middle Ages* (Cambridge, 1992), pp. 130–57

Bynum, Caroline Walker, *Jesus as Mother: Studies in the Spirituality of the High Middle Ages* (Berkeley, 1982)

—— *Fragmentation and Redemption: Essays on Gender and the Human Body in Medieval Religion* (New York, 1992)

Coiner, Nancy, 'The "Homely" and the *Heimliche*: the hidden, doubled self in Julian of Norwich's *Showings*', *Exemplaria*, 5 (1993), 305–23

Colledge, Edmund, and James Walsh, eds., *A Book of Showings to the Anchoress Julian of Norwich*, 2 vols. (Toronto, 1978)

Colledge, Eric, *The Mediaeval Mystics of England* (New York, 1961)

Gillespie, Vincent, and Maggie Ross, 'The Apophatic Image: the poetics of effacement in Julian of Norwich's *Revelation of Love*', in *The Medieval Mystical Tradition in England: Exeter Symposium V* (Cambridge, 1992), pp. 53–77

Glasscoe, Marion, *Medieval English Mystics: Games of Faith* (London, 1993), pp. 215–67

Harries, Richard, 'On the Brink of Universalism', in *Julian, Woman of Our Day*, ed. Robert Llewelyn (London, 1985), pp. 41–60

Holdsworth, C. J., 'Visions and Visionaries in the Middle Ages', *History*, 48 (1963), 141–53

Jacoff, Rachel, 'God as Mother: Julian of Norwich's theology of love', *University of Denver Quarterly*, 18 (1983–4), 134–9

Jantzen, Grace M., *Julian of Norwich: Mystic and Theologian* (London, 1987)

Johnson, Lynn Staley, 'The trope of the scribe and the question of literary authority in the works of Julian of Norwich and Margery Kempe', *Speculum*, 66 (1991), 820–38

Knowles, David, *The English Mystical Tradition* (London, 1961)

McNamer, Sarah, 'The exploratory image: God as Mother in Julian of Norwich's *Revelations of Divine Love*', *Mystics Quarterly*, 15 (1989), 21–8

Molinari, Paul, *Julian of Norwich: The Teaching of a Fourteenth-Century English Mystic* (London, 1958)

Pelphrey, Brant, *Love Was His Meaning: The Theology and Mysticism of Julian of Norwich* (Salzburg, 1982)

Peters, Brad, 'Julian of Norwich and her conceptual development of evil', *Mystics Quarterly*, 17 (1991), 181–8

Riddy, Felicity, '"Women talking about the things of God": a late medieval sub-culture', in *Women and Literature in Britain, 1150–1500*, ed. Carole M. Meale (Cambridge, 1993), pp. 104–27

Robertson, Elizabeth, 'Medieval medical views of women and female spirituality in the *Ancrene Wisse* and Julian of Norwich's *Showings*', in *Feminist Approaches to the Body in Medieval Literature*, ed. Linda Lomperis and Sarah Stanbury (Philadelphia, 1993), pp. 142–67

Tanner, Norman P., *The Church in Late Medieval Norwich, 1370–1532* (Toronto, 1984)

(Ward), Sr Benedicta, 'Julian the Solitary', in *Julian Reconsidered*, ed. Kenneth Leech and Sr Benedicta (Oxford, 1988), pp. 10–31

—'Lady Julian and her audience: "Mine Even-Christian"', in *The English Religious Tradition and the Genius of Anglicanism*, ed. Geoffrey Rowell (Oxford, 1992), pp. 47–63

Watson, Nicholas, 'The trinitarian hermeneutic in Julian of Norwich's *Revelation of Love*', in *The Medieval Mystical Tradition in England: Exeter Symposium V* (Cambridge, 1992), pp. 79–100

—'The composition of Julian of Norwich's *Revelation of Love*', *Speculum*, 68 (1993), 637–83

—'"Yf wommen be double naturelly": remaking "woman" in Julian of Norwich's *Revelation of Love*', *Exemplaria*, 8 (1996), 1–34

Windeatt, B. A., 'Julian of Norwich and her audience', *Review of English Studies*, n.s. 28 (1977), 1–17
— 'The art of mystical loving: Julian of Norwich', in *The Medieval Mystical Tradition in England: Exeter Symposium I* (Exeter, 1980), pp. 55–71

TRANSLATOR'S NOTE

The manuscripts containing both texts of Julian's *Revelations of Divine Love* all date from after her lifetime. ST survives in only one manuscript, copied in the mid-fifteenth century from an original dated 1413. This is British Library MS Add. 37790, an anthology of late-medieval religious writings, including selections from works by mystics such as Rolle, Ruysbroek, Suso and Saint Bridget of Sweden. My translation is taken from this manuscript, as edited by Barry Windeatt, whose chapter divisions I follow.[1]

LT survives in three manuscripts, all much later, made after the Reformation for English Catholics in exile on the continent. One of these, British Library Sloane MS 3705 (S2), is copied from another, Sloane MS 2499 (S1) (or else is an inferior copy of a common original), so the editorial choice is between S1 and the third manuscript, Paris, Bibliothèque Nationale, fonds anglais 40 (P). S1 and S2 are seventeenth-century manuscripts. P may be somewhat earlier, but is more sophisticated; some editors prefer it,[2] while others regard the sophistication as scribal. We take the latter view, and my translation of LT is generally based on Glasscoe's edition,[3] which takes S1 as its copy-text. But the S1 scribe often had real difficulty in understanding the manuscript to be copied, and there remain numerous places where editors and translators will differ as to what Julian wrote and what she meant by it. It is not certain how many layers of scribal copying separate S1 from Julian's autograph, nor how accurate the copyists were, nor how far scribal misunderstanding of a treatise difficult in both language and thought obscures Julian's original words. Glasscoe presents a conservative text of S1; we believe that an ideal edition of a manuscript so manifestly corrupt would risk more emendation, and in various places, where the manuscript of ST (over a century closer to Julian herself) runs parallel and offers better readings, I have emended accordingly; occasionally too I have borrowed readings from P where these manifestly make better sense. An example of emendation of LT in accordance with ST is as follows: in LT chapter 65 (p. 150: 'it sets all other fears . . . apprehensions') S1 reads 'All our dreds he setteth among passions and bodely sekenes and imaginations'; the parallel passage in ST chapter 20 (p. 31) reads 'alle othere dredes sette tham emange passyons and bodelye sekeness and ymagynacions'; since Julian is distinguishing between the fear of God and other fears that have no spiritual value, *our dreds* must almost certainly be a scribal error for *othere dredes*, so I have translated 'other fears'. An example of the substitution of a P reading occurs in LT chapter 56 (p. 133: 'he is the means . . . kept together'), where S1 reads 'he is mene that kepith the substance and the sensualite to God'. P has *togeder* in place of *to God*; P's reading seems obviously preferable, because Julian is referring to what prevents the two aspects of the soul from being separated, so I have translated 'together'.

The chapter headings may or may not be by Julian herself; and in our view the afterword, with its determination to appropriate Julian's teaching for orthodoxy, is probably by a writer other than Julian. But, given that complete certainty is unattainable, and that both headings and afterword have long been accepted as part of the text of the *Revelations*, I have not omitted them from the translation and have kept them in their traditional places.

The texts of the *Revelations* are written in an oral register; they may even have been taken down from Julian's spoken words. When translating I have tried to keep the sound of a woman's speaking voice, which runs constantly through the Middle English.[4] Julian's language is largely vernacular, and I have avoided as far as possible introducing Latinate words and phrases where she uses everyday ones – often concrete, simple and domestic. It would be all too easy to produce a text with overtones of a Victorian bishop. Nor have Julian's words been changed for the sake of changing them; when the original presents no problems to the understanding of an average modern reader, I have done no more than modernize the spelling. It has occasionally seemed desirable to add or omit a few words for the sake of clarity, or to clarify the sense of a consciously used ambivalent word in the original. In some cases a difficulty arises not just from changes in the meaning of words, but from larger cultural changes. There is difficulty with the vocabulary of lordship, for example; Julian lived in a world where fear of and obedience to a superior could be perceived as natural and beautiful, and where 'condescension' had no negative tones.

A number of Julian's words express crucial concepts, but have no one modern equivalent. As noted above,[5] *homely* and various allied forms are frequently applied to God; the word is important to our understanding of Julian, for the fusion of the domestic and the transcendental is one of the most important elements in her vision; but 'homely' would often sound odd and misleading in modern English and American. I have tried to convey Julian's meaning cumulatively by using such terms as 'close', 'friendly', 'familiar', 'intimate', as well as 'homely' itself; it seems more important to give an impression of what Julian may really have meant than to choose one word throughout for the sake of consistency. On the other hand, changing a word in some instances can destroy the cumulative effect of a simple term used repeatedly in one passage. This repetition of key words can be very important, and sometimes has to affect the translator's choice, even if the same word does not sound quite right at every occurrence. 'Grace' and related terms such as 'gracious(ly)' are repeated in this way; and while they can evoke secular meanings such as *The Oxford English Dictionary*'s sense 6.a, 'favour or goodwill', and sense 1, 'the quality of producing favourable impressions; attractiveness, charm', it is important to recognize, yet almost impossible for a translator to convey, that in Julian their fundamental reference is always to the important theological concept of the grace of God: 'The divine influence which operates in men to regenerate and sanctify, to inspire virtuous impulses, and to impart strength to endure trial and resist temptation' (*OED* sense 11.b). Again, Julian's word 'kind' incorporates the senses of a wide range of modern terms that I have often had to substitute for it: 'generous' and (secular) 'gracious', but also 'natural'.

I have tried to keep as much of the original syntax as possible; it conveys Julian's vision much better than modern syntax would. There are sometimes grammatical inconsistencies, but that is the nature of the spoken word, and indeed sometimes a consequence of the overflow of multiple significance from her showings. The distinctive rhythm of the original, especially in LT, comes partly from what nowadays seem very long sentences, with clauses accumulating one after the other, and frequent repetition of conjunctions; but this is part of Julian's voice. A full stop and the break it brings would often disrupt the intensity and wonder of her vision, distancing the reader from her experience, and long though some of the sentences may be, they are rarely confusing. The accumulated clauses often have a deliberate pattern, working up to the most important point at the end. Julian very rarely ends with an insignificant word or phrase. Her words can modulate into language which is on the edge of poetry – metrical, rhythmic, alliterative: 'for as the body is cladde in the cloth, and the flesh in the skyne, and the bonys in the flesh, and the herte in the bouke, so arn we, soule and body, cladde in the goodnes of God . . .'; 'for all these may wasten and weren away'; 'many mervel how it might be'; 'fairhede of heavyn, flowre of erth and the fruite of the mayden wombe'.[6] I have attempted to preserve the rhythm and flow and some ghostly echo of the original language. (I have, for example, added alliteration in some places to compensate for its loss in others.) Corresponding phrases in ST and LT are not invariably translated in precisely the same words, because in translating each text I have had to consider the flow of its own sentences and paragraphs. The punctuation, since it cannot be Julian's own, I have felt free to change, sometimes to reflect the pace and emphasis of speech, and the work has been divided into paragraphs.

One translator suggested the desirability of pruning and giving paragraphs and sentences 'a sharper edge',[7] but mysteries do not come with sharp edges. The work deals with mysteries and miracles and experiences which Julian herself found hard to follow and interpret, and it seems wrong to oversimplify, to make her book too easy and clear. The past struggle to understand and the present struggle to express sometimes merge together, and a certain degree of effort and confusion may be a necessary element in receiving the text. Saint Augustine described certain passages of Scripture as 'covered with a most dense mist', and suggested that this situation was 'provided by God', as what is grasped quickly is insufficiently valued.[8] Julian too conveys what she believed to be God's own utterances, and we should not be able to skim quickly through her writings.

In matters of gender, I have frequently made such changes as that of 'men' to 'people' to conform with modern usage, but have sometimes used 'mankind' and 'man' as Julian does, as a neuter noun, encompassing male and female, singular and plural. 'Man and God' has more impact than 'people and God' or other attempts to avoid a word which is now more gendered than it could have been to her. Similarly with pronouns: I have used non-gendered forms where this could be done without awkwardness, but have made no systematic attempt to impose modern sensitivities on a medieval writer.

Though translation must always be a matter of compromise, I have tried to preserve Julian's text rather than making it my own, while removing obstacles to clear reception – not just obsolete language, but any quaintnesses added by the passage of time which might seem obtrusive enough to modify a reader's response. I hope my version is close enough to the original to be of use as an aid for those who would like to read Julian's own words and are not familiar with Middle English, and to make it accessible not just to those interested in literature, theological ideas or the voice of a medieval woman, but also as it was originally intended: a devotional text. Readers interested in the original will find two sample extracts in Appendix II.

Finally, it is obvious that Julian herself was extremely familiar with her material: she frequently quotes from other chapters and refers forwards and back; I hope that Appendix I will be a useful guide for such cross-references.

NOTES

1 *English Mystics of the Middle Ages*, ed. Barry Windeatt (Cambridge, 1994), pp. 181–213.
2 Notably Colledge and Walsh (see Further Reading).
3 Marion Glasscoe, ed. *Julian of Norwich: A Revelation of Love*, rev. edn. (Exeter, 1993).

4 Cf. ibid., p. xviii.

5 See Introduction, p. xix.

6 Chapters 6 and 10; ed. Glasscoe, pp. 9 and 15.

7 *Revelations of Divine Love*, trans. Clifton Wolters (Harmondsworth, 1966), p. 20.

8 *On Christian Doctrine*, II. VI, trans. D. W. Robertson, Jr. (Indianapolis, 1958), p. 37. Julian describes the parable of the lord and servant as being *mysty*, which means 'cloudy' as well as 'mysterious'.

Revelations of Divine Love

(THE SHORT TEXT)

This is a vision shown, through God's goodness, to a devout woman, and her name is Julian, and she is a recluse at Norwich and is still alive in the year of our Lord 1413; in this vision there are many comforting and very moving words for all those who wish to be lovers of Christ.

1

I asked for three graces of God's gift. The first was vivid perception of Christ's Passion, the second was bodily sickness and the third was for God to give me three wounds. I thought of the first as I was meditating: it seemed to me that I could feel the Passion of Christ strongly, but yet I longed by God's grace to feel it more intensely. I thought how I wished I had been there at the crucifixion with Mary Magdalene and with others who were Christ's dear friends, that I might have seen in the flesh the Passion of our Lord which he suffered for me, so that I could have suffered with him as others did who loved him. Nevertheless, I firmly believed in all the torments of Christ as Holy Church reveals and teaches them, and also in the paintings of crucifixes that are made by God's grace in the likeness of Christ's Passion, according to the teaching of Holy Church, as far as human imagination can reach.

In spite of all this true faith, I longed to be shown him in the flesh so that I might have more knowledge of our Lord and Saviour's bodily suffering and of our Lady's fellow-suffering and that of all his true friends who have believed in his pain then and since; I wanted to be one of them and suffer with him. I never wished for any other sight or showing of God until my soul left my body, for I faithfully trusted that I would be saved, and my intention was this: that afterwards, because of the showing, I would have a truer perception of Christ's Passion.

As for the second gift, there came to me with contrition, freely, without any effort on my part, a strong wish to have of God's gift a bodily sickness. And I wanted this bodily sickness to be to the death, so that I might in that sickness receive all the rites of Holy Church, that I might myself believe I was dying and that everyone who saw me might believe the same, for I wanted no hopes of fleshly or earthly life. I longed to have in this sickness every kind of suffering both of body and soul that I would experience if I died, with all the terror and turmoil of the fiends,[1] and all other kinds of torment, except for actually giving up the ghost, because I hoped that it might be to my benefit when I died, for I longed to be soon with my God.

I longed for these two things – the Passion and the sickness – with one reservation, for it seemed to me that they went beyond the common course of prayers; and therefore I said, 'Lord, you know what I would have. If it is your will that I should have it, grant it to me. And if it is not your will, good Lord, do not be displeased, for I only want what you want.' I asked for this sickness in my youth, to have it when I was thirty years old.

As for the third gift, I heard a man of Holy Church tell the story of Saint Cecilia; from his description I understood that she received three sword wounds in the neck from which she slowly and painfully died.[2] Moved by this I conceived a great longing, praying our Lord God that he would grant me three wounds in my lifetime: that is to say, the wound of contrition, the wound of compassion and the wound of an earnest longing for God. Just as I asked for the other two with a reservation, so I asked for the third with no reservation.

The first two of the longings just mentioned passed from my mind, and the third stayed with me continually.

2

And when I was thirty and a half years old, God sent me a bodily sickness in which I lay for three days and three nights; and on the fourth night I received all the rites of Holy Church and did not believe that I would live until morning. And after this I lingered on for two days and two nights. And on the third night I often thought that I was dying, and so did those who were with me. But at this time I was very sorry and reluctant to die, not because there was anything on earth that I wanted to live for, nor because I feared anything, for I trusted in God, but because I wanted to live so as to love God better and for longer, so that through the grace of longer life I might know and love God better in the bliss of heaven. For it seemed to me that all the short time I could live here was as nothing compared with that heavenly bliss. So I thought, 'My good Lord, may my ceasing to live be to your glory!' And I was answered in my reason, and by the pains I felt, that I was dying. And I fully accepted the will of God with all the will of my heart.

So I endured till day, and by then my body was dead to all sensation from the waist down. Then I felt I wanted to be in a sitting position, leaning with my head back against the bedding, so that my heart could be more freely at God's disposition, and so that I could think of God while I was still alive; and those who were with me sent for the parson, my parish priest, to be present at my death. He came, and a boy with him, and brought a cross, and by the time he came my eyes were fixed and I could not speak. The parson set the cross before my face and said, 'Daughter, I have brought you the image of your Saviour. Look upon it and be comforted, in reverence to him that died for you and me.' It seemed to me that I was well as I was, for my eyes were looking fixedly upwards into heaven, where I trusted that I was going. But nevertheless I consented to fix my eyes on the face of the crucifix if I could, so as to be able to do so for longer until the moment of my death; because I thought that I might be able to bear looking straight ahead for longer than I could manage to look upwards. After this my sight began to fail and the room was dim all around me, as

5

dark as if it had been night, except that in the image of the cross an ordinary, household light remained – I could not understand how. Everything except the cross was ugly to me, as if crowded with fiends. After this I felt as if the upper part of my body was beginning to die. My hands fell down on either side, and my head settled down sideways for weakness. The greatest pain that I felt was shortness of breath and failing of life. Then I truly believed that I was at the point of death. And at this moment all my suffering suddenly left me, and I was as completely well, especially in the upper part of my body, as ever I was before or after. I marvelled at this change, for it seemed to me a mysterious work of God, not a natural one. And yet, although I felt comfortable, I still did not expect to live, nor did feeling more comfortable comfort me entirely, for I felt that I would rather have been released from this world, for in my heart I was willing to die.

3

And it suddenly occurred to me that I should entreat our Lord graciously to give me the second wound, so that he would fill my whole body with remembrance of the feeling of his blessed Passion, as I had prayed before; for I wanted his pains to be my pains, with compassion, and then longing for God. Yet in this I never asked for a bodily sight or any kind of showing of God, but for fellow-suffering, such as it seemed to me a naturally kind soul might feel for our Lord Jesus, who was willing to become a mortal man for love. I wanted to suffer with him, while living in my mortal body, as God would give me grace.

And I suddenly saw the red blood trickling down from under the crown of thorns, all hot, freshly, plentifully and vividly, just as I imagined it was at the moment when the crown of thorns was thrust on to his blessed head – he who was both God and man, the same who suffered for me. I believed truly and strongly that it was he himself who showed me this, without any intermediary, and then I said, 'Benedicite dominus!'³ Because I meant this with such deep veneration, I said it in a very loud voice; and I was astounded, feeling wonder and admiration that he was willing to be so familiar with a sinful being living in this wretched flesh. I supposed at that time that our Lord Jesus of his courteous love would show me comfort before the time of my temptation. For I thought it might well be, by God's permission and under his protection, that I would be tempted by fiends before I died. With this sight of the blessed Passion, along with the Godhead that I saw in my mind, I saw that I, yes, and every creature living that would be saved, could have strength to resist all the fiends of hell and all spiritual enemies.

4

And at the same time that I saw this bodily sight, our Lord showed me a spiritual vision of his familiar love. I saw that for us he is everything that is good and comforting and helpful. He is our clothing, wrapping and enveloping us for love, embracing us and guiding us in all things, hanging about us in tender love, so that he can never leave us. And so in this vision, as I understand it, I saw truly that he is everything that is good for us.

And in this vision he showed me a little thing, the size of a hazel-nut, lying in the palm of my hand, and to my mind's eye it was as round as any ball. I looked at it and thought, 'What can this be?' And the answer came to me, 'It is all that is made.' I wondered how it could last, for it was so small I thought it might suddenly disappear. And the answer in my mind was, 'It lasts and will last for ever because God loves it; and in the same way everything exists through the love of God.' In this little thing I saw three attributes: the first is that God made it, the second is that he loves it, the third is that God cares for it. But what does that mean to me? Truly, the maker, the lover, the carer; for until I become one substance with him, I can never have love, rest or true bliss; that is to say, until I am so bound to him that there may be no created thing between my God and me. And who shall do this deed? Truly, himself, by his mercy and his grace, for he has made me and blessedly restored me to that end.

Then God brought our Lady into my mind. I saw her spiritually in bodily likeness, a meek and simple maid, young of age, in the same bodily form as when she conceived. God also showed me part of the wisdom and truth of her soul so that I understood with what reverence she beheld her God who is her maker, and how reverently she marvelled that he chose to be born of her, a simple creature of his own making. For what made her marvel was that he who was her Maker chose to be born of the creature he had made. And the wisdom of her faithfulness, and knowledge of the greatness of her Maker and the littleness of her who was made, moved her to say very humbly to the angel Gabriel, 'Behold, the handmaid of the Lord.'[4] With this sight I really understood that she is greater in worthiness and fullness of grace than all that God made below her; for nothing that is made is above her except the blessed Manhood of Christ. This little thing that is made that is below our Lady Saint Mary, God showed it to me as small as if it had been a hazel-nut. It was so small I thought it might have disappeared.

In this blessed revelation God showed me three nothings.[5] Of these nothings this was the first I was shown, and all men and women who wish to lead the contemplative life need to have knowledge of it: they should choose to set at nothing everything that is made so as to have the love of God who is unmade. This is why those who choose to occupy themselves with earthly business and are always pursuing worldly success have nothing here of God in their hearts and souls: because they love and seek their rest in this little thing where there is no rest, and know nothing of God, who is almighty, all wise and all good, for he is true rest. God wishes to be known, and is pleased that we should rest in him; for all that is below him does nothing to satisfy us. And this is why, until all that is made seems as nothing, no soul can be at rest. When a soul sets all at nothing for love, to have him who is everything that is good, then it is able to receive spiritual rest.

5

And during the time that our Lord was showing in spiritual sight what I have just described, the bodily sight of the plentiful bleeding from Christ's head remained, and as long as I could see this sight I kept saying, 'Benedicite dominus!' In this first showing from our Lord I saw six things in my understanding: the first is the signs of Christ's blessed Passion and the plentiful shedding of his precious blood; the second is the Maiden who is his beloved mother; the third is the blessed Godhead that ever was, is and ever shall be, almighty, all wisdom and all love. The fourth is all that he has made; it is vast and wide, fair and good, but it looked so small to me because I saw it in the presence of him that is Maker of all things; to a soul that sees the Maker of all, all that is made seems very small. The fifth thing I understood is that he made everything that is made for love; and the same love sustains everything, and shall do so for ever, as has been said before. The sixth is that God is everything that is good, and the goodness that is in everything is God. And all these our Lord showed me in the first vision, and gave me time and space to contemplate it. And when the bodily vision stopped, the spiritual vision remained in my understanding. And I waited with reverent fear, rejoicing in what I saw, and longing, as far as I dared, to see more if it was his will, or else to see the same vision for longer.

6

All that I saw concerning myself, I mean to be applied to all my fellow Christians, for I am taught by our Lord's spiritual showing that this is what he means. And therefore I beg you all for God's sake and advise you all for your own advantage that you stop paying attention to the poor, worldly, sinful creature to whom this vision was shown, and eagerly, attentively, lovingly and humbly contemplate God, who in his gracious love and in his eternal goodness wanted the vision to be generally known to comfort us all. And you who hear and see this vision and this teaching, which come from Jesus Christ to edify your souls, it is God's will and my desire that you should receive it with joy and pleasure as great as if Jesus had shown it to you as he did to me.

I am not good because of the showing, unless I love God better, and so may and should everyone that sees it and hears it with good will and true intention; and so my desire is that it should bring everyone the same advantage that I desired for myself, and this is how God moved me the first time I saw it. For it is universal and addressed to all because we are all one, and I am sure I saw it for the advantage of many others. Indeed it was not shown to me because God loved me better than the lowest soul that is in a state of grace, for I am sure that there are very many who never had a showing or vision, but only the normal teaching of Holy Church, and who love God better than I do. For if I look solely at myself, I am really nothing; but as one of mankind in general, I am in oneness of love with all my fellow Christians; for upon this oneness of love depends the life of all who shall be saved; for God is all that is good, and God has made all that is made, and God loves all that he has made.

And if any man or woman ceases to love any of his fellow Christians, then he loves none, for he does not love all; and so at that moment he is not saved, for he is not at peace; and he who loves all his fellow Christians loves all that is; for in those who shall be saved, all is included: that is all that is made and the Maker of all; for in man is God, and so in man is all. And he who loves all his fellow Christians in this way, he loves all; and he who loves in this way is saved. And thus I wish to love, and thus I love, and thus I am saved. (I am speaking in the person of my fellow Christians.) And the more I love with this kind of love while I am here, the more like I am to the bliss that I shall have in heaven without end, which is God, who in his endless love was willing to become our brother and suffer for us. And I am sure that whoever looks at it in this way will be truly taught and greatly comforted if he needs comfort.

But God forbid that you should say or assume that I am a teacher, for that is not what I mean, nor did I ever mean it; for I am a woman, ignorant, weak and frail. But I know well that I have received what I say from him who is the supreme teacher. But in truth, I am moved to tell you about it by love, for I wish God to be known and my fellow Christians helped, as I wish to be helped myself, so that sin shall be more hated and God more loved. Just because I am a woman, must I therefore believe that I must not tell you about the goodness of God, when I saw at the same time both his goodness and his wish that it should be known? And you will see that clearly in the chapters which follow, if they are well and truly understood. Then you must quickly forget me, a paltry creature, you must not let me hinder you, but look directly at Jesus, who is teacher of all. I speak of those who will be saved, for at this time God showed me no others. But in all things I believe what Holy Church teaches, for in all things I saw this blessed showing of our Lord as one who is in the presence of God, and I never perceived anything in it that bewilders me or keeps me from the true teaching of Holy Church.

7

All this blessed teaching of our Lord God was shown me in three parts: that is, by bodily sight, and by words formed in my understanding, and by spiritual sight. But I neither can nor may show you the spiritual vision as openly or as fully as I would like to. But I trust that our Lord God almighty will, out of his own goodness and love for you, make you receive it more spiritually and more sweetly than I can or may tell you; and so may it be, for we are all one in love. And in all this I was much moved with love for my fellow Christians, wishing that they might see and know what I was seeing; I wanted it to comfort them all as it did me, for the vision was shown for everyone and not for any one particular person. And what comforted me most in the vision was that our Lord is so familiar and courteous. And this was what gave me most happiness and the strongest sense of spiritual safety. Then I said to the people who were with me, 'For me, today is the Day of Judgement.' And I said this because I thought I was dying; for

on the day that someone dies, he receives his eternal judgement. I
said this because I wanted them to love God better and set a lower
value on the vanity of the world, to remind them that life is short, as
they might see by my example; for all this time I thought I was dying.

8

And after this I saw with my bodily sight in the face of Christ on the
crucifix which hung before me, which I was looking at continuously,
a part of his Passion: contempt and spitting, which soiled his body,
and blows on his blessed face, and many lingering pains, more than I
can tell, and frequent changes of colour, and all his blessed face covered
at one time in dry blood. I saw this bodily in distress and darkness,
and I wished for better bodily light to see it more clearly. And I was
answered in my reason that if God wanted to show me more he
would, but I needed no light but him.

And after this I saw God in an instant,[6] that is in my understanding,
and in seeing this I saw that he is in everything. I looked attentively,
knowing and recognizing in this vision that he does all that is done.
I marvelled at this sight with quiet awe, and I thought, 'What is sin?'
For I saw truly that God does everything, no matter how small. And
nothing happens by accident or luck, but by the eternal providence
of God's wisdom. Therefore I was obliged to accept that everything
which is done is well done, and I was sure that God never sins.
Therefore it seemed to me that sin is nothing, for in all this vision no
sin appeared. So I marvelled no longer about this but looked at our
Lord to see what he would show me; and at another time God showed
me what sin is, in its naked essence, as I shall recount later.[7]

And after this I saw, as I watched, the body of Christ bleeding
abundantly, hot and freshly and vividly, just as I saw the head before.
And I saw the blood coming from weals from the scourging, and in
my vision it ran so abundantly that it seemed to me that if at that
moment it had been natural blood, the whole bed would have been
blood-soaked and even the floor around. God has provided us on

earth with abundant water for our use and bodily refreshment, because of the tender love he has for us, yet it pleases him better that we should freely take his holy blood to wash away our sins; for there is no liquid created which he likes to give us so much, for it is so plentiful and it shares our nature.

And after this, before God revealed any words, he allowed me to contemplate longer all that I had seen, and all that was in it. And then, without any voice or opening of lips, there were formed in my soul these words: 'By this is the Fiend overcome.' Our Lord said these words meaning overcome by his Passion, as he had shown me earlier. At this point our Lord brought into my mind and showed me some part of the Fiend's wickedness and the whole of his weakness, and to do so he revealed how with his Passion he defeats the Devil. God showed me that he is still as wicked as he was before the Incarnation and works as hard, but he continually sees that all chosen souls escape him gloriously, and that grieves him; for everything that God allows him to do turns into joy for us and into pain and shame for him; and that is because he may never do as much evil as he would wish, for God holds fast all the Devil's power in his own hand. I also saw our Lord scorn his wickedness and set him at nought, and he wants us to do the same.

At this revelation I laughed heartily and that made those who were around me laugh too, and their laughter pleased me. I wished that my fellow Christians had seen what I saw, and then they would all have laughed with me. But I did not see Christ laughing. Nevertheless, it pleases him that we should laugh to cheer ourselves, and rejoice in God because the Fiend has been conquered. And after this I became serious, and said, 'I can see three things: delight, scorn and seriousness. I see delight that the Fiend is defeated; I see scorn because God scorns him and he is to be scorned; and I see seriousness because he is defeated by the Passion of our Lord Jesus Christ and by his death, which took place in all seriousness and with weary hardship.'

After this our Lord said, 'I thank you for your service and your suffering, especially in your youth.'

9

God showed me three degrees of bliss which every soul who has willingly served God shall have in heaven, whatever his degree on earth. The first is the glorious gratitude of our Lord God, which he will receive when he is freed from his sufferings; the gratitude is so exalted and so glorious that it would seem to fill the soul, even if there were no greater bliss; for I thought that all the pain and trouble that could be suffered by all living men could not have deserved the gratitude which one man shall have who has willingly served God. The second degree is that all the blessed beings who are in heaven will see that glorious gratitude of our Lord God, and all heaven will know about his service. And the third degree is that this pleasure will for ever seem as new and delightful as it did when it was first felt. I saw that this was said and revealed to me sweetly and in kind terms: every man's age[8] shall be known in heaven, and he will be rewarded for his willing service and for the time he has served; and more especially the age of those who willingly and freely offered their youth to God is surpassingly rewarded and they are wonderfully thanked.

And our Lord's next showing was a supreme spiritual pleasure in my soul. In this pleasure I was filled with eternal certainty, strongly anchored and without any fear. This feeling was so joyful to me and so full of goodness that I felt completely peaceful, easy and at rest, as though there were nothing on earth that could hurt me. This only lasted for a while, and then my feeling was reversed and I was left oppressed, weary of myself, and so disgusted with my life that I could hardly bear to live. There was no ease or comfort for my feelings but faith, hope and love, and these I had in reality, but I could not feel them in my heart. And immediately after this God again gave me the spiritual rest and comfort, certainty and pleasure so joyful and so powerful that no fear, no sorrow, no bodily or spiritual pain that one might suffer could have distressed me. And then the sorrow was revealed to my consciousness again, and first one, then the other, several times, I suppose about twenty times. And in the moments of joy I might have said with Paul, 'Nothing shall separate me from the love of Christ.' And in the moments of sorrow I might have said with Saint Peter, 'Lord save me, I perish.'[9]

This vision was shown to me, as I understand, to teach me that it is necessary for everybody to have such experiences, sometimes to be strengthened, sometimes to falter and be left by himself. God wishes us to know that he safely protects us in both joy and sorrow equally, and he loves us as much in sorrow as in joy. And to benefit his soul, a man is sometimes left to himself, though not because of sin; for at this time I did not deserve by sinning to be left alone, neither did I deserve the feeling of bliss. But God gives joy generously when he so wishes, and sometimes allows us sorrow; and both come from love. So it is God's will that we should hold on to gladness with all our might, for bliss lasts eternally, and pain passes and shall vanish completely. Therefore it is not God's will that we should be guided by feelings of pain, grieving and mourning over them, but should quickly pass beyond them and remain in eternal joy, which is God almighty, who loves and protects us.

10

After this Christ showed me the part of his Passion when he was near death. I saw that dear face as if it were dry and bloodless with the pallor of death; and then it went more deathly, ashen and exhausted, and still nearer to death it went blue, then darker blue, as the flesh mortified more completely; all the pains that Christ suffered in his body appeared to me in the blessed face as far as I could see it, and especially in his lips; there I saw these four colours, though before they appeared to me fresh and red-tinted, vivid and lovely. It was a sorrowful change to see this extreme mortification; and, as it appeared to me, the nose shrivelled and dried. This long agony made it seem to me that he had been dead for a full week, always suffering pain. And I thought that the drying of Christ's flesh was the greatest agony, and the last, of his Passion. And in this dryness the words that Christ spoke were brought to my mind: 'I thirst';[10] and I saw in Christ a double thirst, one bodily, the other spiritual. In these words was revealed to me the bodily thirst, and the spiritual thirst was revealed to me as I shall say later.[11] And I understood that the bodily thirst was caused by the body's loss of moisture, for the blessed flesh and bones were left altogether without blood and moisture. The blessed body was drying for a long time, becoming distorted because of the nails and the heaviness of the head and its own weight, with the blowing of the wind from without that dried him more and tormented him with cold more than I can imagine, and all other torments. I saw such pains that everything I could say would be quite inadequate, for they were indescribable. But every soul, as Saint Paul says, should feel in himself what was in Jesus Christ.[12] This showing of Christ's pain filled me with pain, though I knew well he only suffered once, yet he wanted to show it to me and fill me with awareness of it as I had wished previously.

My mother, who was standing with others watching me, lifted her hand up to my face to close my eyes, for she thought I was already dead or else I had that moment died; and this greatly increased my sorrow, for in spite of all my suffering, I did not want to be stopped from seeing him, because of my love for him. And yet, in all this time of Christ's presence, the only pain I felt was the pain of Christ. Then I thought to myself, 'I little knew what pain it was that I asked for'; for I thought that my pain was worse than bodily death. I thought, 'Is any pain in hell like this pain?', and I was answered in my mind that despair is greater, for that is spiritual pain, but no bodily pain is greater than this. How could any pain be greater to me than to see him who is my whole life, all my bliss and all my joy, suffering? Here I truly felt that I loved Christ so much more than myself that I thought bodily death would have been a great relief to me.

Here I saw part of the compassion of our Lady Saint Mary, for Christ and she were so united in love that the greatness of her love caused the intensity of her pain; for just as her love for him surpassed that of anyone else, so did her suffering for him; and so all his disciples, and all those who truly loved him, suffered greater pain than they would for their own bodily death; for I am certain, from my own feelings, that the humblest of them loved him much better than themselves.

Here I saw a great union between Christ and us; for when he was in pain, we were in pain. And all creatures who were capable of suffering, suffered with him. And as for those who did not know him, their suffering was that all creation, sun and moon, withdrew their service, and so they were all left in sorrow during that time. And thus those that loved him suffered for love, and those that did not love him suffered from a failure of comfort from the whole of creation.

At this point I wanted to look away from the cross, but I dared not, for I well knew that while I contemplated the cross I was safe and sound; therefore I was unwilling to imperil my soul, for beside the cross there was no safety, but the ugliness of fiends. Then a suggestion came from my reason, as though a friendly voice had spoken, 'Look up to his Father in heaven.' Then I saw clearly with the faith that I felt, that there was nothing between the cross and heaven which could have distressed me, and either I must look up or I must answer. I answered and said, 'No, I cannot, for you are my heaven.' I said this because I did not wish to look up, for I would rather have suffered until Judgement Day than have come to heaven otherwise than by him; for I well knew that he who redeemed me so dearly would unbind me when he wished.

11

Thus I chose Jesus as my heaven, though at that time I saw him only in pain.[13] I was satisfied by no heaven but Jesus, who will be my bliss when I am there. And it has always been a comfort to me that I chose Jesus for my heaven in all this time of suffering and sorrow. And that has been a lesson to me, that I should do so for evermore, choosing him alone for my heaven in good and bad times. And thus I saw my Lord Jesus Christ lingering for a long time; for union with the Godhead gave his Manhood the strength to suffer for love more than anyone could. I do not mean only more pain than any man could suffer, but also that he suffered more pain than all men who ever existed from the very beginning until the very last day. No tongue may tell, nor heart fully imagine, the pains that our Saviour suffered for us, considering the majesty of the highest, most worshipful King and the shameful, insulting and painful death; for he who was highest and most majestic was brought lowest and most truly despised. But the love that made him suffer all this is as much greater than his pain as heaven is above the earth; for the Passion was a deed performed at one particular time through the action of love, but the love has always existed, exists now and will never end. And suddenly I saw, while looking at the same cross, his expression changed into one of bliss. The changing of his expression changed mine, and I was as glad and happy as it was possible to be. Then our Lord made me think happily, 'What is the point of your pain or your sorrow?' And I was very happy.

12

Then our Lord spoke, asking, 'Are you well pleased that I suffered for you?' 'Yes, my good Lord,' I said. 'Thank you, my good Lord, blessed may you be!' 'If you are pleased,' said our Lord, 'I am pleased. It is a joy and a delight and an endless happiness to me that I ever endured suffering for you, for if I could suffer more, I would suffer.' As I became conscious of these words my understanding was lifted up into heaven, and there I saw three heavens, a sight which caused me great amazement, and I thought, 'I saw three heavens, and all of them of the blessed Manhood of Christ;[14] and none is greater, none is lesser, none is higher, none is lower, but they are all equally full of supreme joy.'

For the first heaven Christ showed me his Father, in no bodily likeness, but in his nature and his action. This is how the Father acts: he rewards his son, Jesus Christ. This gift and this reward give Jesus such great joy that his Father could have given no reward that pleased him better. The first heaven, that is the pleasing of the Father, appeared to me like a heaven, and it was full of great joy, for he is greatly pleased with all the deeds he has done to promote our salvation; because of these we do not just belong to Jesus by redemption, but also by his Father's generous gift. We are his joy, we are his reward, we are his glory, we are his crown. What I am describing causes Jesus such great pleasure that he thinks nothing of all his hardship and his bitter suffering and his cruel and shameful death. And in these words, 'If I could suffer more, I would suffer more', I saw truly that if he might die once for each man who shall be saved as he died once for all, love would never let him rest until he had done it. And when he had done it, he would still think nothing of it out of love; for everything seems a trifle to him in comparison with his love. And he showed me this very seriously, saying these words, 'If I could suffer more'. He did not say, 'If it were necessary to suffer more', but 'If I could suffer more'; for if he could suffer more, he would, even if it were not necessary. This deed and this action for our salvation was ordered as well as he could order it, it was done as gloriously as Christ could do it. And here I saw complete joy in Christ, but this joy would not have been as complete if it could have been done any better than it was done.

And in these three sayings, 'It is a joy, a delight and an endless happiness to me', three heavens were shown to me, as follows: by the joy I understood the pleasure of the Father; by the delight, the glory of the Son; and by the endless happiness, the Holy Ghost. The Father is pleased, the Son is glorified, the Holy Ghost rejoices. Jesus wishes us to consider the delight which the Holy Trinity feels in our salvation, and wishes us to delight as much, through his grace, while we are on earth. And this was shown in these words, 'Are you well pleased?' In the other words that Christ spoke, 'If you are pleased, I am pleased', he revealed the meaning, as if he had said, 'It is joy and delight enough to me, and I ask nothing more of you for my hardship but that I give you pleasure.' This was shown to me abundantly and fully. Think hard too about the deep significance of the words 'That I ever endured suffering for you', for in those words was a great sign of love and of the pleasure that he took in our salvation.

13

Very happily and gladly our Lord looked into his side, and gazed, and said these words, 'Look how much I loved you'; as if he had said, 'My child, if you cannot look at my Godhead, see here how I let my side be opened, and my heart be riven in two, and all the blood and water that was within flow out. And this makes me happy, and I want it to make you happy.' Our Lord revealed this to make us glad and joyful.

And with the same mirth and joy he looked down to his right and brought to my mind the place where our Lady was standing during the time of his Passion; and he said, 'Would you like to see her?' And I answered and said, 'Yes, my good Lord, thank you, if it is your will.' I prayed for this repeatedly and I thought I would see her in bodily likeness, but I did not do so. And with these words Jesus showed me a spiritual vision of her; just as I had seen her low and humble before, he now showed her to me high, noble and glorious, and more pleasing to him than any other creature. And so he wants it to be known that all those who rejoice in him should rejoice in her and in the joy that he has in her and she in him. And in these words that Jesus said, 'Would you like to see her?', it seemed to me I had the greatest pleasure that he could have given me, with the spiritual vision of her; for our Lord gave me no special revelation except of our Lady Saint Mary, and he showed her to me three times: the first when she conceived, the second as if she were in her sorrow under the cross and the third as she is now, in delight, honour and joy.

And after this our Lord showed himself to me in even greater glory, it seemed to me, than when I saw him before, and from this revelation I learned that each contemplative soul to whom it is given to look for God and seek him, shall see her and pass on to God through contemplation. And after this friendly and courteous teaching of true and blessed life, our Lord Jesus said to me repeatedly, 'It is I who am highest; it is I you love; it is I who delight you; it is I you serve; it is I you long for; it is I you desire; it is I who am your purpose; it is I who am everything; it is I that Holy Church preaches and teaches you; it is I who showed myself to you before.' I only make these utterances known so that, according to the powers of understanding and loving which are given by the grace of God, everyone may receive them as our Lord intended.

Afterwards, our Lord reminded me of the longing I had had for him;[15] and I saw that nothing kept me from him but sin, and I saw that this is so with all of us. And I thought that if sin had never existed, we should all have been pure and like himself, as God made us; and so I had often wondered before now in my folly why, in his great foreseeing wisdom, God had not prevented sin; for then, I thought, all would have been well. I ought certainly to have abandoned these thoughts, and I grieved and sorrowed over the question in great pride, with no reason or judgement. Nevertheless, Jesus, in this vision, informed me of all that I needed to know. I am not saying that I do not need any more teaching, for our Lord, in this revelation, has left me to Holy Church; and I am hungry and thirsty and needy and sinful and frail, and willingly submit myself to the teaching of Holy Church, with all my fellow Christians, until the end of my life.

He answered with this assurance: 'Sin is befitting.' With this word 'sin' our Lord brought to my mind the whole extent of all that is not good: the shameful scorn and the utter humiliation that he bore for us in this life and in his dying, and all the pains and sufferings of all his creatures, both in body and spirit – for we are all to some extent brought to nothing and should be brought to nothing as our master Jesus was, until we are fully purged: that is to say until our own mortal flesh is brought completely to nothing, and all those of our inward feelings which are not good. He gave me insight into these things, along with all pains that ever were and ever shall be; all this was shown in a flash, and quickly changed into comfort; for our good Lord did not want the soul to be afraid of this ugly sight.

But I did not see sin; for I believe it has no sort of substance nor portion of being, nor could it be recognized were it not for the suffering which it causes. And this suffering seems to me to be something transient, for it purges us and makes us know ourselves and pray for mercy; for the Passion of our Lord supports us against all this, and that is his blessed will for all who shall be saved. He supports us willingly and sweetly, by his words, and says, 'But all shall be well, and all manner of things shall be well.' These words were shown very tenderly, with no suggestion that I or anyone who will be saved was being blamed. It would therefore be very strange to blame or wonder at God because of my sins, since he does not blame me for sinning.

Thus I saw how Christ feels compassion for us because of sin. And just as I was earlier filled with suffering and compassion at the Passion of Christ, so was I now also partly filled with compassion for all my fellow Christians; and then I saw that whenever a man feels kind compassion with love for his fellow Christian, it is Christ within him.

14

But you must apply yourself to this: contemplating these things in general, sad and grieving, in my mind I said to our Lord with great reverence, 'Ah, my good Lord, how could all be well, given the great harm that has been done to humankind by sin?' And here I prayed, as much as I dared, for some clearer explanation to ease my mind over this. And our blessed Lord answered most compassionately and in a very friendly way, and showed me that Adam's sin was the greatest harm that ever was done, or ever shall be, until the end of the world; and he also showed me that this is publicly acknowledged through all Holy Church on earth. Furthermore he taught me that I should consider the glorious atonement; for this atonement is incomparably more pleasing to God and more glorious in saving mankind than Adam's sin was ever harmful.

So what our blessed Lord's teaching means is that we should take heed of the following: 'Since I have turned the greatest possible harm into good, it is my will that you should know from this that I shall turn all lesser evil into good.'

He made me understand two aspects of this. One of them is our Saviour and our salvation; this aspect is blessed and is clear and bright, light and beautiful and abundant, for all men who are or shall be of good will are included in it; we are bidden to it by God, and drawn to it, admonished and taught inwardly by the Holy Ghost and outwardly by Holy Church by the same grace; our Lord wishes our minds to be filled with this, rejoicing in him because he rejoices in us; and the more abundantly we are filled with this, reverently and humbly, the more we deserve his thanks and the more we benefit ourselves, and thus we may say, rejoicing, our Lord is our portion.[16]

The second aspect is closed to us and hidden (that is to say, everything which is not necessary for our salvation); for it is our Lord's privy counsel and it is proper to the royal lordship of God that his privy counsel should be undisturbed,[17] and it is proper for his servants, out of obedience and reverence, not to know his counsel too well. Our Lord feels pity and compassion for us because some people are so anxious to know about it; and I am sure that if we knew how much we would please him and set our own minds at rest by leaving the matter alone, then we would do so. The saints in heaven do not want to know anything except what our Lord wants to reveal to them, and their love and their desires are directed by our Lord's will. We should desire to be like them: then, like the saints, we should wish and desire nothing that is not the will of our Lord; for God's purpose for us all is the same.

And here I was taught that we must rejoice only in our blessed Saviour Jesu and trust in him for everything.

15

And thus our good Lord answered all the questions and doubts I could put forward, saying most comfortingly as follows: 'I will make all things well, I shall make all things well, I may make all things well and I can make all things well; and you shall see for yourself that all things shall be well.' I take 'I may' for the words of the Father, I take 'I can' for the words of the Son and I take 'I will' for the words of the Holy Ghost; and where he says 'I shall', I take it for the unity of the Holy Trinity, three persons in one truth; and where he says, 'You shall see for yourself', I understand it as referring to the union with the Holy Trinity of all mankind who shall be saved. And with these five sayings God wishes to be surrounded by rest and peace; and thus Christ's spiritual thirst comes to an end; for this is the spiritual thirst, the love-longing that lasts and ever shall do until we see that revelation on Judgement Day.

For we that shall be saved, and shall be Christ's joy and his bliss, are still here on earth, and shall be until that last day. Therefore this is the thirst, the incompleteness of his bliss, that he does not have us in himself as wholly as he will have then. All this was shown me as a revelation of compassion, and his thirst will cease on Judgement Day. Thus he has pity and compassion for us, and he has longing to have us, but his wisdom and love do not permit the end to come until the best time.

And thus I understand the five sayings mentioned above – 'I may make all things well', etc. – as a powerful and comforting pledge for all the works of our Lord which are to come; for just as the Holy Trinity made all things from nothing, so the Holy Trinity shall make all well that is not well. It is God's will that we should pay attention to all the deeds he has done, for he wants us to know from them all he will do; and he showed me that when he said, 'And you shall see yourself that all manner of things shall be well.' I understand this in two ways: first, I am well pleased that I do not know it; second, I am glad and happy because I shall know it. It is God's wish that we should know in general terms that all shall be well; but it is not God's wish that we should understand it now, except as much as is suitable for us at the present time, and that is the teaching of Holy Church.

16

God showed me the very great pleasure he takes in men and women who strongly and humbly and eagerly receive the preaching and teaching of Holy Church; for he is Holy Church; he is the foundation, he is the substance, he is the teaching, he is the teacher, he is the goal, he is the prize which every true soul works hard to win; and he is known and shall be known to every soul to whom the Holy Ghost reveals it. And I am sure that all those who are seeking this will succeed, for they are seeking God. All that I have now said, and more that I shall say afterwards, gives strength against sin; for first, when I saw that God does all which is done, I did not see sin, and then I saw that all is well. But when God gave me a revelation about sin, then he said, 'All shall be well.'

And when almighty God had shown his great goodness so fully and abundantly, I requested to know how it would be with a certain person whom I loved. And in this request I stood in my own way, for I was not answered immediately. And then I was answered in my reason as though by a friendly man, 'Take these showings generally, and consider the kindness of your Lord God as he gives them to you; for it honours God more to consider him in all things than in any particular thing.' I assented, and with this I learned that it honours God more to have knowledge of everything in general than to take pleasure in any one thing in particular. And if I were to follow this teaching faithfully I should not rejoice over any one special thing, nor be distressed over anything of any kind, for 'All shall be well.'

God reminded me that I would sin; and because of my pleasure in contemplating him, I was slow to pay attention to that showing. And our Lord very courteously waited till I paid attention; and then our Lord, along with my own sins, reminded me of the sins of all my fellow Christians, in general and not in particular.

17

Although our Lord showed me that I would sin, by me alone I understood everyone. At this I began to feel a quiet fear, and to this our Lord answered me as follows: 'I am keeping you very safe.' This promise was made to me with more love and assurance and spiritual sustenance than I can possibly say, for just as it was previously shown that I would sin, the help was also shown to me: safety and protection for all my fellow Christians. What could make me love my fellow Christians more than to see in God that he loves all who shall be saved as though they were one soul? For just as there is an animal will in our lower nature which can have no good impulses, there is a godly will in our higher nature which, no less than the persons of the Holy Trinity, can will no evil, but only good. And this is what our Lord showed in the completeness of love in which he holds us: yes, that he loves us as much now while we are here as he will do when we are there in his blessed presence.

God also showed me that sin is not shameful to man, but his glory; for in this revelation my understanding was lifted up into heaven; and then there came truly into my mind David, Peter and Paul, Thomas of India and the Magdalene[18] – how they are famous in the Church on earth with their sins as their glory. And it is no shame to them that they have sinned, any more than it is in the bliss of heaven, for there the badge of their sin is changed into glory. In this way our Lord God showed them to me as an example of all others who shall come there.

Sin is the sharpest scourge that any chosen soul can be struck with; it is a scourge which lashes men and women so hard, and batters them and destroys them so completely in their own eyes, that they think they only deserve to sink down into hell. But when the touch of the Holy Ghost brings contrition, it turns the bitterness into hope of God's mercy; and then their wounds begin to heal and the soul begins to revive into the life of Holy Church. The Holy Ghost leads a man on to confession, and he earnestly shows his sins, nakedly and truly, with great sorrow and great shame that he has so befouled the fair image of God. Then, in accordance with the basic teaching which the Church has received from the Holy Ghost, his confessor imposes a penance on him for each sin. By this medicine every sinful soul needs to be healed, especially of sins that are in themselves mortal. Although a man has the scars of healed wounds, when he appears before God they do not deface but ennoble him. And as on the one hand sin is punished here with sorrow and suffering, on the other it shall be rewarded in heaven by the generous love of our Lord God almighty, who does not want the toils and troubles of any who come there to be wasted. The reward we are going to receive there will not be a small one, but great, splendid and glorious. And so all shame will be turned into glory and into greater joy. And I am sure, by what I feel myself, that the more every well-natured soul sees this in the kind and generous love of God, the more loath he is to sin.

18

But if you are moved to say or think, 'Since this is true, then it would be a good idea to sin in order to have the greater reward', beware of this impulse, for it comes from the Enemy, for any soul that chooses to follow this impulse can never be saved until he has been healed of this as if it were a mortal sin. For if there were laid out before me all the sufferings of hell and of purgatory and of earth – death and everything else – and sin, I would choose all those sufferings rather than sin, for sin is so vile and so very hateful that it cannot be compared to any suffering other than the suffering of sin itself. For all things are good but sin, and nothing is wicked but sin. Sin is neither a deed nor a pleasure, but when a soul deliberately chooses to sin (which is punishment in God's eyes), in the end he has nothing at all. That punishment seems to me the hardest hell, for he does not have his God. A soul can have God in all sufferings[19] except sin.

And God is as eager to save man as he is strong and wise; for Christ himself is the foundation of the whole law of Christian men, and he taught us to return good for evil. Here we can see that he himself is love, and he treats us as he wishes us to treat others, for he wants us to be like him in completeness of unending love for ourselves and our fellow Christians. Just as his love for us does not fail because of our sin, he does not want our love for ourselves and our fellow Christians to fail; we must feel naked hatred for sin and unending love for the soul, as God loves it. This assertion of God's is an endless help and comfort, which keeps us very safe.

19

After this our Lord gave a revelation about prayer. I saw two qualities in those who pray, like those I have felt in myself. One is that they do not wish to pray for anything that may be, but only for things which are God's will and his glory. The second thing is that they set themselves strongly and continually to pray for things which are his will and his glory. And that is what I have understood from the teaching of Holy Church. And in this our Lord gave me the same teaching, to have as God's gift faith, hope and love, and hold to them until our lives' end. And so we say 'Pater noster', 'Ave' and the Creed,[20] with devotion, as God may grant. And so we pray for all our fellow Christians, and for all manner of men, according to God's will, for we wish that all manner of men and women were in the same state of virtue and grace that we ought to desire for ourselves. But yet, for all this, often we do not trust God almighty fully for it seems to us that, because of our unworthiness, and because we are feeling absolutely nothing, we cannot be certain that he is hearing our prayers. For often we are as barren and as dry after our prayers as we were before, and so we feel our folly is the cause of our weakness; I have felt like this myself.

And our Lord brought all this suddenly into my mind, strongly and vividly, and, as a comfort to me against this kind of weakness in prayers, he said, 'I am the foundation of your prayers: first it is my will that you should have something, and then I make you desire it, and then I make you pray for it; and if you pray, then how could it be that you should not have what you pray for?' And thus in his first statement, along with the three which follow, our good Lord shows us something immensely helpful. Where he begins by saying, 'If you pray for it', there he reveals the very great joy and unending reward that our prayer will receive from him. And where he says next, 'Then how could it be that you should not have what you pray for?', there he gives a serious rebuke, because we do not trust as strongly as we should.

Thus our Lord wants us both to pray and to trust, for the purpose of the preceding statements is to strengthen us against weakness in our prayers. For it is God's will that we should pray, and he moves us to do so in these preceding words. He wants us to pray with sure trust, for prayer pleases him. Prayer gives man pleasure in himself, and makes him calm and humble, where before he was contentious and troubled. Prayer unites the soul to God; for though the soul is always like God in nature and substance, yet because of sin on man's part, it is often in a state which is unlike God. Prayer makes the soul like God; when the soul wills what God wills, it is then in a state like God, as it is like God in nature. And so God teaches us to pray, and to trust firmly that we shall obtain what we pray for, though everything which is done would be done, even if we never prayed for it. But the love of God is so great that he considers us sharers in his good deed, and therefore he moves us to pray for what it pleases him to do; and for these prayers and for the good will which he grants us, he will reward us and give us an everlasting recompense. And this was shown in these words, 'If you pray for it'. In this statement God revealed to me such great pleasure and so much delight that it seemed as if he was deeply grateful to us for every good deed that we do – and yet it is he who does them – and because we entreat him earnestly to do everything that pleases him; as if he said, 'Then what could please me more than to be entreated earnestly, truly and eagerly to do what I wish to do?' And thus prayer makes accord between God and man's soul, though while man's soul is near to God, there is no need for him to pray, but reverently to contemplate what he says. For during all the time of my showing, I was not moved to pray, but always to have this good in mind for my comfort, that when we see God, we have what we desire, and then we do not need to pray. But when we do not see God, then we need to pray because we lack something, and to make ourselves open to Jesus; for when a soul is tempted, troubled and isolated by distress, then it is time to pray and to make oneself pliable and submissive to God. Unless we are submissive, no kind of prayer can make God bend to us, though his love is always alike; but while man is in a state of sin, he is so enfeebled, so unwise and so unloving, that he can love neither God nor himself.

His worst trouble is blindness, for he cannot see all this. Then the whole love of God almighty, which is ever one, gives him eyes to see himself, and then he supposes that God is angry with him for his sin. And then he is moved to contrition, and by confession and other good deeds to allay God's anger, until he finds rest of soul and ease of conscience. And then it seems to him that God has forgiven his sins, and it is true. And then it seems to the soul that God turns towards it, as though it had been in pain or in prison, saying this: 'I am glad you have come to rest, for I have always loved you, and love you now, and you love me.' And thus with prayers, as I have said before, and with other good works that are customarily taught by Holy Church, is the soul united to God.

20

Before this time I often had a great longing, and desired that as a gift from God I should be delivered from this world and this life, so as to be with my God in bliss where, through his mercy, I hope to be surely for ever. For I often saw the grief which is here and the well-being and bliss which is existence there. And even if there had been no sorrow in this life except for the absence of our Lord, I sometimes thought it more than I could bear, and this made me grieve and earnestly yearn. Then God said to me, to bring me comfort and patience, 'You shall suddenly be taken from all your suffering, from all your pain and from all your woe. And you shall come up above, and you shall have me as your reward, and you shall be filled with joy and with bliss. And you shall have no kind of suffering, no kind of sickness, no kind of displeasure, no unfulfilled desires, but always joy and bliss without end. Why should you fret about suffering for a while, since it is my will and my glory?' And at these words, 'You shall suddenly be taken', I saw how God rewards man for the patience he shows in awaiting God's will in his lifetime, and I saw that man's patience extends throughout the time he has to live, because he does not know the time of his passing. This is a great advantage, for if a man knew his time, he would not have patience over that time. And God wishes that while the soul is in the body it should seem to itself always about to die, for all this life of distress which we have here is only a moment, and when we are suddenly taken from suffering into bliss, then it will be nothing. And this is why our Lord said, 'Why should you fret about suffering for a while, since it is my will and my glory?' It is God's will that we accept his promises and his comfort in as broad and strong a sense as we can take them. And he also wants us to take our waiting and our distress as lightly as we can and to consider them nothing; for the more lightly we take them, the less importance we give them for love, the less we shall suffer from feeling them and the more thanks we shall have for them.

In this blessed revelation I was truly taught that the people who in this life willingly choose God may be sure that they are chosen. Remember this faithfully, for truly it is God's will that we should hope as securely for the bliss of heaven while we are here, as we shall enjoy it securely while we are there. And the more pleasure and joy we take in this security, with reverence and humility, the more it pleases him. For I am sure that if there had been none but I that would be saved, God would have done all that he has done for me. And every soul, knowing how God loves him, should think the same, forgetting if he can all other people, and thinking that God has done for him all that he has done. And it seems to me that this should inspire a soul to love and hold him dear, and fear only him, for he wants us to understand that all the strength of our Enemy is held fast in our Friend's hand. And therefore a soul that knows this truly will fear none but him that he loves, and set all other fears among sufferings and bodily sickness and mental apprehensions.

And therefore if a man is suffering so much pain, so much woe and so much distress, that it seems he can think of nothing but the state he is in and what he is feeling, he should pass over it lightly and set it at nought as soon as he can. And why? Because God wishes to be known. For if we knew him and loved him, we should have patience and be completely at rest, and everything that he does should be pleasing to us. And our Lord revealed this to me in these words: 'Why should you fret about suffering for a while, since it is my will and my

glory?' And that was the end of all that our Lord revealed to me that
day.

21

And after this I soon returned to myself and to my bodily sickness,
understanding that I would live, and like a wretch I tossed and moaned
with the feeling of bodily pain, and I thought it a great weariness that
I should live longer; and I was as barren and dry, through the return
of my pain and my loss of spiritual feeling, as if I had received little
comfort. Then a man belonging to a religious order came to me and
asked me how I was. And I said that I had been delirious today, and
he laughed loud and heartily. And I said, 'The cross which stood at
the foot of my bed, it was bleeding hard.' And as soon as I said this,
the person to whom I was speaking became very serious and marvelled.
And I was immediately very ashamed at my heedlessness, and I thought,
'This man takes my least word seriously, saying nothing in reply.'
And when I saw that he took it so seriously and so reverently, I
became very ashamed, and wanted to be given absolution; but I did
not feel I could tell any priest about it, for I thought, 'How could a
priest believe me? I did not believe our Lord God.' I had truly believed
while I was seeing him, and had then wanted and intended to do so
for ever, but, like a fool, I let it slip from my mind. What a wretch I
was! This was a great sin and very ungrateful, that I, through stupidity,
just because I felt a little bodily pain, should so foolishly lose for the
time being the comfort of all this blessed showing of our Lord God.

Here you can see what I am of myself; but our kind Lord would
not leave me like this. And I lay still till night, trusting in his mercy,
and then I went to sleep. And as soon as I fell asleep it seemed the
Fiend was at my throat, and he tried to strangle me, but he could not.
Then I woke out of my sleep, and I was barely alive. The people who
were with me noticed and bathed my temples, and my heart began
to take comfort. And immediately a little smoke came in through the
door with a great heat and a foul stench. I said, 'Benedicite dominus!

Everything here is on fire!' And I supposed it was a physical fire and would burn us all to death. I asked those who were with me if they smelled any stench. They said no, they smelled none. I said, 'Blessed be God!' for then I knew well it was the Fiend that had come to torment me. And I had recourse at once to all that our Lord had shown me that same day, along with the faith of Holy Church, for I consider both as one, and fled to that as my comfort. And immediately it all vanished completely, and I was brought to a state of great rest and peace without sickness of the body or terrors of the mind.

22

And I was still awake, and then our Lord opened my spiritual eyes and showed me my soul in the middle of my heart. I saw my soul as large as if it were a kingdom; and from the properties that I saw in it, it seemed to me to be a glorious city. In the centre of that city sits our Lord Jesu, true God and true man, glorious, highest Lord; and I saw him dressed imposingly in glory. He sits in the soul, in the very centre, in peace and rest, and he rules and protects heaven and earth and all that is. The Manhood and the Godhead sit at rest, and the Godhead rules and protects without any subordinate or any trouble; and my soul was blissfully filled with the Godhead, which is supreme power, supreme wisdom, supreme goodness. In all eternity Jesus will never leave the position which he takes in our soul; for in us is his most familiar home and his favourite dwelling. This was a ravishing and restful sight, for it is truly so everlastingly. And it is very pleasing to God and extremely helpful to us that we should see this while we are here. And the soul which sees it in this way makes itself like the one seen and unites itself to him in rest and peace. And it was a very great joy and bliss to me that I saw him sitting, for the sight of this sitting gave me certainty that he dwells there eternally. And I knew for certain that it was he who had shown me all that went before. And when I had considered this carefully, our Lord gently revealed words to me, without any voice or opening of his lips, as he had done before, and he said very seriously, 'Know well that what you saw today was no delirium; accept and believe it, and hold to it, and you shall not be overcome.' These last words were said to me to prove with full assurance that it is our Lord Jesu who showed me everything. For just as in the first phrase which our Lord revealed, referring to his blessed Passion – 'By this is the Fiend overcome'[21] – in just the same way he said his last phrase with very great certainty, 'You shall not be overcome.'

And this teaching and true comfort applies without exception to all my fellow Christians, as I said before, and it is God's will that it should be so. And these words, 'You shall not be overcome', were said very loudly and clearly, for security and comfort against all the tribulations that may come. He did not say, 'You shall not be tormented, you shall not be troubled, you shall not be grieved', but he said, 'You shall not be overcome.' God wants us to pay attention to his words and wants our certainty always to be strong, in weal and woe; for he loves and is pleased with us, and so he wishes us to love and be pleased with him and put great trust in him; and all shall be well.

And soon after this it was all over and I saw no more.

23

After this the Fiend came again with his heat and his stench and distressed me greatly, the stench was so vile and so agonizing and the physical heat was terrifying and tormenting. And I also heard a human jabbering as if there were two people, and it seemed to me that both of them were jabbering at once, as if they were having a very tense discussion; and it was all quiet muttering, and I could understand nothing they said. But I thought that all this was to drive me to despair. And I trusted firmly in God and comforted my soul by speaking aloud as I would have done to another person who was distressed like this. I thought that this anxiety could not be compared to any other human anxiety. I set my bodily eyes on the same cross in which I had seen comfort before, and my tongue to speaking of Christ's Passion and reciting the faith of Holy Church, and I fixed my heart on God with all my trust and with all my strength. And I thought to myself, 'You must now be very careful to hold to the faith; if only from now on you could always be so careful to keep yourself from sin, it would be a beneficial and good way of life'; for I truly thought that if I were safe from sin I would be quite safe from all the fiends of hell and enemies of my soul. And so they kept me occupied all that night and in the morning until it was just after sunrise. And then at once they were all gone and passed away, leaving nothing but a stench; and that persisted for a while. And I thought of them with contempt. And thus I was delivered from them by the power of Christ's Passion, for that is how the Fiend is overcome, as Christ said to me before.

Ah, wretched sin! What are you? You are nothing. For I saw that God is all things: I saw nothing of you. And when I saw that God has made all things, I saw nothing of you; and when I saw that God is in all things, I saw nothing of you; and when I saw that God does all things that are done, greater and lesser, I saw nothing of you. And when I saw our Lord Jesu sitting so gloriously in our souls, and loving and liking and ruling and guiding all that he has made, I saw nothing of you. And so I am certain that you are nothing; and all those who love you, and like you, and follow you, and choose you at the end, I am certain that they shall be brought to nothing with you, and endlessly overthrown. God protect us all from you. Amen, for the love of God.

And I will say what vileness is, as I have been taught by the revelation of God. Vileness is all things that are not good: the spiritual blindness which we fall into with our first sin, and all that follows from that vileness: passions and pains of spirit or body, and all that is on earth or in any other place which is not good. And this leads to the question: what are we? And to this I answer: if all that is not good were taken from us, we should be good. When vileness is taken from us, God and the soul are all one, and God and man all one.

What is there on earth which separates us from God? I answer and say: in that it serves us, it is good, and in that it shall perish, it is vile, and for a man to consider it in any other way is sinful. And during the time that a man or woman loves sin, if there are any who do, his suffering is beyond all suffering. And when he does not love sin, but hates it and loves God, all is well. And he who truly does this, though he may sometimes sin through frailty or inexperience, he does not fall, for he will strongly rise again and behold God, whom he loves with all his might. God has made the world to be loved by him or her who is a sinner, but he always loves us, and always longs to have our love. And when we love Jesu strongly and truly, we are at peace.

All the blessed teaching of our Lord God was shown to me in three ways, as I have said before; that is to say, by bodily sight, by words formed in my understanding and by spiritual sight. I have described what I saw with bodily sight as truly as I can; and I have said the words exactly as our Lord revealed them to me; but so far as the spiritual sight is concerned, I have said something about it, but I could never recount it all, and so I am moved to say more if God will give me grace.

24

God showed me that we suffer from two kinds of sickness, of which he wishes us to be cured: one of them is impatience, because we find our trouble and suffering a heavy burden to bear, and the other is despair, or doubtful fear,[22] as I shall explain later. And these two are the ones which most trouble and torment us, according to what our Lord showed me, and the ones it most pleases him if we reform. I am talking of those men and women who for the love of God hate sin and are anxious to do God's will. And these are the two secret sins which threaten us most, so it is God's will that they should be recognized and then we shall reject them as we do other sins.

And our Lord very humbly revealed to me the patience with which he bore his terrible Passion and also the joy and delight which that Passion gave him because of his love. And he showed by his example that we should bear our sufferings gladly and lightly, because that pleases him greatly and benefits us for ever. And we are troubled by them because we do not recognize love. Though the persons of the Holy Trinity are all equal in nature, what was shown me most clearly was that love is nearest to us all.[23] And this is the knowledge of which we are most ignorant; for many men and women believe that God is almighty and has power to do everything, and that he is all wisdom and knows how to do everything, but that he is all love and is willing to do everything – there they stop. And this ignorance is what hinders those who most love God; for when they begin to hate sin, and to mend their ways under the laws of Holy Church, there still remains some fear which moves them to think of themselves and their previous sins. And they take this fear for humility, but it is foul ignorance and weakness. And we cannot despise it, though if we knew it we should immediately despise it, as we do some other sin that we recognize, for it comes from the Enemy, and it is contrary to truth. So, of all the properties of the Holy Trinity, it is God's wish that we should place most reliance on liking and love; for love makes God's power and wisdom very gentle to us; just as through his generosity God forgives our sin when we repent, so he wants us to forget our sin and all our depression and all our doubtful fear.

25

For I saw four kinds of fear. One is fear of attack which suddenly comes to a man through weakness. This fear does good, for it helps to purify, just like bodily sickness or other sufferings which are not sinful; for all such suffering helps if it is endured patiently.

The second fear is that of punishment, whereby someone is stirred and woken from the sleep of sin; for those who are deep in the sleep of sin are for the time being unable to perceive the gentle comfort of the Holy Ghost, until they have experienced this fear of punishment, of bodily death and of spiritual enemies. And this fear moves us to seek the comfort and mercy of God; and this fear serves as an entrance and enables us to be contrite through the blessed teaching of the Holy Ghost.

The third is doubtful fear; for though it may be small in itself, if it were recognized it would be seen as a sort of despair. For I am sure that God hates all doubtful fear, and he wishes us to separate ourselves from it by gaining true knowledge of life.

The fourth is reverent fear; the only fear we can have which pleases God is reverent fear; and it is very sweet and gentle because of the greatness of love. And yet this reverent fear and love are not one and the same. They are two in their nature and their way of working, yet neither of them may be had without the other. Therefore I am certain that those who love also fear, though they may only feel it a little.

Even though they may appear to be holy, all the fears which face us, apart from reverent fear, are not truly so; and this is how we can tell which is which. For reverent fear, the more we have it, the more it softens and comforts and pleases and rests us; and the false fear disquiets, distresses and disturbs. This is the remedy then, to recognize them both and reject the false fear, just as we would a wicked spirit that appeared in the likeness of a good angel. However attractive his company and his behaviour appear to be, he first disquiets and distresses and disturbs the person he speaks with, and hinders him and leaves him thoroughly upset; and the more he has to do with him, the more he disturbs him, and the further he is from peace. Therefore it is God's will and our gain that we should know them apart; for God always wants us to be secure in love, and peaceful and restful, as he is towards us. And in the same way as he is disposed towards us, so he wishes us to be disposed towards ourselves and towards our fellow Christians.   Amen.

Revelations of Divine Love
(THE LONG TEXT)

1

A description of the chapters.

This first chapter lists the series of revelations one by one.

This is a revelation of love that Jesus Christ, our unending joy, gave in sixteen showings or special revelations. The first is of his precious crowning with thorns, and by this was understood and specified the Trinity with the Incarnation and unity between God and the soul of man, with many fair showings of unending wisdom and teaching of love, on which all the showings that follow are founded and in which they are all united. The second is the discolouring of his fair face as a sign of his dear Passion. The third is that our Lord God, almighty wisdom, all love, just as truly as he has made everything that is, so truly he does and brings about all that is done. The fourth is the scourging of his tender body with plentiful shedding of his blood. The fifth is that the Fiend is defeated by the precious Passion of Christ. The sixth is the noble gratitude of our Lord God with which he rewards his blessed servants in heaven. The seventh is frequent experience of joy and sorrow (the feeling of joy is God kindly touching and cheering us, giving us true certainty of everlasting happiness; the feeling of sorrow is temptation caused by the depression and irritations of our bodily lives), all with the spiritual understanding that we are securely protected through love, in joy and sorrow, by the goodness of God. The eighth is Christ's last sufferings and his cruel dying. The ninth is the pleasure taken by the Holy Trinity in the hard agony of Christ and his pitiable dying; in which joy and pleasure he wants us to be comforted and gladdened with him until we come to the fullness of pleasure in heaven. The tenth is our Lord Jesus Christ, lovingly showing his blessed heart, rejoicing

even as it is split in two. The eleventh is a high spiritual showing
of his dear Mother. The twelfth is that our Lord is Being in its
most noble form. The thirteenth is that our Lord wishes us to
consider carefully and admire the splendour of all that he has done
in making all things, and of the excellence of man's making, which
surpasses all his works, and of the precious atonement he made for
our sin, turning all our blame into everlasting glory. And here our
Lord says, 'Behold and see, for by the same mighty wisdom and
goodness I shall make well all that is not well and you shall see
it.' And in this he wants us to trust in the faith and promise of
Holy Church, not wanting to know his secret mysteries now,
except for what rightly concerns us in this life. The fourteenth is
that our Lord is the foundation of our prayers. In this we see two
properties: one of them is true prayer, the other is sure trust, and
he wants both to be abundant; thus our prayers will please him
and in his goodness he will answer them. The fifteenth is that we shall
be immediately taken from all our suffering and from all our sorrow
and, through his goodness, we shall come up above where we shall
have our Lord Jesus as our reward and be filled full of joy and bliss in
heaven. The sixteenth is that the Holy Trinity our Maker lives eternally
in our souls in Christ Jesus our Saviour, gloriously ruling and giving
all things, strongly and wisely saving and protecting us for love, and
we shall not be overcome by our Enemy.

2

Of the time of these revelations, and how she begged for three things.

These revelations were shown to a simple, uneducated[1] creature in
the year of our Lord 1373, on the eighth day of May; she had already
asked God for three gifts: the first was vivid perception of his Passion,
the second was bodily sickness in youth at thirty years of age, the
third was for God to give her three wounds.

As for the first, it seemed to me that I could feel the Passion of

Christ to some extent, but yet I longed by God's grace to feel it more strongly. I thought how I wished I had been there at the crucifixion with Mary Magdalene and with others who were Christ's dear friends, and therefore I longed to be shown him in the flesh so that I might have more knowledge of our Saviour's bodily suffering and of our Lady's fellow-suffering and that of all his true friends who then saw his pain; I wanted to be one of them and suffer with him. I never wished for any other sight or showing of God until my soul left my body. I begged for this so that after the showing I would have a truer perception of Christ's Passion.

The second gift came to me with contrition: I longed eagerly to be on my death-bed, so that I might in that sickness receive all the rites of Holy Church, that I might myself believe I was dying and that everyone who saw me might believe the same, for I wanted no hopes of earthly life. I longed to have in this sickness every kind of suffering both of body and soul that I would experience if I died, with all the terror and turmoil of the fiends,[2] except for actually giving up the ghost. And I thought of this because I wished to be purged by the mercy of God and afterwards to live more to God's glory because of that sickness; and that I should die more quickly, for I longed to be soon with my God. I longed for these two things – the Passion and the sickness – with one reservation, saying, 'Lord, you know what I would have, if it is your will that I should have it; and if it is not your will, good Lord, do not be displeased, for I only want what you want.'

As for the third gift, by the grace of God and the teaching of Holy Church, I conceived a great longing to receive three wounds[3] in my life: that is to say, the wound of true contrition, the wound of kind compassion and the wound of an earnest longing for God. And this last petition was with no reservation.

The first two of the longings just mentioned passed from my mind, and the third stayed with me continually.

3

Of the sickness obtained from God by petition.

And when I was thirty and a half years old, God sent me a bodily sickness in which I lay for three days and three nights; and on the fourth night I received all the rites of Holy Church and did not believe that I would live until morning. And after this I lingered on for two days and two nights. And on the third night I often thought that I was dying, and so did those who were with me. And I thought it was a great pity to die while still young; but this was not because there was anything on earth that I wanted to live for, nor because I feared any suffering, for I trusted God's mercy. I wanted to live so as to love God better and for longer, and therefore know and love him better in the bliss of heaven. For it seemed to me that all the short time I had lived here was as nothing compared with that heavenly bliss. So I thought, 'Good Lord, may my ceasing to live be to your glory!' And I understood, both with my reason and by the bodily pains I felt, that I was dying. And I fully accepted the will of God with all the will of my heart. Thus I endured till day, and by then my body was dead to all sensation from the waist down. Then I felt I wanted to be supported in a sitting position, so that my heart could be more freely at God's disposition, and so that I could think of God while I was still alive.

My parish priest was sent for to be present at my death, and by the time he came my eyes were fixed and I could not speak. He set the cross before my face and said, 'I have brought you the image of your Maker and Saviour. Look upon it and be comforted.' It seemed to me that I was well as I was, for my eyes were looking fixedly upwards into heaven, where I trusted that I was going with God's mercy. But nevertheless I consented to fix my eyes on the face of the crucifix if I could, and so I did, because I thought that I might be able to bear looking straight ahead for longer than I could manage to look upwards. After this my sight began to fail and the room was dark all around me as though it had been night, except for the image of the cross, in which I saw an ordinary, household light – I could not understand how. Everything except the cross was ugly to me, as if crowded with fiends. After this the upper part of my body began to die to such an extent that I had almost no feeling and was short of breath. And then I truly believed that I had died. And at this moment, all my suffering was suddenly taken from me, and I seemed to be as well, especially in the upper part of my body, as ever I was before. I marvelled at this sudden change, for it seemed to me a mysterious work of God, not a natural one. And yet, although I felt comfortable, I still did not expect to live, nor did feeling more comfortable comfort me entirely, for I felt that I would rather have been released from this world.

Then it suddenly occurred to me that I should entreat our Lord graciously to give me the second wound, so that my whole body should be filled with remembrance and feeling of his blessed Passion; for I wanted his pains to be my pains, with compassion, and then longing for God. Yet in this I never asked for a bodily sight or showing of God, but for fellow-suffering, such as a naturally kind soul might feel for our Lord Jesus; he was willing to become a mortal man for love, so I wanted to suffer with him.

4

Here begins the first revelation of the precious crowning of Christ, as listed in the first chapter; and how God fills the heart with the greatest joy; and of his great meekness; and how the sight of Christ's Passion gives sufficient strength against all the temptations of the fiends; and of the great excellency and meekness of the blessed Virgin Mary.

Then I suddenly saw the red blood trickling down from under the crown of thorns, hot and fresh and very plentiful, as though it were the moment of his Passion when the crown of thorns was thrust on to his blessed head, he who was both God and man, the same who suffered for me like that. I believed truly and strongly that it was he himself who showed me this, without any intermediary. And as part of the same showing the Trinity suddenly filled my heart with the greatest joy. And I understood that in heaven it will be like that for ever for those who come there. For the Trinity is God, God is the Trinity; the Trinity is our maker and protector, the Trinity is our dear friend for ever, our everlasting joy and bliss, through our Lord Jesus Christ. And this was shown in the first revelation, and in all of them; for it seems to me that where Jesus is spoken of, the Holy Trinity is to be understood. And I said, 'Benedicite domine!'⁴ Because I meant this with such deep veneration, I said it in a very loud voice; and I was astounded with wonder and admiration that he who is so holy and awe-inspiring was willing to be so familiar with a sinful being living in wretched flesh. I supposed that the time of my temptation had now come, for I thought that God would allow me to be tempted by fiends before I died. With this sight of the blessed Passion, along with the Godhead that I saw in my mind, I knew that I, yes, and every creature living, could have strength to resist all the fiends of hell and all spiritual temptation.

Then he brought our blessed Lady into my mind. I saw her spiritually in bodily likeness, a meek and simple maid, young – little more than a child, of the same bodily form as when she conceived. God also showed me part of the wisdom and truth of her soul, so that I understood with what reverence she beheld her God and Maker, and how reverently she marvelled that he chose to be born of her, a simple creature of his own making. And this wisdom and faithfulness, knowing as she did the greatness of her Maker and the littleness of her who was made, moved her to say very humbly to Gabriel, 'Behold, the handmaid of the Lord.'⁵ With this sight I really understood that she is greater in worthiness and grace than all that God made below her; for, as I see it, nothing that is made is above her, except the blessed Manhood of Christ.

5

How God is everything that is good to us, tenderly enfolding us; and everything
that is made is as nothing compared to almighty God; and how there is no rest
for man until he sets himself and everything else at nought for the love of God.

At the same time, our Lord showed me a spiritual vision of his familiar
love. I saw that for us he is everything that we find good and
comforting. He is our clothing, wrapping us for love, embracing and
enclosing us for tender love, so that he can never leave us, being
himself everything that is good for us, as I understand it.

In this vision he also showed a little thing, the size of a hazel-nut
in the palm of my hand, and it was as round as a ball. I looked at it
with my mind's eye and thought, 'What can this be?' And the answer
came to me, 'It is all that is made.' I wondered how it could last, for
it was so small I thought it might suddenly have disappeared. And the
answer in my mind was, 'It lasts and will last for ever because God
loves it; and everything exists in the same way by the love of God.'
In this little thing I saw three properties: the first is that God made it,
the second is that God loves it, the third is that God cares for it. But
what the maker, the carer and the lover really is to me, I cannot tell;
for until I become one substance with him, I can never have complete
rest or true happiness; that is to say, until I am so bound to him that
there is no created thing between my God and me.

We need to know the littleness of all created beings and to set at
nothing everything that is made in order to love and possess God who
is unmade. This is the reason why we do not feel complete ease in
our hearts and souls: we look here for satisfaction in things which are
so trivial, where there is no rest to be found, and do not know our
God who is almighty, all wise, all good; he is rest itself. God wishes
to be known, and is pleased that we should rest in him; for all that is
below him does nothing to satisfy us; and this is why, until all that is
made seems as nothing, no soul can be at rest. When a soul sets all at
nothing for love, to have him who is everything, then he is able to
receive spiritual rest.

Our Lord God also showed that it gives him very great pleasure when a simple soul comes to him in a bare, plain and familiar way. For, as I understand this showing, it is the natural yearning of the soul touched by the Holy Ghost to say, 'God, of your goodness, give me yourself; you are enough for me, and anything less that I could ask for would not do you full honour. And if I ask anything that is less, I shall always lack something, but in you alone I have everything.' And such words are very dear to the soul and come very close to the will of God and his goodness; for his goodness includes all his creatures and all his blessed works, and surpasses everything endlessly, for he is what has no end. And he has made us only for himself and restored us by his blessed Passion and cares for us with his blessed love. And all this is out of his goodness.

6

How we should pray; of the great and tender love that our Lord has for man's soul; and how he wants us to devote ourselves to knowing and loving him.

This showing was made to teach our souls to be wise and cling to the goodness of God. And at that point our usual way of praying came into my thoughts; how usually, because we do not understand or know about love, we pray indirectly. Then I saw that it really honours God more, and gives more joy, if we ask him to answer our prayers through his own goodness, and cling to it by his grace, with true understanding and loving steadfastness, than if we approach him through all the intermediaries[6] that heart can devise. For all these intermediaries are diminishing, we are not giving God full honour; but his own goodness is everything, there is nothing lacking.

And this is what came into my thoughts at that time: we pray to God by his holy flesh and by his precious blood, his holy Passion, his glorious death and wounds; and all the blessed kindness, the unending life that we have from these is from his goodness. And we pray to him by the love of the sweet Mother who bore him, and all the help we have from her is from his goodness. And we pray by the holy cross upon which he died, and all the strength and help we gain from the cross is from his goodness. And in the same way, all the help that is given to us by special saints and by all the blessed company of heaven, the precious love and unending friendship that we receive from them, we receive from his goodness. For in his goodness, God has ordained a great many excellent means to help us, of which the chief and principal one is the blessed Humanity which he took from the Virgin, with all the means which went before and come afterwards which belong to our redemption and our eternal salvation. Therefore it pleases him that we should seek and worship him in these intermediate ways while understanding and knowing that he is the goodness of all; for the goodness of God is the highest object of prayer and it reaches down to our lowest need. It quickens our soul and gives it life, and makes it grow in grace and virtue. It is nearest in nature and readiest in grace; for it is the same grace which the soul seeks and always will seek until we truly know him who has enclosed us in himself; for he does not despise what he has made, nor does he disdain to serve us in the simplest task that belongs by nature to our bodies, through love of the soul which he has made in his own likeness; for as the body is clad in the cloth, and the flesh in the skin, and the bones in the flesh, and the heart in the chest, so are we, soul and body, clad in the goodness of God and enclosed in it; yes, and more inwardly, because all these may waste and wear away, but God's goodness is always strong, and incomparably near to us; for truly our loving God wants our souls to cling to him with all their might, and wants us to cling to his goodness for ever. For of everything the heart could devise, this is what most pleases God and most readily benefits us; for our soul is so specially loved by him that is highest that it surpasses the knowledge of all beings – that is to say that there is no being made that can know how much and how sweetly and how tenderly our Maker loves us.

And therefore with his grace and his help we may stand and gaze at him in the spirit, with unending amazement at this high, surpassing, inestimable love that almighty God has for us in his goodness. And therefore we may reverently ask our loving friend whatever we wish; for our natural wish is to have God, and God's good wish is to have us. And we can never stop wishing or longing until we fully and joyfully possess him, and then we shall wish for nothing more; for he wants us to be absorbed in knowing and loving him until the time when we reach fulfilment in heaven.

And that is why this lesson of love was shown, with all that follows, as you will see; for the strength and the foundation of everything was shown in the first vision; for of all else, beholding and loving our Maker makes the soul see itself as most puny, and most fills it with reverent awe and true meekness, with abundance of love for its fellow Christians.

7

How our Lady, seeing the greatness of her Maker, thought herself the lowliest; and of the great drops of blood running from beneath the crown of thorns; and how what is most joyful to man is that God, the highest and the mightiest, is also the holiest and the most generous.

And to teach us this, as I understand it, our Lord God showed our Lady Saint Mary at the same time; that is to say he showed her deep wisdom and faith as she beheld her Maker so great, so high, so strong and so good. Seeing the greatness and the nobility of God filled her with reverent awe, and she saw herself so small and so low, so simple and so poor in comparison with her Lord God, that this reverent awe made her feel very humble. And so this formed the foundation, from this she was filled with grace and every kind of virtue, surpassing any other created being.

And all the time that God was showing in spiritual sight what I have just described, the bodily sight of the plentiful bleeding from Christ's head remained. The great drops fell down from under the crown of thorns like pills,[7] as though they had come out of the veins; and as they came out they were dark red, for the blood was very thick; and as it spread it was bright red; and when it reached the brows it vanished, and yet the bleeding continued until many things were seen and understood. The beauty and vividness of the blood are like nothing but itself. It is as plentiful as the drops of water which fall from the eaves[8] after a heavy shower of rain, drops which fall so thickly that no human mind can number them. As for the roundness of the drops, they were like herring scales as they spread on the forehead. These three things occurred to me at the time: pills for roundness as the blood came out; herring scales as it spread on the forehead, for roundness; drops from the eaves, for innumerable plenty. This showing was alive and vivid, horrifying and awe-inspiring, sweet and lovely. And what comforted me most in the vision was that our God and Lord, who is so holy and awe-inspiring, is also so familiar and courteous. And this was what gave me most happiness and the strongest sense of spiritual safety. And to make this easier to understand he gave me this clear example: a majestic king or a great lord can show most respect for a poor servant if he treats him in a familiar way, especially if he does so personally, with real sincerity and a cheerful expression, both in private and in public. Then this poor man thinks, 'Ah! How could this noble lord give me more respect or more pleasure than by treating me, who am so humble, with this marvellous friendliness? In truth, it gives me more joy and pleasure than if he gave me great gifts and behaved in a cold and distant manner.' This human example was so powerfully shown, that a man's heart could be ravished and he could be beside himself with joy at this great friendliness. This is the way that our Lord Jesus treats us; for truly, it seems to me that it is the greatest possible joy that he who is highest and mightiest, noblest and worthiest, is also the lowest and humblest, the most kind and friendly. And truly and certainly this marvellous joy will be made known to all of us when we see him. And this is what our Lord wants us to long for and believe, to rejoice and take pleasure in, to receive comfort and support from, as much as we can, until the time when we can see it for ourselves; for it seems to me that the greatest fullness of joy that we shall have is the marvellous courtesy and intimacy of the Father who made us, through our Lord Jesus Christ who is our brother and saviour. But no man can know this marvellous intimacy during his life here on earth, unless he has a special showing from our Lord, or he is inwardly filled with plentiful grace by the Holy Ghost. But faith and trust with love deserve the reward, and so it is gained through grace; for our life is grounded in faith and hope with love.

The showing, made to whomever God may choose, plainly teaches the same thing as our faith,[9] revealed and explained with many secret details which belong to it and which it is glorious to know. And when the showing, which is given at a moment in time, is hidden and past, then the faith lasts by the grace of the Holy Ghost until our life's end. And thus what the showing reveals is nothing other than the faith, neither more nor less, as may be seen from the meaning our Lord conveys in it by the time it is completed.

8

A recapitulation of what has been said, and how it was shown to her and meant for everybody.

And as long as I could see this sight of the plentiful bleeding from Christ's head I could never stop saying these words, 'Benedicite domine!' From this showing I understood six things: the first is the signs of Christ's blessed Passion and the plentiful shedding of his precious blood; the second is the Maiden who is his beloved mother; the third is the blessed Godhead that ever was, is and ever shall be, almighty, all wisdom, all love. The fourth is all that he has made; for I know well that heaven and earth and all that is made is vast and wide, fair and good, but it looked so small to me because I saw it in the presence of him that is Maker of all things; to a soul that sees the Maker of all, all that is made seems very small. The fifth thing I understood is that he made everything for love; the same love sustains everything, and shall do so for ever; the sixth is that God is everything that is good, it seems to me, and the goodness that is in everything is God. And all these our Lord showed me in the first vision, with time and space to contemplate it. And when the bodily vision stopped, the spiritual vision remained in my understanding. And I waited with reverent fear, rejoicing in what I saw. And as far as I dared, I longed to see more if it was his will, or else to see the same vision for longer.

In all this I was much moved with love for my fellow Christians, wishing that they might see and know what I was seeing; I wanted it to comfort them, for the vision was shown for everyone. Then I said to those who were around me, 'For me, today is the Day of Judgement.' And I said this because I thought I was dying; for on the day that a man dies, he receives his eternal judgement, as I understand it. I said this because I wanted them to love God better, to remind them that life is short, as they might see by my example; for all this time I thought I was dying, and this made me feel wonder – and some sorrow, for I thought this vision was shown for those who were going to live. And what I say of myself, I am saying on behalf of all my fellow Christians, for I was taught in the spiritual showing of our Lord God that this is his purpose; and therefore I beg you all for God's sake and advise you for your own advantage that you stop paying attention to the poor being to whom this vision was shown, and eagerly, attentively and humbly contemplate God, who in his gracious love and eternal goodness wanted the vision to be generally known to comfort us all; for it is God's will that you should receive it with joy and pleasure as great as if Jesus had shown it to you all.

9

Of the humility of this woman, which always keeps her in the faith of Holy Church; and how he who loves his fellow Christian for the sake of God, loves everything.

I am not good because of the showing unless I love God better; and if you love God better, it is meant more for you than for me. I am not saying this to the wise, for they know it well; but I am saying it to those of you who are ignorant, to support and comfort you: we all need support. Indeed I was not shown that God loved me better than the lowest soul that is in a state of grace, for I am sure that there are many who never had a showing or vision, but only the normal teaching of Holy Church, and who love God better than I do. For if I look solely at myself, I am really nothing; but as one of mankind in general, I am, I hope, in oneness of love with all my fellow Christians; for upon this oneness depends the life of all who shall be saved; for God is all that is good, as I see it, and God has made all that is made, and God loves all that he has made, and he who loves all his fellow Christians for God's sake, loves all that is; for in those who shall be saved, all is included: that is to say, all that is made and the Maker of all; for in man is God, and God is in everything. And I hope by the grace of God that he who looks at it in this way will be truly taught and greatly comforted if he needs comfort. I speak of those who will be saved, for at this time God showed me no others.

But I believe everything that Holy Church believes, preaches and teaches; for the faith of Holy Church which I had understood beforehand, and, I hope, by the grace of God, gladly followed and kept in my daily life, was continually before me, and I never wished or intended to receive anything which might be at variance with it. And with this intention I considered the showing as carefully as possible; and I saw it to be as one with the Church's teaching as God intended.

All this was shown in three ways: that is to say, by bodily sight, and by words formed in my understanding, and by spiritual sight. But I neither can nor may show the spiritual vision as openly or as fully as I would like to. But I trust that our Lord God almighty will out of his own goodness and love for you make you receive it more spiritually and more sweetly than I can or may tell it.

10

The second revelation is of the discolouring of Christ's face, of our redemption, and the discolouring of the vernicle;[10] *and how God wants us to seek him eagerly, resting in him steadfastly and trusting him greatly.*

And after this I saw with my bodily sight in the face of Christ on the crucifix which hung before me, which I was looking at continuously, a part of his Passion: contempt and spitting, dirt and blows, and many lingering pains, more than I can tell, and frequent changes of colour. And once I saw how half his face, beginning at the ear, was covered in dry blood until it reached the middle of his face, and after that the other half was covered in the same way, and meanwhile the first part was as before. I saw this bodily, in distress and darkness, and I wished for better bodily sight to see it more clearly. And I was answered in my reason, 'If God wants to show you more, he will be your light. You need no light but him.' For I saw him and sought him; for we are now so blind and so unwise that we never seek God until out of his goodness he shows himself to us, and if he graciously lets us see something of himself, then we are moved by the same grace to seek with a great longing to see him more fully; and thus I saw him and I sought him, I had him and I wanted him. And it seems to me that this is, or should be, our usual way of proceeding.

At one moment my consciousness was taken down on to the sea bed, and there I saw green hills and valleys, looking as though they were covered in moss, with seaweed and sand.[11] Then I understood this: that if a man or a woman were under the wide waters, if he could see God (and God is constantly with us) he would be safe, body and soul, and be unharmed, and furthermore, he would have more joy and comfort than words can say. For God wants us to believe that we can see him constantly, even though we think we see very little of him, and if we believe this he makes us grow in grace continually; for he wants to be seen and he wants to be sought; he wants to be waited for and he wants to be trusted.

This second showing was so humble and so small and so simple that my spirits were greatly troubled as I saw it, grieving and fearing and longing; and I doubted for some time whether it was a showing. And then several times our good Lord let me see more clearly so that I truly understood that it was indeed a showing. It was the form and likeness of the foul, dead covering which our fair, bright, blessed Lord bore when he took on human flesh for our sins. It made me think of the holy vernicle at Rome, on which he printed his own sacred face during his cruel Passion, willingly going to his death, and often changing colour. Many marvel how it may be, the brownness and blackness, the pitifulness and the leanness of this image, considering that he printed it with his sacred face, which is the fairness of heaven, the flower of earth and fruit of the Virgin's womb. Then how could this image be so discoloured and so far from fair? I would like to say how, by the grace of God, I understand this. We know through our faith, and believe by the preaching and teaching of Holy Church, that the Holy Trinity made mankind in his image and in his likeness. In the same way we know that when man fell so deeply and so wretchedly through sin, the only help through whom man could be restored was he who made man. And he who made man for love, by that same love would restore man to the same blessed state, or to one more blessed. And just as we were made like the Trinity when we were first made, our Maker wanted us to be like Jesus Christ our Saviour, in heaven without end, by the miracle of our remaking. Then between these two he wanted, loving and honouring man, to make himself as much like man in this mortal life, in our vileness and our wretchedness, as a man without guilt might be. So this means what was said before: it was the image and likeness of our vile, black, mortal covering which hid our fair, bright, blessed Lord.

But I can boldly say with great confidence, and we ought to believe, that never was man so fair as he until the time his fair colour was changed by his trouble and sorrow and his suffering and final agony. This is spoken of in the eighth revelation, where more is said about the same image. And when I mentioned the vernicle in Rome, I mean that it moves with various changes of colour and expression, sometimes looking more cheerful and animated, sometimes more wretched and deathly, as may be seen in the eighth revelation.

And this vision instructed my understanding that it pleases God a great deal if the soul never ceases to search; for the soul can do no more than seek, suffer and trust, and souls that do this are moved by the Holy Ghost; and the splendour of having found God comes by his special grace when it is his will. Seeking with faith, hope and love pleases our Lord, and finding pleases the soul and fills it with joy. And thus my understanding was taught that seeking is as good as finding for the time that our soul is allowed to labour. It is God's wish that we seek to behold him, for then he will graciously show himself to us when he wills. And God himself will teach how a soul may behold him, and that most honours him and benefits you, leading you to receive the greatest humility and strength by means of the grace and guidance of the Holy Ghost; for if a soul attaches itself solely to God with true trust, either by seeking him or by beholding him, it is honouring him as much as possible, it seems to me.

There are two actions that may be seen in this vision: one is seeking, the other is beholding. The seeking is within everyone's reach; everyone *may* have it by God's grace, and *ought* to have it by the Church's wisdom and teaching. It is God's wish that we should observe three things in our seeking: the first is that our search should be committed and diligent, with no laziness, as it may be through his grace, glad and cheerful without unreasonable depression and unprofitable misery. The second is that for his love we await him steadfastly, without grumbling and struggling against him, until our life's end, for life lasts only a short while. The third is that we should trust him utterly with sure and certain faith, for that is what he wishes. We know that he will appear suddenly and joyfully to all those that love him; for he works secretly, and he wishes to be perceived, and his appearance will be very sudden; and he wants us to trust him, for he is most kind and approachable – blessed may he be!

11

The third revelation, how God does everything except sin, never changing his eternal purpose, for he has made everything in the perfection of excellence.

And after this I saw God in an instant,[12] that is to say, in my understanding, and in seeing this I saw that he is in everything. I looked attentively, seeing and recognizing what I observed with quiet awe, and I thought, 'What is sin?' For I saw truly that God does everything, no matter how small. And I saw that truly nothing happens by accident or luck, but everything by God's wise providence. If it seems to be accident or luck from our point of view, our blindness and lack of foreknowledge is the cause; for matters that have been in God's foreseeing wisdom since before time began (and which he righteously and gloriously and continually brings to the best conclusion as they happen) befall us suddenly, all unawares; and so in our blindness and ignorance we say that this is accident or luck, but to our Lord God it is not so. Therefore I was obliged to accept that everything which is done is well done, because our Lord God does everything; for in that instant the actions of human beings were not shown, but only those of God within human beings; for he is in the centre of everything and he does everything, and I was sure he never sins. And here I saw that sin is really not something which is done, for in all this vision no sin appeared. So I marvelled no longer about this but looked at our Lord to see what he would show. And thus, so far as was possible at that time, the righteousness of God's actions was shown to the soul. Righteousness has two admirable properties: it is just and it is complete[13] (and so are all the works of our Lord God), and it does not need the intervention of either mercy or grace, for it is completely righteous, and lacks nothing. (At another time God gave me a vision of naked sin, as I shall recount later,[14] revealing his use of the operation of mercy and grace.)

And this vision was shown to my understanding because our Lord wants the soul to be moved to consider himself and all his works taken together; for they are wholly good, and all his actions are sweet and comforting and bring great comfort to the soul that turns from considering the blind judgement of man to the fair, sweet judgement of our Lord God; for a man considers some deeds well done and some deeds evil, but our Lord does not consider them in the same way; for as everything which naturally exists is of God's making, so everything which is appropriately done is of God's doing; for it is easy to understand that the best deed is well done; and the lowest deed is done as well as the best and the highest; and all are done appropriately and in the order that our Lord has ordained since before time began, for there is no doer but he. I saw quite certainly that he never changes his purpose in anything, nor ever will, for ever; for nothing has been unknown to him in his just ordinances since before time began, and therefore everything was set in the order in which it would remain for ever before anything was made; and nothing of any kind will fail to conform to this; for he made everything in the perfection of excellence; and therefore the Holy Trinity is always satisfied with all his works.

And God showed all this most gloriously, with this meaning, 'See that I am God. See that I am in everything. See that I do everything. See that I have never stopped ordering my works, nor ever shall, eternally. See that I lead everything on to the conclusion I ordained for it before time began, by the same power, wisdom and love with which I made it. How can anything be amiss?' Thus powerfully, wisely and lovingly was the soul tested in this vision. Then I saw truly that I must comply with great reverence, rejoicing in God.

12

The fourth revelation — how it pleases God better to wash us from sin in his blood rather than in water, for his blood is most precious.

And after this I saw, as I watched, the body of Christ bleeding abundantly, in weals from the scourging. It looked like this: the fair skin was very deeply broken, down into the tender flesh, sharply slashed all over the dear body; the hot blood ran out so abundantly that no skin or wound could be seen, it seemed to be all blood. And when it reached the point where it should have overflowed, it vanished; nevertheless, the bleeding continued for a while so that it could be observed attentively. And it looked so abundant to me that I thought if at that moment it had been real, natural blood, the whole bed would have been blood-soaked and even the floor around.

And then it came to me that God has provided us on earth with abundant water for our use and bodily refreshment, because of the tender love he has for us, yet it pleases him better that we should simply take his holy blood to wash away our sins; for there is no liquid created which he likes to give us so much; it is as plentiful as it is precious by virtue of his holy Godhead. And it shares our nature and pours over and transports us by virtue of his precious love. The beloved blood of our Lord Jesus Christ is as truly precious as it is truly plentiful. Behold and see. The precious plenty of his beloved blood descended into hell and burst their bonds and freed all who were there who belonged to the court of heaven. The precious plenty of his beloved blood overflows the whole earth and is ready to wash away the sins of all people of good will who are, have been or will be. The precious plenty of his beloved blood ascended into heaven to the blessed body of our Lord Jesus Christ, and there in him it bleeds and intercedes for us with the Father – and this shall be as long as there is need. And it flows throughout the heavens for ever, rejoicing in the salvation of all mankind who are there and shall be there, and making up the number that is lacking.

13

The fifth revelation is that the temptation of the Fiend is overcome by the Passion of Christ, to increase our joy and the Fiend's sorrow, eternally.

And afterwards, before God revealed any words, he allowed me to contemplate him for a sufficient time, and all that I had seen, and all the significance which was in it as far as my simple soul might grasp it. Then he, without any voice or opening of his lips, formed these words in my soul: 'By this is the Fiend overcome.' Our Lord said these words meaning overcome by his blessed Passion, as he had shown it earlier. Now our Lord was revealing how with his Passion he defeats the Devil. God showed that the Fiend is still as wicked as he was before the Incarnation and works as hard, but he continually sees that all those to whom salvation is due escape him gloriously through the power of Christ's dear Passion, and that grieves and humiliates him severely; for everything that God allows him to do turns into joy for us and into shame and vexation for him. And he feels as much sorrow when God allows him to work as when he does not work; and that is because he may never do as much evil as he would wish, for God holds all the Devil's power in his own hand.

But it seems to me that there can be no anger in God, for our good Lord is always thinking of his own glory and the good of all who shall be saved. With power and justice he stands up against the reprobates who out of wickedness and malignity work hard to plot and act against God's will. I also saw our Lord scorn the Fiend's wickedness and despise his lack of power, and he wants us to do the same. At this revelation I laughed heartily and that made those who were around me laugh too, and their laughter pleased me. I wished that all my fellow Christians had seen what I saw and then they would all have laughed with me. But I did not see Christ laughing; yet I understood that we may laugh to cheer ourselves and to rejoice in God because the Fiend has been conquered. And when I saw him scorn the Devil's wickedness, it was because my understanding was led within God; that is to say, I received an inward showing of truth, without any change of his outward expression; and it seems to me to be a noble quality of God that he is unchanging.

And after this I became grave, and said, 'I can see three things: delight, scorn and seriousness. I see delight that the Fiend is defeated; I see scorn because God scorns him and he shall be scorned; and I see seriousness because he is defeated by the blessed Passion and death of our Lord Jesus Christ which took place in all seriousness and with weary hardship.' When I said, 'He is scorned', I mean that God scorns the Devil, which is to say that he sees him now as he will do for ever;

for here God showed that the Fiend is damned. And this is what I meant when I said, 'He shall be scorned': I meant by the great body of people who will be saved on Judgement Day, whose consolation he greatly envies; for then he will see that all the sorrow and suffering which he has caused them will be turned into eternal heightening of their joy; and all the sorrow and suffering he would have liked to bring them will go with him eternally to hell.

14

The sixth revelation is of the glorious gratitude with which God rewards his servants; and it has three joys.

After this our good Lord said, 'I thank you for your suffering, especially in your youth.' And at that my understanding was lifted up into heaven where I saw our Lord as a lord in his own house who has invited all his beloved servants and friends to a solemn feast. Then I saw the Lord take no seat in his own house, but I saw him reign royally there, and fill it with joy and delight, himself gladdening and comforting his beloved friends familiarly and courteously, with a marvellous melody of endless love in his own fair, blessed face; the glorious face of the Godhead which fills heaven full of joy and bliss.

God showed three degrees of bliss which every soul who has willingly served God shall have in heaven, whatever his degree on earth. The first is the glorious gratitude of our Lord God which he will receive when he is freed from his sufferings; the gratitude is so exalted and so glorious that it would seem to fill the soul, even if there were nothing more; for I thought that all the pain and trouble that could be suffered by all living men might not deserve the glorious gratitude which one man shall have who has willingly served God. The second degree is that all the blessed beings who are in heaven will see that glorious gratitude, and all heaven will know about his service. And then this example was shown: it is a great honour to a king's servants if he thanks them; and if he makes it known to the whole realm, then the honour is greatly increased. The third degree is that this pleasure will for ever seem as new and delightful as it did when it was first felt. And I saw that this was revealed in a sweet and simple way: every man's age shall be known in heaven, and he will be rewarded for his willing service and for the time he has served; and more especially the age of those who willingly and freely offered their youth to God is surpassingly rewarded and they are wonderfully thanked; for I saw that whenever a man or woman has turned truly to God, even for one day's service with the wish to serve for ever, he shall have all these three degrees of bliss.

And the more the loving soul sees this generosity in God, the gladder he is to serve him all the days of his life.

15

The seventh revelation is about frequent feelings of joy and sorrow; and how it is expedient for man sometimes to be left without comfort, even when he has not sinned.

And God's next showing was a supreme spiritual pleasure in my soul. I was filled with eternal certainty, strongly sustained, and without any tormenting fear. This feeling was so joyful and so inward that I felt completely peaceful and at rest, as though there were nothing on earth that could hurt me. This only lasted for a while, and then my feeling was reversed and I was left to myself, oppressed, weary of my life, and so disgusted with myself that I could hardly bear to live. There was no comfort or ease for me but faith, hope and love, and these I had in reality, but I could not feel them in my heart. And immediately after this, our blessed Lord again gave me the spiritual rest and comfort, with certainty and pleasure so joyful and so powerful that no fear, no sorrow, no bodily pain that one might suffer could have distressed me. And then the sorrow was revealed to my consciousness again, and first one, then the other, several times, I suppose about twenty times. And in the moments of joy I might have said with Saint

Paul, 'Nothing shall separate me from the love of Christ.' And in the moments of sorrow I might have said with Peter, 'Lord save me, I perish.'[15]

This vision was shown to me, as I understand it, because it is helpful for some souls to have such experiences, sometimes to be strengthened, sometimes to falter and be left by themselves. God wishes us to know that he safely protects us in both sorrow and joy equally. And to benefit his soul, a man is sometimes left to himself, though not always because of sin; for at this time the changes were so sudden that I could not have deserved by sinning to be left alone. Neither did I deserve the feeling of bliss. But our Lord gives generously when he so wishes and sometimes allows us sorrow; and both come from the same love. So it is God's will that we should hold on to gladness with all our might, for bliss lasts eternally, and pain passes and shall vanish completely for those who are saved. And therefore it is not God's will that we should be guided by feelings of pain, grieving and mourning over them, but should quickly pass beyond them and remain in eternal joy.

16

The eighth revelation is of the pitiful agony of the dying Christ, and of the discolouring of his face and the drying of his flesh.

After this Christ showed the part of his Passion when he was near death. I saw his dear face as it was then, dry and bloodless with the pallor of death; and then it went more ashen, deathly and exhausted, and, still nearer to death, it went blue, then darker blue, as the flesh mortified more completely; for his sufferings were most distinct to me in his blessed face, and especially in his lips; there I saw these four colours, though before they appeared to me fresh, red-tinted and lovely. It was a sorrowful change to see this extreme mortification, and, as it appeared to me, the nose shrivelled and dried, and the dear body was dark and black, quite transformed from his own fair living

colour into parched mortification; for at the time when our Lord and
blessed Saviour was dying on the cross it seemed to me that there was
a bitter, dry wind and it was wonderfully cold; and it was shown that
while all the precious blood that could bleed from the dear body had
done so, there yet remained some moisture in Christ's dear flesh. Loss
of blood and pain drying him from within, and blasts of wind and
cold coming from without, met together in the dear body of Christ.
And these four, two without and two within, gradually dried the flesh
of Christ as time passed. And though this pain was bitter and sharp,
it seemed to me that it lasted a very long time, and painfully dried up
all the vitality of Christ's flesh. So I saw Christ's dear flesh dying,
seemingly bit by bit, drying up with amazing agony. And as long as
there was any vital spirit in Christ's flesh, so long did he suffer pain.
This long agony made it seem to me that he had been dead for a full
week – dying, on the point of passing away, suffering the final throes
of death. And when I say that it seemed to me as though he had been
dead for a full week, it means that the dear body was as discoloured,
as dry, as withered, as deathly and as pitiful as if he had been dead a
full week, yet dying continually. And I thought that the dying of
Christ's flesh was the greatest agony, and the last, of his Passion.

17

*Of Christ's grievous bodily thirst, caused in four ways; and of his pitiful
crowning; and of the greatest pain to a loving friend.*

And in this dying the words of Christ were brought to my mind: 'I
thirst';[16] and I saw in Christ a double thirst, one bodily, the other a
spiritual one which I shall speak of in the thirty-first chapter; for in
these words was revealed to me the bodily thirst which I understood
was caused by the loss of moisture, for the blessed flesh and bones
were left altogether without blood and moisture. The blessed body
was abandoned and drying for a long time, becoming distorted because
of the nails and its own weight; for I understood that because the dear

hands and the dear feet were so tender, the great size, hardness and grievousness of the nails made the wounds become wider, and the body sagged with its own weight from hanging for such a long time. And the piercing and twisting of the head, bound with the crown of thorns and all baked with dry blood, with the dear hair and the dry flesh clinging to the thorns, and the thorns to the dying flesh; and at first, while the flesh was fresh and bleeding, the continuous grip of the thorns made the wounds wide. And furthermore I saw that the dear skin and the tender flesh, with the hair and the blood, was all raised and loosened from the bone by the thorns where it was slashed through[17] in many pieces, like a sagging cloth, as if it would soon have fallen off, it was so heavy and loose while it still had its natural moisture; and that caused me great sorrow and fear, for I thought I would not for my life have seen it fall off. How this was done I did not see, but understood that it was with the sharp thorns and the rough and grievous way the crown was pressed on to his head, mercilessly and without pity.

This continued for a while and soon it began to change, and I watched and marvelled how it might be. And then I saw that it was because it began to dry, and to lose some of its weight and congeal about the garland of thorns. And so it surrounded his head, like one garland upon another. The garland of thorns was dyed with the blood, and the other garland of wounds, and the head, all was one colour, like dry, clotted blood. Where the skin of the flesh of his face and body appeared, it was fine and wrinkled, with a tanned colour, like a dry board when it has been scorched; and the face darker than the body. I saw four ways in which it had been dried up: the first was loss of blood; the second was the torment which then followed; the third, being hung in the air, as a cloth is hung to dry; the fourth, that his bodily nature needed liquid, and he was given no kind of help in all his grief and pain. Ah! His pain was hard and grievous, but it was much more hard and grievous when the moisture was exhausted and everything began to dry and shrink. The pains that were revealed in the blessed head were these: the first done to the dying body while it was moist; and the second a slow pain as the body dried and shrank with the blowing of the wind from without that dried him more, and tormented him with cold as much as I could imagine, and other torments, from which I saw that everything I could say would be quite inadequate, for they were indescribable.

This showing of Christ's pain filled me with pain, though I knew well he only suffered once, yet he wanted to show it to me and fill me with awareness of it as I had wished previously. And in all this time of Christ's pain the only pain I felt was for the pain of Christ. Then I thought to myself, 'I little knew what pain it was that I asked for', and repented like a wretch, thinking that if I had known what it would be like, I would have been loath to pray for it; for I thought that it was worse than bodily death, my pain. I thought, 'Is any pain like this?', and I was answered in my reason, 'Hell is another pain, for there is despair. But of all the pains which lead to salvation, this is the greatest pain: to see your love suffer.' How could any pain be greater to me than to see him who is my whole life, all my bliss and all my joy, suffering? Here I truly felt that I loved Christ so much more than myself that there was no pain that could be suffered comparable to the sorrow I felt to see him in pain.

18

Of the spiritual martyrdom of our Lady and other lovers of Christ; and how everything suffered with him, good and bad.

Here I saw part of the compassion of our Lady Saint Mary, for Christ and she were so united in love that the greatness of her love for him caused the intensity of her pain; in this I saw the essential character of the love, natural but maintained by grace, which all creation has for him; this natural love was shown in his dear Mother most abundantly, and indeed supremely, for just as her love for him surpassed that of anyone else, so did her suffering for him; for the higher, the stronger, the dearer that love is, the greater the sorrow that the lover feels to see the beloved body in pain. And all his disciples, and all those who truly loved him, suffered greater pain than they would for their own bodily death; for I am certain, from my own feelings, that the humblest of them loved him so much better than themselves, that it goes beyond all that I can say.

Here I saw a great union between Christ and us, as I understand it; for when he was in pain, we were in pain. And all creatures who were capable of suffering, suffered with him, that is to say, all the creatures that God has made to serve us. At the time of Christ's dying, the firmament and the earth failed for sorrow, each according to their nature. For it is their natural property to recognize as their God him in whom all their natural power is grounded; when he failed then by their very natures they had as far as possible to fail with him from sorrow at his pain. And so those who were his friends suffered pain from love. And everyone without exception – that is to say even those who did not know him – suffered from a failure of all comfort except the strong and mysterious care of God. I am thinking of two sorts of people, who can be represented by the example of two men: one was Pontius Pilate, the other was Saint Denis of France,[18] who at that time was a pagan; for when he saw the marvellous sorrows and terrors which happened at that time, he said, 'Either the world is coming to an end, or else he who made all nature is suffering.' Therefore he had this written on an altar: 'This is the altar of the unknown God.'[19] God in his goodness makes the planets and the elements function according to their nature both for the blessed and for the damned, but at that time this goodness was withdrawn from both. And that is how it was that people who did not know him were sorrowful at that time.

Thus was our Lord Jesus brought low for us, and we are all brought low like him; and so we shall remain until we come to his bliss, as I shall explain later.

19

Of the comforting contemplation of the crucifix; and how desire of the flesh without consent of the soul is no sin; and man's flesh must be in pain and suffer until both flesh and spirit are united in Christ.

At this point I wanted to look up from the cross, but I dared not, for I well knew that while I contemplated the cross I was safe and sound; therefore I was unwilling to imperil my soul, for beside the cross there was no safety but the horror of fiends. Then a suggestion came from my reason, as though a friendly voice had spoken, 'Look up to his Father in heaven.' And then I saw clearly with the faith that I felt, that there was nothing between the cross and heaven which could have distressed me. Either I must look up, or I must answer. I answered inwardly with all the strength of my soul and said, 'No, I cannot, for you are my heaven.' I said this because I did not wish to look up, for I would rather have suffered until Judgement Day than come to heaven otherwise than by him; for I well knew that he who bound me so painfully would unbind me when he wished. Thus was I taught to choose Jesus as my heaven, though at that time I saw him only in pain.[20] I was satisfied by no heaven but Jesus, who will be my bliss when I go there. And it has always been a comfort to me that I chose Jesus for my heaven, through his grace, in all this time of suffering and sorrow. And that has been a lesson to me, that I should do so for evermore, choosing Jesus alone for my heaven in good and bad times.

And though like a wretch I had repented – I said before that if I had known what suffering it would cause me, I would not have prayed to share Christ's Passion – I now saw that really this was the grumbling and cursing of the flesh, without the agreement of the spirit, and to this God attaches no blame. Regret and conscious choice are opposites, which I then felt both at the same time. And these two are divided, one part outward and the other inward. The outward part is our mortal flesh, which now suffers pain and grief, and shall while this life lasts; I felt it greatly at this time, and it was this part of me that regretted the prayer. The inward part is a high, blessed state of being, full of peace and love, and this was a more mysterious experience; and it was in this part that I strongly, surely and eagerly chose Jesus for my heaven. And here I saw truly that the inward part is master and ruler of the outward one, and does not consider or heed the desire of the flesh, but all the intention and desire of the spirit is set for ever upon being united with our Lord Jesus. It was not revealed to me that the outward part would draw the inward into agreement, but that the inward should draw the outward, through grace, and both shall be united in everlasting bliss through the power of Christ: this is what was shown.

20

Of the indescribable Passion of Christ, and of three things about his Passion which must always be remembered.

And so I saw our Lord Jesus Christ lingering for a long time; for union with the Godhead gave his Manhood the strength to suffer for love more than anyone who was completely and only a man could suffer. I do not mean only more pain than any man could suffer, but also that he suffered more pain than could be reckoned or fully imagined by any of those who are saved, who have ever lived from the very beginning until the last day, considering the majesty of the highest, most worshipful king and the shameful, insulting, painful death; for he who is highest and most majestic was brought lowest and most utterly despised; for the very summit of what we can see in the Passion is to think and know what he is who suffered.

And God now brought to my mind some part of the height and nobility of the glorious Godhead, and with it the excellence and tenderness of the blessed body, these two being united in Christ, along with our natural reluctance to suffer pain; for he was as tender and pure as he was strong and indomitable in suffering; and he suffered for the sins of every man who shall be saved; and he saw every man's sorrow and desolation and sorrowed for kindness and love. And just as our Lady sorrowed for his suffering, he suffered as much for her sorrow, and more, because his dear humanity was by nature more worthy. For as long as he was capable of suffering, he felt pain and sorrow for us; and now that he has ascended into heaven and is beyond human pain, he is still suffering with us.

And I, contemplating all this through his grace, saw that his love for our souls is so strong that he chose the pain willingly and eagerly, and suffered it meekly and was well-pleased to do so; for the soul who contemplates it in this way, when touched by grace, shall truly see that the pain of Christ's Passion surpasses all pain: that is to say, it surpasses the pains which will be turned into supreme and everlasting joys by virtue of Christ's Passion.

21

Of three ways of regarding the Passion of Christ; and how we are now dying on the cross with Christ; but his face banishes all pain.

It is God's will, as I understand it, that we should contemplate his blessed Passion in three different ways. The first is the cruel pain that he suffered, which we should consider with contrition and compassion; at this time our Lord revealed that to me, and gave me the power and grace to see it. And I watched for the last breath with all my might and expected to see the body completely dead, but I did not see him like that. And just at the very moment when it seemed to me that to all appearances his life could last no longer and the end must be revealed, suddenly I saw, while looking at the same cross, that his blessed expression changed. The changing of his blessed expression changed mine, and I was as glad and happy as it was possible to be. Then our Lord made me think happily, 'Where is there now one jot of your pain or your sorrow?' And I was very happy. I understood that we are now, as our Lord intends it, dying with him on his cross in our pain and our passion; and if we willingly remain on the same cross with his help and his grace until the final moment, the countenance he turns on us will suddenly change, and we shall be with him in heaven. There will be no time between one moment and the next, and everything will be turned to joy; and this is what he meant in this showing: 'Where is there now one jot of your pain or your sorrow?' And we shall be entirely blessed.

And here I truly saw that if he showed us his blessed countenance now, there is no pain on earth, nor in any other place, that could hurt us, but everything would cause us joy and bliss. But because he shows us a time of suffering, like the suffering he bore in this life and on his cross, we are in distress and suffer with him the hardships which belong to our frailty. And the reason why he suffers is that of his goodness he wants to raise us higher with him in his bliss, and in return for the little pain we suffer here on earth we shall have an exalted, endless knowledge of God, which we could never have without that. And the worse the pain we have suffered with him on his cross, the greater the glory we shall enjoy with him in his kingdom.

22

The ninth revelation is of Christ's happiness in suffering; of three heavens; and of the infinite love of Christ who is eager to die for us every day if he could, although it is not necessary.

Then our good Lord Jesus Christ spoke, asking, 'Are you well pleased that I suffered for you?' I said, 'Yes, my good Lord, thank you. Yes, my good Lord, blessed may you be!' Then Jesus, our kind Lord, said, 'If you are pleased, I am pleased. It is a joy, a delight and an endless happiness to me that I ever endured suffering for you, and if I could suffer more, I would suffer more.' As I became conscious of these words my understanding was lifted up into heaven, and there I saw three heavens, a sight which caused me great amazement. And though I saw three heavens, and all of them in the blessed Manhood of Christ,[21] none is greater, none is lesser, none is higher, none is lower, but they are all equally full of supreme joy.

For the first heaven Christ showed me his Father, in no bodily likeness, but in his nature and his action: that is to say, I saw in Christ what the Father is. This is how the Father acts: he rewards his son, Jesus Christ. This gift and this reward give Jesus such great joy that his father could have given him no reward that could have pleased him better. The first heaven, that is the pleasing of the Father, appeared to me like a heaven, and it was full of great joy, for he is greatly pleased with all the deeds Jesus has done to promote our salvation; because of these we do not just belong to Jesus by his buying[22] of us, but also by his Father's generous gift. We are his joy, we are his reward, we are his glory, we are his crown — and this was a special marvel and a thrilling vision, that we should be his crown.

What I am describing causes Jesus such great pleasure that he thinks nothing of all his hardship and his bitter suffering and his cruel and shameful death. And in these words, 'If I could suffer more, I would suffer more', I truly saw that he was willing to die as often as he was able to die, and love would never let him rest until he had done it. And I watched very carefully to see how often he would die if he could, and truly the number of times passed my understanding and my senses by so much that my reason neither would nor could comprehend it. And if he had died, or was going to die, so often, he would still think nothing of it out of love. For his love is so great that everything seems a trifle to him in comparison. For although the dear humanity of Christ could only suffer once, his goodness makes him always ready to do so again; he would do it every day if it were possible; and if he said that for love of me he would make new heavens and a new earth, it would be but little in comparison, for he could do this every day if he so wished, without any hardship; but to offer to die for love of me so often that the number of times passes human comprehension, that is the most glorious present that our Lord God could make to man's soul, it seems to me.

Then his meaning is this: 'How should I not do all that I can for love of you? — for doing so does not grieve me, since I would die for love of you so often with no concern for my bitter pain.' And here I saw the second insight into this blessed Passion: the love that made him suffer is as much greater than his pain as heaven is above the earth; for the Passion was a noble, glorious deed performed at one particular time through the action of love, love which has always existed and will never end; because of this love, he very affectionately said these words, 'If I could suffer more, I would suffer more.' He did not say, 'If it were necessary to suffer more', for if he could suffer more, he would, even if it were not necessary. This deed and this action for our salvation was ordered as well as God could order it. And here I saw complete joy in Christ; for if God could have ordered it any better, his joy could not have been complete.

23

How Christ wishes us to rejoice greatly with him in our redemption and to pray that by his grace we may do so.

And in these three sayings, 'It is a joy, a delight and an endless happiness to me', three heavens were shown, as follows: by the joy I understood the pleasure of the Father; and by the delight, the glory of the Son; and by the endless happiness, the Holy Ghost. The Father is pleased, the Son is glorified, the Holy Ghost rejoices. And here what I saw was the third insight into his blessed Passion; namely, the joy and the delight which cause him to take pleasure in it; for our kind Lord showed me five aspects of his Passion: the first of these is the bleeding of the head, the second is the discolouring of his face, the third is the abundant bleeding of the body in weals from the scourging, the fourth is the solemn dying. These four have already been mentioned as the pains of the Passion – and the fifth is what was shown as the joy and delight of the Passion; for God wishes us to take true pleasure with him in our salvation, and in this he wishes us to be greatly comforted and strengthened, and so he wants our souls to be happily filled with this, through his grace; for we are his delight; he takes pleasure in us eternally, and so shall we in him, through his grace. And all that he has done for us, and all that he does, and ever will do, was never a loss or a burden to him, nor ever could be; except what he did in our human form, beginning at the precious incarnation and lasting until the blessed resurrection on Easter morning; that was the only loss and burden that he bore to accomplish our redemption, a redemption in which he rejoices eternally, as I have already said.

Jesus wishes us to consider the delight which the Holy Trinity feels in our salvation and wishes us to long for as much spiritual pleasure, through his grace, as has already been described; that is to say, that our pleasure in salvation should be, as far as is possible here on earth, like the joy Christ has in our salvation. The whole Trinity took part in the Passion of Christ, dispensing an abundance of virtues and fullness of grace to us through him, but only the son of the Virgin suffered; and because of this the whole blessed Trinity is eternally joyful. And this was shown in these words, 'Are you well pleased?' and by Christ's other words, 'If you are pleased, I am pleased', as if he said, 'It is joy and delight enough to me, and I ask nothing more of you for my hardship but that I give you pleasure.'

And with these words he brought to mind the nature of a glad giver: a glad giver pays little attention to the thing he is giving, but his whole desire and intention is to please and comfort the one to whom he gives it; and if the receiver values the gift highly and takes it gratefully, then the generous giver thinks nothing of all his hardship and the price he had to pay, because of the joy and delight that he feels at having pleased and comforted the one he loves. This was shown abundantly and fully.

Think hard too about the deep significance of this word 'ever';[23] for it was a great sign of the love he shows in our salvation, with the numerous joys that follow from the Passion of Christ; one is that he rejoices that he has indeed done it, and he will suffer no more; another, that he has brought us up to heaven and made us his crown and his endless delight; another is that he has by this means bought us from the endless torments of hell.

24

The tenth revelation is that our Lord Jesus, rejoicing, lovingly shows his sacred heart riven in two.

Then, with a glad face, our Lord looked into his side, and gazed, rejoicing; and with his dear gaze he led his creature's understanding through the same wound[24] into his side. And then he revealed a beautiful and delightful place which was large enough for all mankind who shall be saved to rest there in peace and love. And with this he brought to mind the precious blood and water which he allowed to pour out completely for love. And in this dear vision he showed his sacred heart quite riven in two. And with this sweet rejoicing he revealed to my understanding some part of the blessed Godhead, arousing the poor soul to understand, so far as it may be expressed, the meaning of the endless love that has always existed and is and ever shall be. And with this our good Lord said most blessedly, 'Look how much I loved you'; as if he had said, 'My darling, look and see your Lord, your God, who is your maker and your eternal joy. See what pleasure and delight I take in your salvation, and for my love rejoice with me now.' And also, to make it plainer, these blessed words were said: 'Look how I loved you. Look and see that I loved you so much before I died for you that I was willing to die for you; and now I have died for you, and willingly suffered as much as I can for you. And now all my bitter torment and painful hardship has changed into endless joy and bliss for me and for you. How could it now be that you could make any request that pleased me that I would not very gladly grant you? For my pleasure is your holiness and your endless joy and bliss with me.' This is the meaning, as simply as I can explain it, of these blessed words, 'Look how much I loved you.' Our good Lord revealed this to make us glad and joyful.

25

The eleventh revelation is a special spiritual showing of his Mother.

And with the same expression of mirth and joy our good Lord looked down to his right and brought to my mind the place where our Lady was standing during the time of his Passion; and he said, 'Would you like to see her?' And with these sweet words it was as if he had said, 'I know very well that you long to see my blessed Mother, for after myself she is the most supreme joy that I could reveal to you, and that which most delights and honours me; and it is she that my blessed creatures most long to see.'

And because of the supreme, marvellous, singular love that he feels for this sweet Virgin, his blessed Mother, our Lady Saint Mary, he showed her very joyful, and that is what these sweet words mean, as if he said, 'Do you want to see how I love her, so that you can rejoice with me in the love that I have for her and she for me?' And also, to explain these sweet words more clearly, our Lord God is speaking to all mankind who will be saved as though to one person, as if he said, 'Would you like to see in her how you are loved? For love of you I made her so high, so noble and so excellent; and this makes me glad, and I want it to gladden you.' For after himself, she is the most blessed sight. But concerning this I am not taught to long to see her bodily presence while I am here on earth, but the virtues of her blessed soul: her truth, her wisdom, her love, so that through these I may learn to know myself and reverently fear my God. And when our good Lord had shown this and said these words, 'Would you like to see her?', I answered and said, 'Yes, my good Lord, thank you. Yes, my good Lord, if it is your will.' I prayed for this repeatedly and I thought I would see her bodily presence, but I did not do so. And with these words Jesus showed me a spiritual vision of her; just as I had seen her low and humble before, he now showed her to me high, noble and glorious, and more pleasing to him than any other creature. And he wants it to be known that all those who rejoice in him should rejoice in her and in the joy that he has in her and she in him. And to make it clearer he gave this example: if a man loves someone uniquely, more than all other creatures, he wants to make all creatures love and rejoice in that person he loves so much. And these words that Jesus said, 'Would you like to see her?', seemed to me the most pleasing words about her that he could have given me with the spiritual vision of her; for our Lord gave me no special revelation except of our Lady Saint Mary, and he showed her three times: the first when she conceived, the second in her sorrow under the cross, the third as she is now, in delight, honour and joy.

26

The twelfth revelation is that the Lord our God is supreme Being.

And after this our Lord showed himself in even greater glory, it seemed to me, than when I saw him before, and from this revelation I learned that our soul will never rest until it comes to him knowing that he is the fullness of joy, of everyday and princely blessedness and the only true life. Our Lord Jesus said repeatedly, 'It is I, it is I; it is I who am highest; it is I you love; it is I who delight you; it is I you serve; it is I you long for; it is I you desire; it is I who am your purpose; it is I who am all; it is I that Holy Church preaches and teaches you; it is I who showed myself to you here.' The number of these utterances went beyond my wit and all my understanding and all my powers, and it is supreme, it seems to me, for there is included within it – I cannot tell how much; but the joy that I perceived as they were revealed surpasses all that the heart may wish and the soul may desire; and therefore the utterances are not fully explained here, but, according to the powers of understanding and loving which are given by the grace of God, may everyone receive them as our Lord intended.

27

The thirteenth revelation is that our Lord God wishes us to hold in high account all that he has done in making all things with such nobility; and of other things; and how sin can only be recognized by suffering.

After this, our Lord reminded me of the longing I had had for him;[25] and I saw that nothing kept me from him but sin, and I saw that this is so with all of us. And I thought that if sin had never existed, we should all have been pure and like himself, as God made us; and so I had often wondered before now in my folly why, in his great foreseeing wisdom, God had not prevented the beginning of sin; for then, I thought, all would have been well. I ought certainly to have abandoned these thoughts, but nevertheless I grieved and sorrowed over the question with no reason or judgement. But Jesus, who in this vision informed me of all that I needed to know, answered with this assurance: 'Sin is befitting, but all shall be well, and all shall be well, and all manner of things shall be well.'

With this bare word 'sin' our Lord brought to my mind the whole extent of all that is not good, and the shameful scorn and the utter humiliation that he bore for us in this life, and his dying, and all the pains and sufferings of all his creatures, both in body and spirit – for we are all to some extent brought to nothing and shall be brought to nothing as our master Jesus was, until we are fully purged: that is to say until our mortal flesh is brought completely to nothing, and all those of our inward feelings which are not truly good. He gave me insight into these things, along with all pains that ever were and ever shall be; and compared with these I realize that Christ's Passion was the greatest pain and went beyond them all. And all this was shown in a flash, and quickly changed into comfort; for our good Lord did not want the soul to be afraid of this ugly sight.

But I did not see sin; for I believe it has no sort of substance nor portion of being, nor could it be recognized were it not for the suffering which it causes. And this suffering seems to me to be something transient, for it purges us and makes us know ourselves and pray for mercy; for the Passion of our Lord supports us against all this, and that is his blessed will. And because of the tender love which our good Lord feels for all who shall be saved, he supports us willingly and sweetly, meaning this: 'It is true that sin is the cause of all this suffering, but all shall be well, and all shall be well, and all manner of things shall be well.' These words were said very tenderly, with no suggestion that I or anyone who will be saved was being blamed. It would therefore be very strange to blame or wonder at God because of my sin, since he does not blame me for sinning.

And in these same words I saw a marvellous great mystery hidden in God, a mystery which he will make openly known to us in heaven; in which knowledge we shall truly see the reason why he allowed sin to exist; and seeing this we shall rejoice eternally in our Lord God.

28

How the children of salvation shall be shaken by sorrows, but Christ rejoices in compassion; and a remedy for tribulation.

Thus I saw how Christ feels compassion for us because of sin. And just as I was earlier filled with suffering and compassion at the Passion of Christ, so was I now also partly filled with compassion for all my fellow Christians, for those well-beloved people who shall be saved; that is to say, God's servants, Holy Church, will be shaken in sorrows and anguish and tribulation in this world, as men shake a cloth in the wind. And to this God answered as follows: 'I shall make some great thing out of this in heaven, something eternally worthy and everlastingly joyful.'

Yes, I saw as far as this – that our Lord rejoices in the tribulations of his servants with pity and compassion; in order to bring to bliss each person that he loves he lays on each of them something which in his sight is no cause of blame, something for which they are blamed and despised in this world, scorned, violently treated and cast out; and this he does to prevent the damage that would be done to them by the pomp and vainglory of this wretched life, and to prepare their path to heaven, and to raise them to his bliss which lasts without end; for he says, 'I shall shatter you for your vain passions and your vicious pride; and after that I shall gather you together and make you humble and meek, pure and holy, by uniting you with me.' And then I saw that whenever a man feels kind compassion with love for his fellow Christian, it is Christ within him.

That same humiliation which was revealed in his Passion was revealed again here in this compassion, in which there were two ways of understanding our Lord's meaning: one was the bliss to which we are bought and in which he will rejoice, the other is for strength in our suffering; for he wants us to know that it will all be turned into glory and profit by virtue of his Passion, and to know we do not suffer alone, but with him, recognizing that we are grounded in him, and he wants us to see that his pain and his humiliation go so far beyond all that we may suffer that it cannot be fully conceived. And consideration of this will save us from grumbling and despair as we experience suffering; and if we truly see that our sin deserves it, his love will nevertheless excuse us, and in his great kindness he takes away all our blame and watches over us with compassion and pity, like children, not hateful but innocent.

29

Adam's sin was the greatest of all, but the atonement for it is more pleasing to God than the sin was ever harmful.

But I paused at this, contemplating these things in general, sad and grieving, and in my thought I said to our Lord with great reverence, 'Ah, my good Lord, how could all be well, given the great harm that has been done to humankind by sin?' And here I prayed, as much as I dared, for some clearer explanation to ease my mind over this. And our blessed Lord answered most compassionately and in a very friendly way, and showed that Adam's sin was the greatest harm that ever was done, or ever shall be, until the end of the world; and he also showed that this is publicly acknowledged through all Holy Church on earth. Furthermore he taught that I should consider the glorious atonement; for this atonement is incomparably more pleasing to God and more glorious in saving mankind than Adam's sin was ever harmful.

So what our blessed Lord's teaching means is that we should take heed of the following: 'Since I have turned the greatest possible harm into good, it is my will that you should know from this that I shall turn all lesser evil into good.'

30

How we should rejoice and trust in our Saviour Jesus, and not presumptuously seek to know his privy counsel.

He made me understand two aspects of this. One of them is our Saviour and our salvation; this aspect is blessed and is clear and bright, light and beautiful and abundant, for all men who are and shall be of good will are included in it; we are bound to it by God, and drawn to it, admonished and taught inwardly by the Holy Ghost and outwardly by Holy Church through the same grace; our Lord wishes our minds to be filled with this, rejoicing in him because he rejoices in us; and the more abundantly we are filled with this, reverently and humbly, the more we deserve his thanks and the more we benefit ourselves, and thus we may say, rejoicing, our Lord is our portion.[26]

The second aspect is hidden and closed to us (that is to say, everything which is not necessary for our salvation); for it is our Lord's privy counsel and it is proper to the royal lordship of God that his privy counsel should be undisturbed,[27] and it is proper for his servant, out of obedience and reverence, not to know his counsel too well. Our Lord feels pity and compassion for us because some people are so anxious to know about it; and I am sure that if we knew how much we would please him and set our own minds at rest by leaving the matter alone, then we would do so. The saints in heaven do not want to know anything except what our Lord wants to reveal to them, and their love and their desires are directed by our Lord's will; our desires should be like theirs: then, like the saints, we should wish and desire nothing that is not the will of our Lord; for God's purpose for us all is the same.

And here I was taught that we must rejoice only in our blessed Saviour Jesus and trust in him for everything.

31

Of the longing and the spiritual thirst of Christ, which lasts and shall last till Judgement Day; and how, because of his body, he is not yet in full glory nor quite beyond suffering.

And thus our good Lord answered all the questions and doubts I could put forward, saying most comfortingly, 'I may make all things well, I can make all things well and I will make all things well and I shall make all things well; and you shall see for yourself that all manner of things shall be well.' I take 'I may' for the words of the Father, I take 'I can' for the words of the Son and I take 'I will' for the words of the Holy Ghost; and where he says 'I shall', I take it for the unity of the Holy Trinity, three persons and one truth; and where he says, 'You shall see for yourself', I understand it as referring to the union with the Holy Trinity of all mankind who shall be saved. And with these five sayings God wishes to be surrounded by rest and peace; and thus Christ's spiritual thirst will come to an end; for this is the spiritual thirst of Christ, the love-longing that lasts and ever shall do until we see that revelation on Judgement Day.

For some of us that shall be saved, and shall be Christ's joy and his bliss, are still here on earth, and some are yet to come, and it shall be so until that last day. Therefore it seems to me that this is his thirst: a love-longing to have us all together, wholly in himself for his delight; for we are not now as wholly in him as we shall be then.

For we know through our faith, and it was also revealed in all the showings, that Jesus Christ is both God and man. And as far as the Godhead is concerned, he is himself the highest bliss, and was from eternity and shall be so to eternity; and this endless bliss may never in itself be heightened or diminished; this was abundantly seen in every showing, and especially in the twelfth, where he says, 'It is I who am highest.' And as far as Christ's Manhood is concerned, it is known through our faith and also from the showings that through the power of his Godhead, and to bring us to his bliss for love, he endured pains and suffering and died; and these are the works of Christ's Manhood in which he rejoices, and he showed this in the ninth revelation where he said, 'It is a joy, a delight and an endless happiness to me that I ever endured suffering for you.' And this is the bliss of Christ's works and this is what he means where he says in the same showing that we are his joy, we are his reward, we are his honour, we are his crown. For regarding Christ as our head, he is in glory and beyond suffering, but as regards his body, in which all his members are joined, he is not yet in full glory or beyond suffering; for that same longing and thirst which he had on the cross – a longing and thirst which it seems to me had been in him from eternity – those he still has, and shall have until the time when the last soul which is to be saved has come up into his bliss.

For as truly as there is a property of compassion and pity in God, so there is as truly a property of thirst and longing in God. And because of the strength of this longing in Christ it is for us in turn to long for him, and without this no soul comes to heaven. And this property of longing and thirst comes from his endless goodness, just as the property of pity comes from his endless goodness, yet, as I see it, the longing and the pity are two separate properties; and this is what distinguishes the spiritual thirst which lasts in him as long as we are in need, drawing us up to his bliss; and all this was shown as a revelation of compassion, and his thirst will cease on Judgement Day.

Thus he has pity and compassion for us, and he has longing to have us, but his wisdom and love do not permit the end to come till the best time.

32

How everything shall be well, and Scripture fulfilled; and we must remain steadfast in the faith of Holy Church, as Christ desires.

At one time our good Lord said, 'All manner of things shall be well'; and at another time he said, 'You shall see for yourself that all manner of things shall be well'; and the soul understood these two sayings differently. On the one hand he wants us to know that he does not only concern himself with great and noble things, but also with small, humble and simple things, with both one and the other; and this is what he means when he says, 'All manner of things shall be well'; for he wants us to know that the smallest thing shall not be forgotten. But another thing understood is this: deeds are done which appear so evil to us and people suffer such terrible evils that it does not seem as though any good will ever come of them; and we consider this, sorrowing and grieving over it so that we cannot find peace in the blessed contemplation of God as we should do; and this is why: our reasoning powers are so blind now, so humble and so simple, that we cannot know the high, marvellous wisdom, the might and the goodness of the Holy Trinity. And this is what he means where he says, 'You shall see for yourself that all manner of things shall be well', as if he said, 'Pay attention to this now, faithfully and confidently, and at the end of time you will truly see it in the fullness of joy.' And thus I understand the five sayings mentioned above – 'I may make all things well', etc. – as a powerful and comforting pledge for all the works of our Lord God which are to come.

It appears to me that there is a deed which the Holy Trinity shall do on the last day, and when that deed shall be done and how it shall be done is unknown to all creatures under Christ, and shall be until it has been done. And he wants us to know this because he wants us to feel more ease in our souls and more at peace in love, rejoicing in him and no longer considering all the tumults which might keep us from the truth. This is the great deed ordained by our Lord God from eternity, treasured up and hidden in his blessed breast, only known to himself, and by this deed he shall make all things well; for just as the Holy Trinity made all things from nothing, so the Holy Trinity shall make all well that is not well.

And I wondered greatly at this revelation, and considered our faith, wondering as follows: our faith is grounded in God's word, and it is part of our faith that we should believe that God's word will be kept in all things; and one point of our faith is that many shall be damned – like the angels who fell out of heaven from pride, who are now fiends, and men on earth who die outside the faith of Holy Church, that is, those who are heathens, and also any man who has received Christianity and lives an unChristian life and so dies excluded from the love of God. Holy Church teaches me to believe that all these shall be condemned everlastingly to hell. And given all this, I thought it impossible that all manner of things should be well, as our Lord revealed at this time. And I received no other answer in showing from our Lord God but this: 'What is impossible to you is not impossible to me. I shall keep my word in all things and I shall make all things well.'

Thus I was taught by the grace of God that I should steadfastly remain in the faith, as I had previously understood, and at the same time that I should firmly believe that all things should be well as our Lord God revealed on the same occasion. For this is the great deed that our Lord shall do, the deed by which he will keep his word in all things and shall make all well that is not well. And how the deed shall be done there is no creature under Christ that knows or shall know until it is done, so far as I understood our Lord's meaning at this time.

33

All damned souls are condemned like the Devil in the sight of God; and these
revelations do not cancel out the faith of Holy Church, but strengthen it; and
the more anxious we are to know God's mysteries, the less we know.

And yet in all this I desired, as far as I dared, to have a complete vision
of hell and purgatory. But it was not my intention to put to the test
anything which belongs to our faith – for I firmly believed that hell
and purgatory have the purpose taught by Holy Church – but my
idea was that I might have seen them so that I could learn everything
belonging to my faith that could help me to live to the greater glory
of God and to my greater spiritual profit. But as for this desire, I could
learn nothing about it, except what I have previously said in the fifth
showing, where I saw that the Devil is scorned by God and endlessly
damned; and, seeing this, I understood that all beings who live their
lives in a state of sin, like the Devil, and who die in this state, are
never again mentioned before God and all his holy ones any more
than the Devil is mentioned, even though they are human beings,
whether or not they have been christened.

For though my revelation was of goodness, and there was little
mention of evil, yet I was not drawn by it from a single detail of the
faith which Holy Church teaches us to believe.[28] I saw the Passion of
Christ in several different showings – in the first, in the second, in
the fifth and in the eighth – as I have said before, and although I felt
some of the sorrow of our Lady and of the true friends who saw him
suffer, yet I did not see the Jews who did him to death specified
individually, although I knew by my faith that they were cursed and
damned for ever except for those who are converted through grace.[29]
And I was taught and instructed to observe every detail of the faith
with no exceptions, in every respect as I had previously understood
it, hoping that I was observing the faith with God's mercy and grace,
and begging and praying inwardly that I might continue in it until
the end of my life.

And it is God's will that we should pay attention to all the deeds he has done, for he wants us to know from them all that he will do, but we must always stop ourselves from considering what the great deed will be. And we must pray to be like our brothers and sisters who are saints in heaven and who only want what God wants, then all our joy will be in God and we shall be content both with what is hidden and with what is shown; for I saw our Lord's purpose quite clearly: the more anxious we are to discover his secret knowledge about this or anything else, the further we shall be from knowing it.

34

God shows the mysteries necessary to those who love him; and how much they please God who diligently receive the preaching of Holy Church.

Our Lord God showed two kinds of mysteries: one of them is this great mystery, with all the secret details which belong to it, and these mysteries he wants us to recognize as hidden until the time when he shows them to us clearly; the other kind are the mysteries which he wants to make open and known to us; for he wants us to recognize that it is his will that we know them. Some mysteries are hidden from us because God wants them to be hidden, but some mysteries are hidden from us because of our blindness and ignorance; and he feels great pity because of this, and therefore he himself wants to make them more open to us so that we may know him and love him and cling to him; for everything that is helpful for us to understand and to know – our Lord will generously show us what these things are, through the preaching and teaching of Holy Church.

God showed the very great pleasure that he takes in men and women who strongly and humbly and eagerly receive the preaching and teaching of Holy Church; for it is his Holy Church; he is the foundation, he is the substance, he is the teaching, he is the teacher, he is the goal, he is the prize which every naturally good soul works hard to win; and this is known and shall be known to every soul to whom the Holy Ghost makes it clear. And I truly expect that he will help all those who are seeking this, for they are seeking God.

All that I have now said, and more that I shall say afterwards, gives strength against sin; for in the third showing, when I saw that God does all that is done, I saw no sin, and then I saw that all is well. But when God gave me a revelation about sin, then he said, 'All shall be well.'

35

How God does all that is good and in his mercy patiently and nobly tolerates everything, and how this shall cease when sin is no longer suffered.

And when almighty God had shown his great goodness so fully and so abundantly, I requested to know whether a certain person whom I loved would continue to lead a good life, as I hoped that she had already begun to do through God's grace. And in this personal request it seemed that I stood in my own way, for I was not answered immediately. And then I was answered in my reason as though by a friendly intermediary, 'Take these showings generally, and consider the kindness of the Lord God as he gives them to you; for it honours God more to consider him in all things than in any particular thing.' I assented, and with this I learned that it honours God more to have knowledge of everything in general than to take pleasure in any one thing in particular. And if I were to follow this teaching faithfully I should neither rejoice over any one special thing, nor be greatly distressed over any thing of any kind, for 'All shall be well'; the fullness of joy is to see God in everything; for by the same power, wisdom and love with which he made all things, our good Lord is continually leading all things to the same end and he himself shall bring this about; and when the time comes we shall see it. And the foundation of this was shown in the first revelation and it was shown more openly in the third where it says, 'I saw God in an instant.'

All that our Lord does is right and all that he endures[30] is praiseworthy; and in these two are contained good and evil, for our Lord does everything which is good and he endures everything which is evil. I am not saying that any evil is to be praised, but I am saying that our Lord God's willingness to endure evil is praiseworthy, and through this his goodness will be recognized for ever in his wonderful compassion and kindness, through the operation of mercy and grace. Righteousness is the thing which is so good that it cannot be better than it is; for God himself is true righteousness and all his deeds are rightly done as they have been ordained since before time began by his great power, his great wisdom, his great goodness. And just as he ordained what is for the best, in the same way he continues to work and lead everything to the same end; and he always takes great pleasure in himself and all his works. And the sight of this blessed accord is very sweet to the soul that sees it through grace.

All the souls which shall be saved everlastingly in heaven are made righteous in the sight of God, and through his own goodness; and in this righteousness we are everlastingly and marvellously preserved, above all other creatures. And mercy is a work which comes from the goodness of God, and it will go on operating as long as sin is allowed to pursue righteous souls; and when sin is no longer allowed to pursue, then the operation of mercy will cease; and then all shall be brought to righteousness and so remain for ever. And he allows us to fall; and in his blessed love we are preserved by his strength and wisdom; and through mercy and grace we are raised to a greater abundance of joys. And thus God wants to be known and loved now and for ever in his righteousness and in his mercy. And the soul that truly sees this through grace takes pleasure in both and rejoices without end.[31]

36

Of another excellent deed our Lord will do, which through his gracious kindness may be partly revealed here, and how we should rejoice over it; and how God still performs miracles.

Our good Lord showed that a deed shall be done, and he himself shall do it; and though I do nothing but sin, my sin shall not prevent the working of his goodness. And I saw that to contemplate this is a sublime joy to a reverent soul who naturally by grace longs always for God's purpose to be fulfilled. This deed shall begin here, and it will be to the glory of God and of immense profit to those on earth who love him; and whenever we come to heaven we shall see it with extraordinary joy, and this is how it will continue to operate until the last day; and the glory and the bliss of that deed will continue in heaven before God and all his holy ones for ever and ever. For this is how the deed was seen and understood according to our Lord's intention, and he revealed this to make us rejoice in him and in all that he does. When I saw that his showing continued, I understood that it was shown for the sake of a great thing which was to come, a thing which God showed that he would do himself; a deed which had the properties already described; and this was very blessedly shown, with the intention that I should take it truly, faithfully and confidently. But what this deed would be, that remained a mystery to me.

And in this I saw that God does not want us to be afraid of knowing the things that he shows us; he shows them because he wants us to know them, and through this knowledge he wants us to love him and be happy and rejoice in him for ever. And because of his great love for us he shows us everything which it is valuable and useful for us to know in this world; and the things which he wants to remain a mystery for the time being, he nevertheless, because of his great kindness, shows us in a veiled way, and from this showing he wants us to believe and understand that we shall really see them in his everlasting bliss. So we ought to rejoice in him for all that he shows and all that he hides; and if we do this willingly and humbly we shall find great pleasure in it and he will look kindly on us for ever because of it.

And this is how that promise is to be understood: what will be done for me – that is, for mankind in general (that is to say, for all who shall be saved) – will be full of glory and wonder and generosity, and God himself will do it. And this will be the greatest of all possible joys, to see the deed that God himself will do even when man does nothing else but sin.

Then what our Lord God means is this: it is as if he said, 'Behold and see. Here you have cause for patience; here you have cause for love; here you have cause to humble yourself; here you have cause to rejoice in me; and rejoice in me for my love, for of all things that is how you can give me most pleasure.' And for as long as we live this earthly life, whenever in our folly we turn to consider the reprobate, our God touches us tenderly and blessedly calls us, saying in our soul, 'Consider me alone my precious child, make me your object, I am enough for you, rejoice in your Saviour and your salvation.' And I am certain that this is how our Lord works within us; the soul which through grace is made aware of this will see it and feel it. And even though this deed of our Lord's truly relates to mankind in general, it still does not exclude the individual; as for what our good Lord will do for his poor creatures, it is now unknown to me. But this deed and the one mentioned before are not the same, but two separate ones. But this deed shall be done sooner, done as we come to heaven, and, to those to whom our Lord grants it, may be partly known here on earth; but the great deed mentioned before shall be known neither in heaven nor on earth until it is done.

And moreover, God gave special understanding and instruction about the operation of miracles, as follows: 'It is known that I have performed miracles before now, many and various, high and marvellous, glorious and great; and as I have done, so I now do continually and shall do in time to come.' It is known that sorrow and anguish and tribulation come before miracles; and that is so that we may recognize our own feebleness and the wickedness into which we have fallen through sin, making us humble and making us fear God, crying out for help and grace. Miracles come after that, they come from the great power, wisdom and goodness of God, showing his excellence and the joys of heaven as far as is possible in this transitory life, so as to strengthen our faith and increase our hope through love; because of this he chooses to be known and honoured through miracles. This then is what he intends: he does not want us to be brought too low by the storms and sorrows that befall us, for it has always been so before the coming of a miracle.

37

God keeps those he has chosen in great safety even though they sin, for in them is a godly will that never assented to sin.

God reminded me that I would sin; and because of my pleasure in contemplating him, I was slow to pay attention to that showing. And our Lord very kindly waited and gave me the grace to pay attention. And I took this showing as applying particularly to myself, but by all the kind help which follows, as you will see, I was taught to apply it to all my fellow Christians in general and not to myself in particular; though our Lord showed me that I would sin, by me alone he meant everyone. And at this I began to feel a quiet fear, and to this our Lord answered, 'I am keeping you very safe.' This promise was made with more love and assurance and spiritual sustenance than I can possibly say, for just as it was shown that I would sin, the help was also shown: safety and protection for all my fellow Christians. What could make me love my fellow Christians more than to see in God that he loves all who shall be saved as though they were one soul? For in every soul that shall be saved there is a godly will which never consented to sin and never shall; just as there is an animal will in our lower nature which can have no good impulses, there is a godly will in our higher nature which is so good that it can never will evil but only good; and that is why God loves us and why we do what pleases him for ever. And this is what our Lord showed in the completeness of the love in which he holds us: yes, that he loves us as much now while we are here as he will do when we are there in his blessed presence. Failure of love on our part is the only cause of all our suffering.

38

How the sins of the chosen shall be turned into joy and glory, with the examples of David, Peter and Saint John of Beverley.

God also showed that sin shall not be shameful to man, but his glory; for in the same way as God's justice gives every sin a suitable punishment, so God's love gives the same soul a joy for every sin. Just as various sins receive various punishments according to how serious they are, in the same way they will be rewarded with various joys in heaven according to how much pain and grief they caused the soul on earth, for the soul that will come to heaven is precious to God, and the place so full of glory that God's goodness never allows any soul that is to come there to sin unless the sin is rewarded; and the sin is made famous for ever and blissfully restored to grace by surpassing glory; for in this revelation my understanding was lifted up into heaven; and then God brought cheeringly into my mind David and innumerable others of the old Jewish Law, and in the new Christian Law he made me think first of Mary Magdalene, Peter, Paul, Thomas of India and Saint John of Beverley,[32] and also innumerable others: how they are famous in the church on earth with their sins, which are not shameful for them, but are all turned into glory. And therefore our kind Lord gives us a partial vision here on earth of their perfection in heaven; for there the badge of their sin is changed into glory.

And as for Saint John of Beverley, our Lord showed him very clearly to encourage us by his familiarity, and he reminded me that he is a very near neighbour and we know him well; and God referred to him as 'Saint John of Beverley' quite straightforwardly as we do, and in a very pleasant, affectionate way, showing that in heaven he is a great and blessed saint in the sight of God; and at the same time he reminded me that as a child and as a young man he was God's much-loved servant, loving and fearing God greatly, and nevertheless God allowed him to fall, mercifully protecting him so that he did not perish or lose his chance; and afterwards God raised him into a state of infinitely more grace, and he lived in such contrition and humility that in heaven God has given him infinite joys, surpassing those he would have had if he had not fallen. And on earth God shows that this is true by the abundant miracles which are continually performed around his body. And this was all to make us glad and happy in love.

39

Of the sharpness of sin and the goodness of contrition, and how our kind Lord does not want frequent falls to make us despair.

Sin is the sharpest scourge that any chosen soul can be struck with; it is a scourge which lashes men and women so hard and damages them so much in their own eyes that sometimes they think they only deserve to sink down into hell, until the touch of the Holy Ghost brings contrition and turns the bitterness into hopes of God's mercy; and then they begin to heal their wounds and the soul begins to revive into the life of Holy Church. The Holy Ghost leads a man on to confession, and he earnestly shows his sins, nakedly and truly, with great sorrow and great shame that he has befouled the fair image of God. Then, in accordance with the basic teaching which the Church has received from the Holy Ghost, his confessor imposes a penance on him for each sin. And this is one way of humbling oneself which pleases God very much; and so does bodily sickness sent by God, and also sorrow and shame from without, and worldly scorn and censure with all the various injuries and temptations which will be flung at him both physically and spiritually.

Our Lord takes tender care of us when we feel that we are almost forsaken and cast away because of our sin and because we have deserved

REVELATIONS OF DIVINE LOVE

it. And because of the humility which we gain through this, we are raised by God's grace right up high in his sight, with great contrition, with compassion and with a true longing for God. Then we are immediately freed from sin and suffering and taken up into bliss and even made exalted saints. By contrition we are made pure, by compassion we are made ready and by true longing for God we are made worthy. As I understand it, these three are the means by which all souls come to heaven – that is to say, all that have been sinners on earth and are to be saved – for every soul needs to be healed by these medicines. Although a man has the scars of healed wounds, when he appears before God they do not deface but ennoble him.

And as on the one hand we are punished here with sorrow and suffering, on the other we shall be rewarded in heaven by the generous love of our Lord God almighty who does not want the toils and troubles of any that come there to be wasted in the least degree; for he considers sin to be the sorrow and suffering of those who love him and out of love he does not blame them. The reward we are going to receive will not be a small one, but great, splendid and glorious. And so shame will be turned into glory and greater joy; for our generous Lord does not want his servants to despair because they fall into sin often or grievously; our falling does not prevent him from loving us.

Peace and love always live in us, being and working, but we do not always live in peace and love; so God wants us to pay attention to this: he is the foundation of our whole life in love, and moreover he watches over us for ever and is a powerful defence against our enemies, who attack us fiercely and furiously; and our need is the greater because we give them the opportunity when we fall.

40

We need to long for love with Jesus, avoiding sin for love; the vileness of sin surpasses all punishment. God loves us tenderly while we are in a state of sin, and so we should love our neighbour in the same way.

It is a supreme favour from our kind Lord, that he should watch over us so tenderly while we are in a state of sin; and furthermore he secretly touches our inner hearts and shows us our sin by the pure, sweet light of mercy and grace. But when we see how filthy we are, then we think that God must be angry with us for our sins and then the Holy Ghost moves us through contrition to prayers and a longing to amend our life with all our might, to lessen God's anger, until the time we find rest for our soul and comfort for our conscience; and then we hope that God has forgiven us our sins; and it is true. And then our kind Lord reveals himself, very joyfully and looking very pleased, with a friendly welcome, as though the soul had been in pain and in prison, sweetly saying this: 'My darling, I am glad you have come to me. I have always been with you in all your misery and now you can see how much I love you and we are united in bliss.' This is how sins are forgiven through mercy and grace and our souls gloriously received in joy, just as they will be when they come to heaven, whenever this occurs through the gracious working of the Holy Ghost and the power of Christ's Passion.

Here I really understood that all manner of things are made ready for us by the great goodness of God, so much so that when we are ourselves in a state of peace and love we are truly safe. But because this cannot be fully so while we are here, it is fitting for us to live with our Lord Jesus in loving prayer and tender longing; for he always longs to bring us to the fullness of joy, as has been said before when his spiritual thirst was shown.[33]

But now, if because of all this spiritual help that has been mentioned, any man or woman is foolishly moved to say or think, 'If this is true, then it would be a good idea to sin in order to have a greater reward', or else to give less weight to sin, beware of this impulse, for in truth, if any such impulse is felt, it is false and comes from the Enemy of that same true love which offers us all this help and comfort. The same blessed love tells us that we should hate sin only because of love. And I am sure, by what I feel myself, that the more every well-natured soul sees this in the generous love of our Lord God, the more loath he is to sin and the more he is ashamed; for if we could see laid out before us all the sufferings of hell and of purgatory and of earth – death and everything else – and sin, we would choose all those sufferings rather than sin, for sin is so vile and so very hateful that it cannot be compared to any suffering other than the suffering of sin itself. And I was shown no harder hell than sin, because for a well-natured soul there is no hell but sin.

If we try to be loving and humble, we are made all fair and pure through the working of mercy and grace. And God is as eager to save man as he is strong and wise; for Christ himself is the foundation of all the laws of Christian men and he taught us to return good for evil. Here we can see that he himself is love, and he treats us as he wishes us to treat others, for he wants us to be like him in completeness of unending love for ourselves and our fellow Christians. Just as his love for us does not fail because of our sin, he does not want our love for ourselves and our fellow Christians to fail; we must feel naked hatred for sin and unending love for the soul, as God loves it. Then we shall hate sin as God hates it and love the soul as God loves it; for this assertion of God's is an endless help and comfort: 'I am keeping you very safe.'

41

The fourteenth revelation concerns what has been said before, that it is impossible that we should pray for mercy and not receive it; and how God always wants us to pray, although we may be dry and barren, because prayer is welcome and pleasing to him.

After this our Lord gave a revelation about prayer; in this showing I saw two qualities in what our Lord conveyed: one is righteousness, another is sure trust. But yet often we do not trust him fully for it seems to us that because of our unworthiness, and because we are feeling absolutely nothing, we cannot be certain that God is hearing our prayers. For often we are as barren and dry after our prayers as we were before, and so we feel our folly is the cause of our weakness; I have felt like this myself. And our Lord brought all this suddenly into my mind and these words were shown and spoken: 'I am the foundation of your prayers: first it is my will that you should have something, and then I make you desire it, and then I make you pray for it; and if you pray for it, then how could it be that you should not have what you pray for?' And thus in his first statement, along with the three which follow, our good Lord shows us something immensely helpful, as can be seen in his very words. Where he begins by saying, 'If you pray for it', there he reveals the very great joy and unending reward that our prayer will receive from him. And where he says next, 'Then how could it be . . .', this is said as an impossibility; for it is quite impossible that we should pray for mercy and grace and not have them; for everything which our good Lord makes us pray for is what he himself has ordained for us since before time began. Here we can see that our prayer is not the cause of God's goodness; and he shows that beyond any doubt in all these precious words when he says, 'I am the foundation.' And our good Lord wants this to be known to those on earth who love him, and the more that we know it, the more we should pray for, if we understand it wisely; and this is what our Lord intends. Prayer is a new, gracious, lasting will of the soul united and fast-bound to the will of God by the precious and mysterious working of the Holy Ghost. Our Lord, he is the chief receiver[34] of our prayers, it seems to me, and he accepts them very gratefully and with much delight; and he sends them up above and puts them in a treasury where they will never perish. They are there in the presence of God and all his holy ones, being received continually, always helping us in our need, and when we finally receive our bliss they will be given to us as a stage in our joy, with endless and glorious thanks from God.

Our Lord is very glad and happy that we should pray, and he expects it and wants it; for, through his grace, when we pray he makes us like him in quality as we are like him in nature, and this is his sacred will; for this is what he says: 'Pray earnestly even though you do not feel like praying, for it is helping you even if you do not feel it doing you good, even if you see nothing, yes, even if you think you cannot pray; for in dryness and in barrenness, in sickness and weakness, then your prayers give me great pleasure, even if you feel that they are hardly pleasing to you at all. And it is so in my sight with all your trustful prayers.' For the sake of the reward and the unending thanks which he wishes to give us, he longs for us to pray continually before him. God accepts the good intentions and the effort of those who serve him, whatever we are feeling; that is why he is pleased when we try hard and through our prayers and through living well, with his help and his grace, we incline towards him with all our strength (but reasonably and prudently) until we possess him we seek in the fullness of joy, that is, Jesus. And he revealed that in the fifteenth showing, where these words stand foremost: 'You shall have me as your reward.'

And thanksgiving is also part of prayer. Thanksgiving is a new inward awareness, accompanied by great reverence and loving fear, when we apply ourselves with all our might to whatever action[35] our good Lord inspires, rejoicing and giving inward thanks. And sometimes thanksgiving is so abundant that it breaks out into words and says, 'Good Lord, thank you; blessed may you be!' And sometimes, when the heart is dry and does not feel anything, or else because of the temptation of our Enemy, it is driven by reason and grace to cry out loud to our Lord, calling on his blessed Passion and his great goodness.

And the power of our Lord's word enters the soul, enlivens the heart and through his grace makes it move properly, and makes it pray very blessedly and truly to rejoice in our Lord; such prayer is truly blessed thanksgiving in the eyes of God.

42

Of three things which belong to prayer, and how we should pray; and of the goodness of God which always makes up for our imperfections and weakness when we do what we should.

Our Lord God wants us to have true understanding, and especially of three things which belong to our prayers. The first is through whom and how our prayers arise; he shows through whom when he says, 'I am the foundation'; and he shows how, through his goodness, for he says, 'First it is my will.' The second thing is in what manner and how we should be accustomed to pray; which is that our will should be joyfully transformed into the will of our Lord, rejoicing; and this is what he means when he says, 'I make you desire it.' As for the third, it is that we should know the fruit and end of our prayers, that is, to be united with and like our Lord in every way. And for this purpose and to this end all this precious teaching was revealed; and he will help us and we shall make what he says come to pass – blessed may he be!

For this is what our Lord wants – that both our prayers and our trust should be equally abundant; for if we do not trust as much as we pray, our prayers do not fully honour our Lord and we also hinder and harm ourselves; and I believe that the reason is this: we do not truly know that our Lord is the foundation from which our prayers arise and neither do we know that this is given to us by the grace of his love; for if we knew this, it would make us confident that our Lord would give us everything we desire; for I am sure that no man asks for mercy and grace with true sincerity unless mercy and grace have already been given to him. Sometimes it seems to us that we have prayed for a long time and yet, we think, we have not received what we asked for; but we should not let this sadden us; for I am sure, according to our Lord's purpose, that we should wait for a better time, for more grace or for a better gift. He wants us to have a true knowledge that he himself is Being, and he wants our understanding to be rooted with all our might and all our will-power and all our thought in this knowledge, and on this foundation he wants us to build our home and our dwelling place.

And by his own gracious light he wants us to understand the following things: the first is our noble and excellent creation; the second our costly and precious redemption; the third, everything which he has made beneath us to be of use to us and which he sustains out of love for us. So this is what he means, as if he said, 'Behold and see that I have done all this before your prayers, and now you exist and you pray to me.' And so he means that it befits us to know that the greatest deeds have been done, as Holy Church teaches. And in contemplating this with thanksgiving we should pray for the deed which is now being done: that is, we pray that he should rule and guide us to his greater glory in this life and bring us to his bliss; and he has done everything to this end.

So this is what he means: we must see that he is doing it, and we must pray for it. One of these alone is not enough; for if we pray and do not see that he is doing it, we become sad and full of doubts, which is not to God's glory; and if we see that he is doing it and do not pray, we are not doing what we owe him; and that must not happen, that is to say, it is not as God sees it; but for us to see that he is doing it and to pray for it, that is to his greater glory and to our advantage. It is God's will that we should pray for everything which he has ordained to be done, either specifically or in general; and it seems to me that the thanks and glory that we shall receive for this are beyond the understanding of any creature; for prayer is a true understanding of that fullness of joy which is to come, with sure trust and great longing for it. Lack of the bliss for which we have been ordained by nature makes us long, and true understanding and love, with sweet thoughts of our Saviour, by God's grace make us trust. And our Lord watches us continually as we perform these two actions; they are what we owe him, and his goodness allows him to allot us no lesser duties. Then we are under an obligation to try as hard as possible: and when we have done so we shall still think it is nothing – and indeed it is. But if we do the best we can, and sincerely pray for mercy and grace, we shall find in him all that we lack; and this is what he means where he says, 'I am the foundation of your prayers.'

And so in this blessed statement, with the showing, I saw how all our weakness and all our doubtful fears are fully overcome.

43

What prayer does when ordered according to God's will; and how the goodness of God delights in the deeds that he does through us, as though he were indebted to us, doing everything most lovingly.

Prayer unites the soul to God; for though the soul, restored through grace, is always like God in nature and substance, yet because of sin on man's part, it is often in a state which is unlike God. Then prayer testifies that the desire of the soul is the desire of God, and it comforts the conscience and fits man to receive grace. And so God teaches us to pray, and to trust firmly that we shall obtain what we pray for; because he regards us with love and wishes to make us sharers in his good deed, and therefore he moves us to pray for what it pleases him to do; and for these prayers, and for the good will that he wishes us to show him, he will reward us and give us an everlasting recompense. And this was shown in these words, 'If you pray for it'. In this statement God revealed such great pleasure and so much delight that it seemed as if he was deeply grateful to us for every good deed that we do – and yet it is he who does them – and because we entreat him very strongly to do everything that pleases him; as if he said, 'Then what could please me more than to be entreated very strongly, truly and eagerly to do what I wish to do?' And thus through prayer the soul is in accord with God.

But when our courteous Lord shows himself to our soul through his grace, we have what we long for; and then for a time we are unaware of anything to pray for; our only aim and our whole strength is set entirely on beholding God; and to me this seems an exalted, imperceptible prayer; for the whole purpose of our prayer is concentrated into the sight and contemplation of him to whom we pray, feeling marvellous joy, reverent fear and such great sweetness and delight in him that at that moment we can only pray as he moves us. And I know very well that the more the soul sees of God, the more it longs for him, through his grace. But when we do not see him in this way, then we feel a need to pray for a particular purpose, because we lack something, and so as to make ourselves open to Jesus; for when the soul is tormented, troubled and isolated by distress, then it is time to pray and make oneself pliable and submissive to God. But no kind of prayer can make God bend to the soul, for God's love is always the same. And so I saw that when we see something we need to pray for, then our good Lord follows us, helping us in our entreaty. And when through his special grace we behold him plainly, seeing no other need, then we follow him and he draws us into him by love; for I saw and felt that his marvellous and abundant goodness fills up all our faculties; and then I saw that his continual operation in all manner of things is done so kindly, so wisely and so powerfully that it surpasses all our imagining and all that we can believe and think; and then we can do no more than contemplate him, rejoicing, with a great and powerful longing to be completely united with him, resting in his dwelling, enjoying his love and delighting in his kindness. And then we shall, with this precious grace, through our own humble and continual prayers, come to him now in this life by many mysterious touches of precious spiritual revelations and feelings, apportioned to us as our simplicity can bear it; and this is done and shall be done, by the grace of the Holy Ghost, until we die in longing for love. And then we shall all enter into our Lord, clearly knowing ourselves and fully possessing God. And we shall all be unendingly held in God, seeing him truly, feeling him fully, hearing him spiritually, smelling him delectably and swallowing him sweetly; and then we shall see God face to face, fully and familiarly; the creature that is made shall see and endlessly contemplate God, who is the Maker; for no man can see God like this and continue to live, that is to say in this mortal life, but when through his special grace God wishes to show himself here, he strengthens the created being beyond its own nature, and he apportions the showing according to his own purpose, as much as is good for it at that moment.

44

Of the qualities of the Trinity; and how man's soul, God's creation, has the same qualities when it does what it was made for – seeing, contemplating and marvelling at its God; so that, compared with God, the soul seems as nothing to itself.

God showed again and again in all the revelations that man works his will and worships him for ever and unceasingly. And what this work is was shown in the first revelation, supported by a wonderful example, for it was shown in the working of the soul of our blessed Lady Saint Mary – truth and wisdom; and how this was shown, I hope, by the grace of the Holy Ghost, to tell as I saw it. Truth sees God, and wisdom contemplates God, and from these two comes the third, a holy and wonderful delight in God, who is love.[36] Where truth and wisdom truly are, there is truly love coming from both of them, and all of God's making; for he is supreme unending truth, supreme unending wisdom, supreme unending love, uncreated; and man's soul is a creature within God which has these same qualities in a created form, and it always does what it was made for: it sees God, it contemplates God and it loves God; so God rejoices in his creature and his creature rejoices in God, marvelling for ever; and in this marvelling he sees his God, his Lord, his Maker, so high, so great and so good in comparison with him that he made, that the creature hardly seems of any value to himself, but the brightness and purity of truth and wisdom make him see and recognize that he is made for love, in which God holds him for ever.

45

Of the stable and deep judgement of God and the wavering judgement of man.

God judges us in terms of our natural essence, which is always preserved unchanged in him, whole and safe for ever; and this judgement comes from his righteousness. And men judge in terms of our changeable sensory being, which seems now one thing, now another, according to the various influences on it and its outward appearance. And this judgement is mixed; for sometimes it is good and lenient, and sometimes it is harsh and painful. And in so far as it is good and lenient it belongs to God's righteousness; and in so far as it is harsh and painful, our good Lord Jesus corrects it by mercy and grace through the power of his blessed Passion, and so changes it into righteousness. And though these two are reconciled and united, yet both shall be known everlastingly in heaven.

The first judgement, from God's righteousness, comes from his exalted, everlasting love, and this is the kind and lovely judgement which was shown throughout the precious revelation in which I saw him assign us no kind of blame. And though this was sweet and delectable, yet I could not be quite freed from anxiety just by contemplating this, because of the judgement of Holy Church, which I had understood before and of which I was always aware. And according to this judgement it seemed to me that I had to acknowledge myself a sinner, and by the same judgement I understood that sinners deserve blame and anger one day; and I could see no blame and anger in God, and then I felt a longing greater than I can or may tell; for God himself revealed the higher judgement at the same time, and therefore I was bound to accept it; and the lower judgement had been taught me before by Holy Church, and therefore I could in no way abandon the lower judgement.

So this was what I longed for: that through him I might see how what is taught in this matter by the judgement of Holy Church is true in the sight of God, and how it befits me to know it truly; so that both judgements might be preserved to the glory of God and in the right way for me. And the only answer I had to this was a wonderful parable of a lord and a servant, very strikingly shown, as I shall recount later.[37] And yet I still long, and shall until my dying day, through God's grace to understand these two judgements as they apply to me; for all heavenly things, and all earthly ones which belong to heaven, are included in these two judgements. And the more understanding we have of these two judgements through the gracious guidance of the Holy Ghost, the more we shall see and recognize our failings. And the more we see them, the more we shall naturally long through grace to be filled with unending joy and bliss; it is what we are made for, and our natural essence is now blessed in God, and has been since it was made, and shall be without end.

46

We cannot know ourselves in this life except through faith and grace, but we must know ourselves to be sinners; and God is never angry, for he is close to the soul, protecting it.

But in our transitory life that we live here in our sensory being we do not know what we are; later we shall truly and clearly see and know our Lord God in the fullness of joy. And therefore it must needs be that the nearer we are to our bliss, the greater will be our longing, both through nature and through grace. We may have knowledge of ourselves in this life through the continuing help and strength of our higher nature, a knowledge which we may develop and increase with the help and encouragement of mercy and grace, but we can never know ourselves completely until the last moment, the moment in which this transitory life and customary grief and pain will come to an end. And therefore it is right and proper for us both by nature and by grace to long and to pray with all our might to know ourselves in the fullness of everlasting joy.

And yet in all this time, from the beginning to the end, I had two kinds of perception: one of them was of endless continuing love with certainty of protection and blessed salvation, for the entire showing revealed this; the other was the general teaching of Holy Church which I was previously instructed in and acquainted with, willingly applying and understanding it. And perception of this did not leave me, for the showing did not move or lead me from it in a single detail, but in it I was taught to love and like it, so that I might, through our Lord's help and grace, grow and rise to more heavenly knowledge and higher love. And from all that I saw it seemed to me that it was necessary for us to see and to acknowledge that we are sinners; we do many evil things which we ought not to do and leave undone many good deeds which we ought to do, and for this we deserve punishment and anger. And in spite of all this I saw truly that our Lord was never angry and never will be angry, for he is God: goodness, life, truth, love, peace; and his loving-kindness does not allow him to be angry, nor does his unity; for I saw truly that it is against the nature of strength to be angry, and against the nature of his wisdom and against the nature of his goodness. God is the goodness that cannot be angry, for he is nothing but goodness; our soul is united to him, unchangeable goodness, and in God's eyes there can be neither anger nor forgiveness between him and our soul; for through his own goodness our soul is completely united with God, so that nothing can come between God and soul.

And in every showing the soul was led to this understanding by love and drawn by strength; in his great goodness our Lord showed truly that it is so and how it is so; and he wants us to desire to know it, that is to say, so far as it is proper for us to know it; for everything that the simple soul understood, God wants to be revealed and known;[38] for the things which he wishes to remain secret, he himself hides them strongly and wisely out of love; for I saw in the same showing that many mysteries are hidden which may never be known until the time when God of his goodness has made us worthy of seeing them. And I am well-satisfied with this, submitting to our Lord's will in this great wonder. And for now I submit to my mother Holy Church as a simple child should do.

47

We must marvel reverently and suffer meekly, always rejoicing in God; and how our blindness in not seeing God is the cause of sin.

There are two points which are the duty of our soul: one is that we should wonder reverently, the other that we should suffer meekly, always rejoicing in God; for he wants us to know that in a short time we shall see clearly in him all that we desire. And in spite of this I considered things and wondered very much what the mercy and forgiveness of God really is; for from what I had already learned, I understood that the mercy of God would be the remission of his anger after our time of sin; for I thought that to a soul whose whole intention and desire is to love, the anger of God would be harsher than any other punishment, and therefore I took it that the remission of his anger would be one of the principal points of his mercy. But however hard I looked and longed, I could not see this anywhere in the whole showing.

But with his grace I shall say a little of what I saw and understood of the works of God's mercy. I understood that we men are changeable in this life and through frailty and accident we fall into sin. Man is naturally weak and foolish, and his will is smothered; and in this world he suffers storm and sorrow and woe, and the cause is his own blindness – he does not see God; for if he saw God continually he would have no evil feelings, nor any sort of impulse towards the craving which leads to sin. I saw and felt this at the same moment; and the sight and the feeling I was given seemed to me exalted and generous in comparison with our usual feelings in this life; but yet I thought they were low and mean in comparison with the great longing which the soul has to see God. For I felt in myself five kinds of emotion: joy, mourning, desire, fear and sure hope; joy, because God allowed me to understand and recognize that it was he himself I saw; mourning, because I was bereft of him; desire, which was always to see him more and more, understanding and recognizing that we shall never be completely at rest until we see him truly and clearly in heaven; fear, because it seemed to me during all that time that the vision would fail and I would be left to myself; my sure hope was in his endless love, so I saw that I would be protected by his mercy and brought to his bliss. And rejoicing in his sight with this sure hope of his merciful protection gave me understanding and comfort so that the mourning and fear were not very painful.

And yet in all this I saw from God's showing that this kind of sight of him cannot continue in this life – cannot for his own glory and the augmentation of our endless joy. And therefore we often lack the sight of him, and we are immediately thrown back into ourselves, where we find no right feelings, nothing but our own contrariness, and that of the ancient root of our first sin with all those contrived by ourselves that follow from it; and in this we are tossed and troubled with all the many different feelings of sin and suffering, both of the body and the soul, which are known to us in this life.

48

Of mercy and grace and their properties; and how we shall be glad that we bore sorrow patiently.

But our good Lord the Holy Ghost, who is eternal life dwelling in our souls, keeps us safe, and brings peace to our souls, giving them comfort through grace and harmony with God and making them pliant. And this is his mercy and the direction in which he always leads us for as long as we are here in this changeable life; for the only anger that I saw was man's, and he forgives us for that; for anger is nothing but contrariness and antagonism to peace and love, and it comes from lack of strength, or from lack of wisdom, or from lack of goodness – and it is not God who lacks these things but we who lack them; for through sin and vileness we have in us a vile and continual antagonism to peace and love, and he showed this again and again in his affectionate expression of pity and compassion; for the source of mercy is love, and the action of mercy is to hold us safely in love; and this was shown in such a way that, at least as it appeared to me, I could not discern where mercy was to be found if it were not in love alone.

Mercy works through tenderness and grace blended with abundant pity; for by the work of mercy we are held safe and by the work of mercy everything is turned to good for us. Through love mercy allows us to fail to some extent, and in so far as we fail, so far we fall, and in so far as we fall, so far we die; for we really must die in so far as we fail to see and feel God who is our life. Our failing is full of fear and our falling of shame and our dying of sorrow; but through all this the sweet eye of pity and love never leaves us, nor does mercy cease to work. For I saw the property of mercy and I saw the property of grace, which have two ways of working in one love. Mercy is a pitiful property which belongs to motherhood in tender love, and grace is an honourable property which belongs to royal lordship in the same love; mercy works – protecting, tolerating, reviving and healing, and all through the tenderness of love; and grace works – raising, rewarding and going infinitely beyond what our love and our effort deserve, spreading far and wide, and showing the great and abundant generosity of God's royal lordship through his marvellous courtesy. And this comes from the abundance of love; for through the working of grace our fearful failing is transformed into abundant, eternal comfort, and through the working of grace our shameful falling is transformed into high, noble rising, and through the working of grace our sorrowful dying is transformed into holy, blessed life; for I saw quite certainly that just as our contrariness brings us pain, shame and sorrow here on earth, so, on the contrary, grace brings us comfort, honour and bliss in heaven; and so far beyond measure that when we come up and receive the sweet reward which grace has prepared for us, then we shall thank and bless our Lord, rejoicing eternally that ever we suffered grief. And that will be because of a property of blessed love which we shall recognize in God, which we might never have known without first suffering grief.

And when I saw all this, I had to admit that the effect of God's mercy and forgiveness is to lessen and wear away our anger.

49

Our life is grounded in love, without which we perish; yet God is never angry, but in our anger and sin he mercifully keeps us safe and ordains peace in us, rewarding our tribulations.

Now this was a great marvel to the soul, continually shown in everything and considered with great attentiveness: that in regard to himself our Lord God cannot forgive, for he cannot be angry – it would be an impossibility. For this is what was shown: that our life is all grounded and rooted in love, and without love we cannot live; and therefore to the soul which through God's special grace sees so much of his great and marvellous goodness, and sees that we are joined to him in love for ever, it is the greatest impossibility conceivable that God should be angry, for anger and friendship are two contraries. It must needs be that he who wears away and extinguishes our anger and makes us gentle and kind is himself always consistently loving, gentle and kind, which is the contrary of anger; for I saw quite clearly that where our Lord appears, everything is peaceful and there is no place for anger; for I saw no kind of anger in God, neither for a short time nor for a long one; indeed, it seems to me that if God could be even slightly angry we could never have any life or place or being; for as truly as we have our being from the eternal strength of God and from the eternal wisdom and from the eternal goodness, so truly are we sustained in the eternal strength of God, in the eternal wisdom and in the eternal goodness; though we feel vengeful, quarrelsome and contentious, yet we are all mercifully enclosed in the kindness of God and in his gentleness, in his generosity and in his indulgence; for I saw quite certainly that our eternal support, our dwelling, our life and our being are all in God; for as his endless goodness protects us when we sin so that we do not perish, the same endless goodness continually negotiates a peace in us in place of our anger and our contentious falling, and makes us see that what is needed is that with true fear we should heartily beseech God for forgiveness with a gracious longing for our salvation; for we cannot be blessedly saved until we are truly in a state of peace and love, for that is what our salvation means.

And though we, through the anger and contrariness which is in us, are now in a state of tribulation, distress and grief, as our blindness and weakness deserve, yet through God's merciful care we are certainly safe so that we shall not perish. But we are not blessedly safe in the possession of our eternal joy until we are in a state of peace and love; that is to say, taking full pleasure in God and in all his works and in all his decrees, and loving and peaceful within ourselves, towards our fellow Christians and towards all whom God loves, as is pleasing to his love. And this is what God's goodness does in us.

Thus I saw that God is our true peace, and he is our sure support when we are ourselves unpeaceful, and he is continually working to bring us into eternal peace. And thus when, through the working of mercy and grace, we are made humble and gentle, we are surely safe. The soul is quickly united to God when it truly finds inner peace, for in God no anger can be found. And I saw that when we are all peaceful and loving we shall find no contrariness, nor shall we be hindered in any way by whatever contrariness is already in us. Our Lord of his goodness makes this contrariness beneficial to us; for it is the cause of all our grief and tribulations, and these our Lord Jesus takes and sends up to heaven, and there they are made more sweet and delectable than heart can think or tongue can tell, and when we come to heaven we shall find them waiting there, all turned into beautiful and eternal glory. So God is our firm ground, and he shall be our bliss and make us as unchangeable as he is when we are there.

50

How the chosen soul was never dead in the sight of God, and how she wondered
about this; and three things which emboldened her to ask God to explain it
to her.

And in this mortal life mercy and forgiveness are our path and keep
leading us on to grace. And through the distress and sorrow that we
ourselves fall into, the earthly judgement of men often considers us
dead, but in the sight of God the soul that shall be saved was never
dead, nor ever shall be. But yet at this point I was amazed and marvelled
most earnestly in my soul, thinking as follows: 'My good Lord, I see
that you are truth itself and I know for certain that we sin grievously
every day and deserve to be bitterly blamed; and I can neither give
up the knowledge of this truth, nor can I see that you show us any
kind of blame. How can this be?' For I knew through the universal
teaching of Holy Church and through my own experience that the
guilt of our sin weighs us down continually, from Adam, the first
man, until the time when we come up into heaven; then this was
what amazed me, that I saw our Lord God blaming us no more than
if we were as pure and as holy as angels in heaven. And between these
two contraries my reason was greatly tormented by my blindness, and
could not rest for fear that God's blessed presence should pass from
my sight and I should be left not knowing how he regards us in our
sin; for either I needed to see in God that sin was all done away with,
or else I needed to see in God how he sees it, so that I might truly
know how it befits me to see sin and what sort of blame is ours.

My longing endured as I looked continually towards him, and yet
my trouble and perplexity were so great that I could not be patient,
thinking, 'If I suppose that we are not sinners nor do we deserve
blame, my good Lord, how can it then be that I cannot see this
certainty in you, who are my God, my Maker, in whom I long to
see all truths? Three reasons give me the courage to ask this: the first
is because it is such a humble thing, for if it were exalted I should be
afraid; the second is that it is so universal, for if it were special and

secret, that would also make me afraid; the third is that it seems to me that I need to know it if I am to live here, in order to recognize good and evil, so that I may through reason and through grace distinguish between them more clearly, and love goodness and hate evil, as Holy Church teaches.' I cried inwardly with all my might, beseeching God for help, thinking as follows: 'Ah! Lord Jesus, king of bliss, how can I be helped? Who can show me and tell me what I need to know if I cannot see it now in you?'

51

The answer to the previous doubt through a marvellous parable of a lord and a servant; and how God wishes us to wait for him, for it was nearly twenty years later before she understood this example fully; and how it is understood that Christ sits at the right hand of the Father.

And then our kind Lord answered by showing in very mysterious images a wonderful parable of a lord who has a servant, and he gave me sight to aid my understanding of both. And this sight was shown twofold in the lord and twofold in the servant: on the one hand it was shown spiritually in bodily likeness, on the other it was shown more spiritually with no bodily likeness.

The first kind of vision was this: the bodily likeness of two people, a lord and a servant, and with this God gave me spiritual understanding. The lord sits with dignity, in rest and peace: the servant stands, waiting reverently in front of his lord, ready to do his will. The lord looks at his servant lovingly and kindly, and he gently sends him to a certain place to do his will. The servant does not just walk, but leaps forward and runs in great haste, in loving anxiety to do his lord's will. And he falls immediately into a slough and is very badly hurt. And then he groans and moans and wails and writhes, but he cannot get up or help himself in any way. And in all this I saw that his greatest trouble was lack of help; for he could not turn his face to look at his loving lord, who was very close to him, and who is the source of all help; but, like a man who was weak and foolish for the time being, he paid attention to his own senses, and his misery continued, and in this misery he suffered seven great torments. The first was the grievous bruising which he received when he fell, which was a torment he could feel. The second was the weight of his body. The third was the weakness caused by these two. The fourth that his reason was blinded and his mind stunned to such an extent that he had almost forgotten his own love for the lord. The fifth was that he could not rise. The sixth was the most astonishing to me, and it was that he lay alone; I looked hard all around, and far and near, high and low, I could see no one to help him. The seventh torment was that the place where he lay was long, hard and full of difficulties. I marvelled at how this servant could humbly suffer all that misery. And I watched carefully to see if I could perceive any fault in him, or if the lord would blame him at all; and in truth there was no fault to be seen, for his good will and his great longing were the only cause of his fall; and he was as willing and inwardly good as when he stood before his lord ready to do his will.

And this is how his loving lord tenderly continued to consider him, and now in two ways. Outwardly he regarded him gently and kindly, with great sorrow and pity, and this was the first way; the second was more inward, more spiritual, and this was shown when my understanding was led into the lord. I saw him rejoicing greatly because of the honourable rest and nobility to which he would and must bring his servant through his plentiful grace. This was the second kind of showing; and now my understanding took me back to the first, while keeping both in my mind. Then this kind lord said within himself, 'Look, look at my beloved servant, what injury and distress he has received in my service for love of me, yes, and all because his will was good! Is it not reasonable that I should compensate him for his terror and his dread, his hurt and his injury and all his misery? And not only this, but would it not be proper for me to give a gift that would be better for him and give him more glory than if he had never been injured? Otherwise it seems to me that I would do him no favour.' And then an inward, spiritual explanation of the lord's purpose penetrated my soul. I saw that, given his own greatness and glory, it needs must be that his dear servant whom he loved so much should be truly and blissfully rewarded for ever, more than he would have been if he had not fallen; yes, and to such an extent that his fall and the misery it caused him should be transformed into great and surpassing glory and eternal bliss.

And at this point the showing of the parable vanished, and our good Lord guided my understanding as to the appearance and meaning of the revelation to the end. But in spite of this guidance, I never lost my sense of wonder at the parable. It seemed that it was given me as an answer to my longing, and yet at that time I could not grasp it fully to my own satisfaction; for in the servant who represented Adam, as I shall explain, I saw many different properties which could in no way be attributed just to Adam. And so for the moment I was in a state of great bewilderment; for a full understanding of this marvellous parable was not given to me at that time.

In this mysterious parable, three aspects of the revelation remain largely hidden; yet I saw and understood that each of the showings is full of mysteries, and so I ought now to enumerate these three aspects and the limited progress I have made in understanding them. The first is the early stage of teaching which I understood from it while it was being shown to me; the second is the inner learning which I have come to understand from it since then; the third is the whole revelation from beginning to end, as set out in this book, which our Lord God in his goodness often shows freely to the eyes of my mind. And these three are so united in my mind that I neither can nor may separate them.[39]

And through these three, united as one, I have been taught how I ought to believe and trust in our Lord God: that just as he showed it out of his goodness and for his own purpose, so out of the same goodness and for the same purpose he will explain the vision to us when he so wishes. Because twenty years after the time of the showing, all but three months, I received inner teaching, as follows: 'You need to pay attention to all the properties and conditions of what you were shown in the parable, though they may seem mysterious and insignificant in your eyes.' I accepted this willingly and with great eagerness, looking inwardly with great care at all the details and properties which were shown at the time of the vision, so far as my wit and understanding would serve. I began by looking at the lord and the servant, and the way the lord was sitting, and the place where he sat, and then the colour of his clothing and the way it was shaped, and his outward appearance, and the nobility and goodness within; I looked at the way the servant stood and where and how, at the sort of clothing he wore, its colour and shape, at his outward behaviour and at his inner goodness and his readiness.

The lord who sat with dignity, in rest and peace, I understood to be God. The servant who stood in front of the lord, I understood that he represented Adam, that is to say, that one man and his fall were shown in that vision to make it understood how God considers any man and his fall; for in the sight of God, all men are one. This man's strength was broken and enfeebled; and his understanding was numbed, for he turned away from looking at his lord. But in the sight of God his purpose remained undiminished; for I saw our Lord commend and approve his purpose, but the man himself was obstructed and blind to the knowledge of this purpose, and this causes him great sorrow and grievous misery; for neither can he clearly see his loving lord, who is most gentle and kind to him, nor can he see truly how he himself appears to his loving lord. And I am quite certain that if we really and truly see these two things, then we shall attain rest and peace partially here on earth and the full bliss of heaven, through his plentiful grace. And this was the beginning of the teaching revealed to me at this same time, through which I might come to know God's attitude to us in our sin. And then I saw that only suffering blames and punishes, and our kind Lord comforts and grieves; he always considers the soul cheerfully, loving and longing to bring us to bliss.

The place where our Lord sat was humble, on the barren earth, deserted, alone in a wilderness. His clothing was full and ample, as befits a lord; the cloth was as blue as azure, most sober and comely. His expression was merciful, the colour of his face a comely brown with pronounced features; his eyes were black, most comely and handsome, appearing full of tender pity; and within him there was a great refuge, long and wide and all full of endless heavens.[40] And his tender expression as he kept looking at his servant, especially when he fell, I thought it could melt our hearts with love and break them in two with joy. The comely expression showed a handsome mixture which was wonderful to look at: it was partly sorrow and pity, partly joy and bliss. The joy and bliss are as far beyond sorrow and pity as heaven is above earth. The pity was earthly and the bliss was heavenly. The sorrow in the Father's pity was for the fall of Adam, his most loved creature; the joy and bliss was for his beloved Son, who is equal to the Father. The merciful gaze of his tender expression filled the whole earth and went down with Adam into hell, and this unending pity kept Adam from everlasting death. And this mercy and pity remain with mankind until the time we come up into heaven. But man is blind in this life, and therefore we cannot see our Father, God, as he is. And when, out of his goodness, he wants to show himself to man, he shows himself in a familiar way, like a man; nevertheless I saw truly that we should know and believe that the Father is not a man. But his sitting on the barren earth in a deserted place means this: he made man's soul to be his own city and his dwelling-place, the most pleasing to him of all his works; and once man had fallen into sorrow and pain he was not fit to serve that noble purpose, and therefore our kind Father would prepare no other place for himself but sit upon the earth waiting for mankind, who is mixed with earth, until the time when, through his grace, his beloved Son had bought back his city and restored its noble beauty with his hard labour.

The blue of his clothing signifies his steadfastness. The brown of his fair face with the handsome blackness of the eyes was most suited to showing his holy gravity. The fullness of his clothing, which was fair, glowing brightly about him, signifies that he has enclosed within him all the heavens and all joy and bliss. And a glimpse of this was given where I said, 'My understanding was led into the lord',[41] when I saw him rejoicing greatly because of the glorious Resurrection to which he wills to bring and shall bring his servant through his plentiful grace.

And yet I marvelled as I considered the lord and the aforementioned servant. I saw the lord sitting with dignity, and the servant standing reverently in front of his lord; and there is a double meaning in this servant, one without and another within. Outwardly, he was simply dressed, as a labourer might be who was ready to work, and he stood very near the lord, not right in front of him, but a little to one side, on the left. His clothing was a white tunic, unlined, old and all spoilt, stained with the sweat of his body, tight-fitting and short on him, only reaching about a hand's breadth below the knee, threadbare, looking as if it would soon be worn out – in rags and tatters. And I was very surprised about this, thinking, 'Now this is unsuitable clothing for such a well-loved servant to wear in front of such an honourable lord.'

Love was shown deep within him, and this love which he had for the lord was just like the love which the lord had for him. His servant's wisdom saw inwardly that there was one thing he could do which would be to the lord's honour. And the servant for love, with no regard for himself or for anything that might happen to him, leapt quickly forward and ran at his lord's command to perform his will and serve his glory. For it looked from his outer clothing as if he had been a labourer continuously for a long time; yet from the inward sight that I had of both the lord and the servant, it seemed that he was a new one, that is to say, newly beginning to labour, a servant who had never been sent out before. There was a treasure in the earth which the lord loved. I marvelled and wondered what it could be. And I was answered in my understanding, 'It is a food which is sweet and pleasing to the lord.' For I saw the lord sit like a man, and I saw neither food nor drink to serve him; this was one marvel. Another marvel was that this dignified lord had only the one servant, and him he sent out. I watched, wondering what kind of labour it could be that the servant should do. And then I understood that he would do the greatest labour and the hardest toil of all – he would be a gardener, digging and ditching, toiling and sweating, and turning the earth upside down, and delving deeply and watering the plants at the right time. And this would continue to be his work, and he would make fresh water flow, and noble and plentiful fruits spring up, which he would bring before the lord and serve him as he wished. And he should never turn back until he had prepared this food all ready as he knew it pleased the lord, and then he should take this food, with the drink as part of it, and carry it very reverently to the lord. And all this time the lord would sit in the same place, waiting for the servant whom he had sent out.

And yet I wondered where the servant came from; for I saw that the lord has within himself eternal life and every kind of goodness, except for the treasure which was in the earth – and that had its origin in the lord in wonderful depths of endless love – but it was not entirely to his glory until this servant had prepared it nobly in this way, and brought it to him, into his own presence; and without the lord there was nothing but a wilderness. And I did not understand all that this parable meant, and that was why I wondered where the servant came from.

In the servant is comprehended the second person of the Trinity, and in the servant is comprehended Adam, that is to say, all men. And therefore when I say 'the Son', it means the Godhead, which is equal with the Father, and when I say 'the servant', it means Christ's Humanity, which is truly Adam. The servant's nearness represents the Son, and his standing on the left side represents Adam. The lord is the Father, God; the servant is the Son, Christ Jesus. The Holy Ghost is the equal love which is in both of them. When Adam fell, God's son fell; because of the true union made in heaven, God's son could not leave Adam, for by Adam I understand all men. Adam fell from life to death into the valley of this wretched world, and after that into hell. God's son fell with Adam into the valley of the Virgin's womb (and she was the fairest daughter of Adam), in order to free Adam from guilt in heaven and in earth; and with his great power he fetched him out of hell.

The wisdom and goodness in the servant represent God's son. That he was poorly dressed as a labourer and standing near the left-hand side represents Christ's Humanity and Adam, with all the consequent trouble and weakness; for in this parable our good Lord showed his own son and Adam as but one man. The strength and the goodness which we have come from Jesus Christ, the weakness and the blindness which we have come from Adam, and these two were represented in the servant.

And thus our good Lord Jesus has taken upon himself all our guilt;

and therefore our Father neither may nor will assign us any more guilt than he does to his own son, dearly loved Christ. Thus the Son was the servant before he came to earth, standing ready before the Father, waiting until the time when he would send him to do that glorious deed by which mankind was brought back to heaven; that is to say that in spite of the fact that he is God, equal with the Father as regards the Godhead, yet because of his providential purpose to become man to save man in fulfilment of his Father's will, he stood in front of his Father like a servant, willingly taking all our burden upon himself. And then he leapt forward eagerly at the Father's will and immediately he fell low into the Virgin's womb, with no regard to himself or to his harsh suffering. The white tunic is the flesh; the single thickness shows that there was nothing at all between the Godhead and the Humanity; the tightness shows poverty; it was old because Adam wore it; it was sweat-stained from Adam's toil; it was short to show the servant must labour.

And this is how I saw the Son standing, and what he said inwardly was, 'Look, my dear Father, I am standing before you in Adam's tunic, all ready to leap forward and to run. It is my wish to be on earth to work for your glory whenever it is your wish to send me. How long must I linger?' The Son knew very well when it would be his Father's will and how long he had to linger, that is to say, in so far as he is the Godhead, for he is the Wisdom of the Father. Therefore what was conveyed was in respect of the Manhood of Christ; for all mankind who shall be saved by Christ's precious Incarnation and blessed Passion, all are Christ's Manhood. He is the head and we are his limbs; and these limbs do not know the day and the time when every passing grief and sorrow will come to an end, and everlasting joy and bliss will be accomplished, the day and time which all the company of heaven longs to see. And all those under heaven who shall come there shall do so by longing and wishing; and this wish and longing was shown in the servant standing in front of the lord, or, to put it differently, in the Son standing in front of the Father in Adam's tunic; for the wish and the craving of all mankind that shall be saved appeared in Jesus; for Jesus is all who shall be saved and all who shall be saved are Jesus; and all through God's love, along with the obedience, humility and patience, and other virtues which pertain to us.

Also this wonderful parable gives me some teaching, as if it were the beginning of an ABC, through which I may have some understanding of our Lord's purpose, for the mysteries of the revelation are hidden in it, though indeed all the showings are full of mysteries. That the Father was sitting signifies his Godhead, in that it shows rest and peace; for there may be no labour in the Godhead. And that he showed himself as lord has meaning in relation to our humanity. That the servant was standing signifies labour; that he was to one side and on the left signifies that he was not quite worthy to stand right in front of the lord. His leaping up belonged to the Godhead and his running to Christ's Manhood; for the Godhead leapt from the Father into the Virgin's womb, falling when he took on our nature; and in this fall he was grievously hurt; the hurt he received was our flesh in which he soon felt deathly pain. That he stood in awe before the lord but not quite in front of him signifies that his clothing was not respectable enough to stand right before the lord; nor could or should that be his duty while he was a labourer; neither could he sit in rest and peace with the lord until he had justly earned his peace with his hard labour; that he was on the left side shows that the Father deliberately left his own Son in human form to suffer all man's pains without sparing him. By the fact that his tunic would soon be in rags and tatters is understood the blows and the scourging, the thorns and the nails, the pulling and the dragging, tearing his tender flesh; as I saw in part, the flesh was torn from the skull, falling in shreds until the bleeding stopped; and then it began to dry again, clinging to the bone.[42] And by the tossing and turning, groaning and moaning, it is understood that he could never rise again in his full power from the time that he fell into the Virgin's womb until his body was slain and he died, yielding his soul into the Father's hands with all mankind for whom he was sent. And at this point he first began to show his power; for he went into hell, and when he was there he raised up out of the deep depths the great root[43] of those who were truly united with him in high heaven. The body was in the grave until Easter morning, and from that time he lay down no more; for then was truly ended the tossing and turning, the groaning and moaning; and our foul mortal flesh which God's son took upon himself, which was Adam's old tunic, tight, bare and short, was then made by our Saviour newly beautiful, white and bright and eternally pure, full and ample, fairer and richer than the clothing which I saw on the Father, for that clothing was blue, and Christ's clothing is now of a comely, handsome mixture which is so wonderful that I cannot describe it; for it is all glory. Now the lord does not sit in a wilderness on earth, but sits in the noblest seat in heaven, which he made to his own liking. Now the Son does not stand in awe in front of the Father like a servant, plainly dressed and partly naked, but he stands immediately before the Father, richly dressed in holy munificence, with a crown of inestimable richness on his head; for it was shown that we are his crown, and that this crown is the Father's joy, the Son's glory, the Holy Ghost's delight, and unending and wonderful bliss to all who are in heaven. Now the Son does not stand before the Father on his left, like a labourer, but he sits at his Father's right hand in eternal rest and peace. This does not mean that the Son sits on the Father's right hand, side by side with him, as one person sits by another in this world; for as I see it there is no such sitting in the Trinity; but he sits on his Father's right hand, which is to say in the highest rank of the Father's joys. Now the spouse, God's son, is at peace with his beloved bride, who is the fair Virgin of eternal joy.[44] Now the Son sits, true God and man, in his city in rest and peace, which his Father has eternally held in preparation for him; and the Father in the Son, and the Holy Ghost in the Father and in the Son.

52

God rejoices that he is our father, mother and spouse; and how the chosen have here a mixture of weal and woe, but God is with us in three ways; and how we may avoid sin, but never perfectly as in heaven.

And so I saw that God rejoices that he is our father, and God rejoices that he is our mother, and God rejoices that he is our true spouse, and our soul is his much-loved bride. And Christ rejoices that he is our brother, and Jesus rejoices that he is our saviour. These are five great joys, as I understand it, in which he wishes us to rejoice, praising him, thanking him, loving him, endlessly blessing him.

All people who shall be saved, while we are in this world, have in us a marvellous mixture of both weal and woe. We have in us our risen Lord Jesus; we have in us the misery of the harm of Adam's falling and dying. We are steadfastly protected by Christ, and by the touch of his grace we are raised into sure trust of salvation. And by Adam's fall our perceptions are so shattered in various ways, by sins and by different sufferings, that we are so darkened and blinded that we can hardly find any comfort. But inwardly we wait for God and trust faithfully that we shall receive mercy and grace; and this is God's own operation within us. And in his goodness he opens the eye of our understanding and by this we gain sight, sometimes more and sometimes less, according to the ability that God gives us to receive it. And at one moment we are raised into weal, and at another we are allowed to fall into woe. And so there is such a wonderful mixture within us that we hardly know how we ourselves or our fellow Christians stand because of the wonder of these varied feelings; but that same holy accord which we accord to God when we feel him, truly wishing to be with him with all our heart, with all our soul and with all our strength, leads us to hate and despise our evil impulses and everything which might be the occasion of bodily or spiritual sin. And yet nevertheless when this sweetness is hidden, we fall back into our blindness, and so into woe and tribulation in various ways. But then this is our comfort: that through our faith we know that by the power of Jesus Christ, our protector, we never consent to it, but we are discontented with it, and endure pain and woe, praying until the time when he shows himself to us again.

And so we remain in this mixed state all the days of our life. But he wants us to have faith that he is unfailingly with us, and in three ways. He is with us in heaven, true man in his own person drawing us upwards, and that was shown in the holy thirst;[45] and he is with us on earth, leading us, and that was shown in the third revelation, where I saw God in an instant; and he is with us in our souls, dwelling there for ever, guiding and caring for us, and that was shown in the sixteenth revelation, as I shall describe.

And so in the servant was shown the trouble and blindness of Adam's fall, and in the servant was shown the wisdom and goodness of God's son. And in the lord was shown the sorrow and pity of Adam's woe; and in the lord was shown the exalted magnificence and endless glory to which mankind attains through the power of the Passion and the death of God's much-loved son. For this reason he rejoices greatly in his fall, because of the great exaltation and fullness of bliss that mankind attains, surpassing what we should have if he had not fallen; and so it was to see this surpassing magnificence that my understanding was led into God at the same time that I saw the servant fall. And so now we have reason for grief, because our sin is the cause of Christ's suffering; and we have reason for lasting joy, because endless love made him suffer. And therefore the person who sees and feels the working of love through grace hates nothing but sin; for it seems to me that, of all things, love and hate are the hardest and most immeasurable contraries. And in spite of all this, I saw and understood that our Lord's meaning was that in this life we may not keep from sin in such full and complete purity as we shall in heaven. But through grace we may well keep ourselves from the sins which, as Holy Church teaches us, will lead us to eternal suffering, and avoid venial sin, as far as our strength allows;[46] and if through our blindness and our wretchedness we ever fall, we are taught to rise again quickly, recognizing the sweet touch of grace, and earnestly amend our life on the basis of Holy Church's teaching according to the grievousness of the sin, and go at once to God in love. We should not on the one hand fall too low, inclining to despair, nor on the other hand be too reckless, as if we did not care, but should recognize our own weakness without concealment, knowing that we cannot stand even for the twinkling of an eye unless we are protected by grace. We should cling reverently to God, trusting in him alone; for man and God regard things in two quite different ways; it is proper for man humbly to accuse himself, and it is proper for God in his natural goodness kindly to excuse man.

These are the two aspects of the double expression with which the lord watched the fall of his loved servant. The first was shown outwardly, very gentle and kind, with great sorrow and pity, and that was the aspect of eternal love. And the way our Lord wants us to accuse ourselves is this: earnestly and truly seeing and recognizing our fall and all the troubles that come from it, seeing and knowing that we can never make it good, but at the same time we should earnestly and truly see and know the everlasting love which he has for us, and his abundant mercy. And seeing and knowing both together in this way is the humble self-accusation which our Lord asks of us, and where it exists, he himself has brought it about. And this is the lower level of man's life and it was shown in the lord's outward appearance; and I saw two aspects of the showing: one is man's pitiable fall, the other is the glorious atonement that our Lord has made for man.

The second expression was shown inwardly; it was more elevated but it was all one with the first; for the life and the virtue which we have on the lower level comes from the higher, and it comes down to us from our natural self-love through grace. Nothing comes between the first and the second, for all is one love, and this one blessed love now works doubly in us; for on the lower level there are pains and passions, sorrows and pities, mercies and forgiveness, and many similar benefits; but on the higher level there are none of these, but all one great love and wonderful joy, and in the wonderful joy there is great compensation for all suffering. And in this our good Lord showed not only our forgiveness, but also the glorious height to which he will bring us, turning all our guilt into endless glory.

53

The kindness of God assigns no blame to those he has chosen, for in them is
a godly will which can never consent to sin; for it befits God's pity to be so
bound to them that a higher nature is preserved which can never be separated
from him.

And I saw that God wants us to recognize that he does not take the
fall of any human being that shall be saved more harshly than he took
the fall of Adam, who we know was eternally loved and securely
protected in the time of his need, and is now blissfully compensated
with great surpassing joys; for our Lord God is so good, so noble, so
generous that he can never blame anyone who will be blessed and
praised in the end.

And what I have just said was part of the answer to my entreaty,
and my great concern was somewhat eased by the kind, gracious
showing of our good Lord; a showing in which I saw and understood
very clearly that in every soul that will be saved there is a godly will
which never agreed to sin, nor ever shall; this will is so good that it
can never intend evil, but always and constantly it intends good and
does good in the sight of God. Therefore our Lord wants us to know
this as a matter of faith and belief, and most especially to know that
we all have this blessed will kept safe and whole in our Lord Jesus
Christ; for beings of the kind that will people heaven must needs, by
God's justice, be so bound and united to him that there would always
remain a higher nature in them which never could nor should be
separated from God; and this is through his own good will in his
eternal foreseeing purpose. And in spite of this just binding and this
everlasting union, the redemption and the buying back of humankind
is necessary and useful in all things, as it is done with the same intention
and for the same purpose that Holy Church teaches us in our faith.

I saw that God never began to love humankind, for just as humankind shall be in eternal bliss, completing the joy of God in his own
works, so has that same humankind been, in God's foresight, known
and loved according to God's righteous purpose since before time

began. And by the eternal consent and agreement of the whole Trinity, Christ would be the ground and the head of these fair beings, he from whom we all come, in whom we are all enclosed, into whom we shall all return; finding in him our full heaven of everlasting joy through the foreseeing purpose of the whole blessed Trinity since before time began. Before he made us he loved us, and when we were made we loved him; and this is a love made of the essential goodness natural to the Holy Ghost, mighty by reason of the might of the Father, and wise in accordance with the wisdom of the Son. Thus man's soul is made of God and bound to God by the same ties.

And thus I understood that man's soul is made of nothing, that is to say, it is made, but of nothing that is made, and in this way: when God was going to make man's body, he took the slime of the earth, which is a substance mixed and gathered from all bodily things, and from this he made man's body; but for the making of man's soul he did not wish to take anything at all, he simply made it. And so created nature is justly united to the Creator, who is essential uncreated nature, that is, God. And that is why there neither can nor shall be anything at all between God and man's soul. And in this eternal love man's soul is kept whole, as the contents of the revelations mean and show; and in this eternal love we are guided and protected by God and shall never be lost; for he wants us to know that our soul is a living creature, which, through his goodness and grace, will last in heaven for ever, loving him, thanking him, praising him. And just as we shall be eternally, so we were treasured and hidden in God, known and loved since before time began.

Therefore he wants us to know that the noblest thing he ever made is humankind, and its supreme essence and highest virtue is the blessed soul of Christ. And furthermore he wants us to know that his precious soul was beautifully bound to him in the making[47] with a knot which is so subtle and so strong that it is joined into God; and in this joining it is made eternally holy. Furthermore, he wants us to know that all the souls which will be eternally saved in heaven are bound and united in this union and made holy in this holiness.

54

We ought to rejoice that God dwells in our soul and our soul in God, so that between God and our soul there is nothing, but as though it were all God; and how faith is the ground of all virtue in our soul, through the Holy Ghost.

And in the great and endless love which God has for all mankind, he makes no distinction in love between the blessed soul of Christ and the least soul that will be saved; for it is very easy to believe that the dwelling of the blessed soul of Christ is most high in the glorious Godhead, and truly, as I understand in what our Lord conveyed, where the blessed soul of Christ is, there is the essential being of all the souls that will be saved in Christ. We ought to rejoice greatly that God dwells in our soul, and we ought to rejoice much more greatly that our soul dwells in God. Our soul is made to be God's dwelling place, and the dwelling place of the soul is God, who is not made. It shows deep understanding to see and know inwardly that God, who is our maker, dwells in our soul; and deeper understanding to see and know that our soul, which is made, dwells in God's being; through this essential being – God – we are what we are.

And I saw no difference between God and our essential being, it seemed to be all God, and yet my understanding took it that our essential being is in God: that is to say that God is God, and our essential being is a creation within God; for the almighty truth of the Trinity is our father, he who made us and keeps us within him; and the deep wisdom of the Trinity is our mother, in whom we are all enclosed; and the great goodness of the Trinity is our lord and in him we are enclosed and he in us. We are enclosed in the Father, and we are enclosed in the Son, and we are enclosed in the Holy Ghost; and the Father is enclosed in us, and the Son is enclosed in us, and the Holy Ghost is enclosed in us: almighty, all wisdom, all goodness, one God, one Lord.

And our faith is a virtue which comes from the essence of our nature into our sensory being through the Holy Ghost, and in this virtue all virtues come to us, for without it no man may receive virtue:

it is no less than a right understanding with true belief and sure trust of what we cannot see, that in our essence we are in God, and God in us. And this virtue, and all the others within it which God has ordained for us, works great things in us; for Christ works mercifully within us and we are in accord with him by divine grace through the gifts and virtues of the Holy Ghost; it is this working which makes us Christ's children and makes us lead Christian lives.

55

Christ is our way, leading and presenting us to the Father; and as soon as the soul is infused into the body, mercy and grace begin to work; and how the second person of the Trinity took on our sensory being to deliver us from double death.

And so Christ is our way, leading us surely in his laws, and Christ in his own body bears us powerfully up to heaven; for I saw that, having within him all of us that shall be saved by him, he presents us with due honour to his Father in heaven; a present which his Father receives gratefully, and kindly gives to his son Jesus Christ; and this gift and action is joy to the Father, bliss to the Son and delight to the Holy Ghost. And out of everything about us, what pleases our Lord most is that we rejoice in this joy at our salvation which is in the Holy Trinity. And this was seen in the ninth showing where more is said of this matter. And in spite of all our feelings, weal and woe, God wants us to understand and believe that we are more truly in heaven than on earth.

Our faith comes from the natural love of our soul and from the bright light of our reason and from the steadfast perception of God which we have when we are first made. And when our soul is breathed into our body, at the moment when we become sensory beings, mercy and grace immediately begin to work, taking care of us and protecting us with pity and love; and as they do so the Holy Ghost shapes in our faith the hope that we shall rise up again to our essential being, into the virtue of Christ, increased and accomplished through the Holy

Ghost. Thus I understand that the sensory being is grounded in nature, in mercy and in grace, and this ground enables us to receive gifts which lead us to eternal life; for I saw quite certainly that our essential being is in God, and I also saw that God is in our sensory being; for at the very point that our soul is made sensory, at that point is the city of God, ordained for him since before time began; a dwelling place to which he comes and which he will never leave, for God never leaves the soul in which he dwells blissfully for ever. And this was seen in the sixteenth showing where it says, 'Jesus will never leave the position which he takes in our soul.'

And all the gifts which God can give to those he creates he has given to his son Jesus for us; and he, dwelling in us, has enclosed these gifts within himself until such time as we have grown and matured, our soul with our body and our body with our soul, neither of them receiving help from the other, until by the operation of nature we achieve our full stature; and then, on the basis of nature and with the operation of mercy, the Holy Ghost graciously breathes into our body gifts leading to eternal life.

And so my understanding was led by God to see into him and to understand, to recognize and to know, that our soul is a created trinity, like the uncreated Holy Trinity, known and loved since before time began, and in the making united to the Maker as has been explained previously. This insight was very sweet and wonderful to contemplate, peaceful and restful, sure and delectable. And because of the glorious union which was thus made by God between the soul and the body, it must needs be that mankind shall be redeemed from double death – a redemption which could never have taken place before the time when the second Person of the Trinity had taken on the lower part of humanity, the higher part having been united to him at the time of humanity's first creation. These two parts were in Christ, the higher and the lower, one soul. The higher part was at one with God in peace, in full joy and bliss; the lower part, which is sensory being, suffered for the salvation of mankind. And these two parts were seen and felt in the eighth showing, in which my body was filled with perception and awareness of Christ's Passion and his death. And yet there came with this a subtle feeling and mysterious inward sight of the higher part which I was shown at the same time, although I could not follow the suggestion made to me that I should look up to heaven;[48] and that was because of the power of my contemplation of the inner life – by which I mean that exalted essential being, that precious soul of Christ, which rejoices eternally in the Godhead.

56

It is easier to know God than our soul, for God is nearer to us than that, and therefore if we want to have knowledge of it, we must look in God; and he wants us to long for knowledge of natural mercy and grace.

And thus I saw quite certainly that it is easier for us to attain knowledge of God than to know our own soul; for our soul is so deeply grounded in God, and so eternally treasured, that we cannot attain knowledge of it until we first know God, the Maker to whom it is united. But in spite of this, I saw that for complete understanding we have to long to know our own soul wisely and truly; and for this reason we are taught to search for it where it is to be found, and that is in God. And so by the gracious guidance of the Holy Ghost we should know them both at once, whether we are moved to know God or our soul; they are both good and true.

God is nearer to us than our own soul, for he is the ground on which our soul stands and he is the means by which essential being and sensory being are kept together, so that they shall never be separated; for our soul sits in God in complete rest and our soul stands in God in complete strength and our soul is naturally rooted in God in eternal love. And therefore if we want knowledge of our soul and intercourse and communion with it, it behoves us to search in our Lord God in whom it is enclosed. And I saw and understood more of this enclosure in the sixteenth showing, as I shall explain.

And so far as our essential being and sensory being are concerned, they may rightly be called our soul, and that is because they are united in God. The noble city in which our Lord Jesus sits is our sensory being, in which he is enclosed; and our essential being is enclosed in Jesus, with the blessed soul of Christ sitting and resting in the Godhead. And I saw quite certainly that we must needs be in a state of longing and suffering until the time when we are led so deeply into God that we really and truly know our own soul. And indeed I saw that into these great depths our good Lord himself leads us, in the same love with which he made us, and in the same love with which he bought us through mercy and grace by virtue of his blessed Passion. And in spite of all this we can never attain full knowledge of God until we first know our own soul clearly, for until our soul reaches its full strength we cannot reach full holiness, and that will happen when through the power of Christ's Passion our sensory being is raised to our essential being, with all the profit which our Lord through mercy and grace will enable us to gain from our tribulations.

I had some degree of insight into this, and it is a process grounded in nature, that is to say, our reason is grounded in God, who is the summit of essential being. From this essential nature, mercy and grace spring and spread into us, influencing all things in fulfilment of our joy. These are the grounds in which we grow and reach our fulfilment, for in nature we have our life and our being, and in mercy and grace we have our growth and our fulfilment; nature, mercy and grace are three aspects of a single goodness, and where one works they all work in the things which concern us in this life. God wants us to understand, longing with all our heart and with all our strength to know more and more of them until the time when we reach fulfilment; for to know them fully and see them clearly is none other than the eternal joy and bliss which we shall have in heaven. God wants this to begin here in the knowledge of his love; for we cannot profit from our reason alone, unless we also have perception and love; nor can we be saved just because we are naturally grounded in God, unless we have knowledge of this ground and of his mercy and grace, for from these three, working all together, we receive all our goodness. The first of these are the goods of nature; for when we were first made, God gave us abundance of natural goods, but also greater goods such as we could receive only in spirit, for in his eternal wisdom his foreseeing purpose wanted us to have this double nature.[49]

57

Our essential being is complete, and though we are lacking in our sensory being it will be replenished by mercy and grace; and how the higher part of our nature is bound to God in its creation, and in taking on our flesh Jesus is bound to the lower part of our nature; and how other virtues spring from faith; and Mary is our mother.

And so far as our essential being is concerned, God made us so noble and so rich that we always work his will and his glory. When I say 'we', I mean those who will be saved; for I saw truly that we are what he loves and we always do what pleases him, without limit; and from the great riches and exalted nobility of our essential being, virtues come to our soul in due measure when it is bound to our body and we become sensory beings. And so in our essential being we are complete and in our sensory being we are lacking, but God will remedy this by making mercy and grace flow abundantly into us from his own natural goodness. And so his natural goodness makes mercy and grace work within us; and the natural goodness which we have from him enables us to receive the workings of mercy and grace.

I saw that our nature is complete in God, and he makes diverse qualities flow into it from him to do his will, and these are sustained by nature, and restored and completed by mercy and grace. And none of these shall be lost; for the higher part of our nature is bound to God in its creation; and God is bound to the lower part of our nature in taking on our flesh. Thus the two parts of us are united in Christ; for the Trinity is included in Christ in whom the higher part of our nature is grounded and rooted, and the second Person of the Trinity has taken on the lower part, a nature which was ordained for him from the beginning; for I saw quite certainly that all the works which God has done or ever shall do were fully known to him and foreseen since before time began; and he made mankind for love, and for the same love chose to be man himself.

The next good which we receive is our faith, in which our profit begins; and it comes from the great riches of our essential being into our sensory soul; and it is grounded in us and we in it through the natural goodness of God by the operation of mercy and grace. And from this come all the other goods by which we are guided and saved; for from it come God's commandments, of which we should have two sorts of understanding. These are first to love and obey what he bids, and second to know what he forbids and to hate and reject it. Everything we do is included in these two. The seven sacraments[50] are also included in our faith, following each other in order as God has ordained them for us. So are all manner of virtues; for through the goodness of God, the same virtues which we have received from our essential being, given to us by nature, are also by the operation of mercy given to us through grace, renewed by the Holy Ghost. These virtues and gifts are treasured up for us in Jesus Christ; for at the same time that God bound himself to our body in the Virgin's womb, he took on our sensory soul, and in doing so he enclosed us all within himself and united the sensory soul with our essential being, a union in which he was perfect man; for Christ, having bound into himself each man who shall be saved, is perfect man.

Thus our Lady is our mother in whom we are all enclosed and we are born from her in Christ; for she who is mother of our Saviour is mother of all who will be saved in our Saviour. And our Saviour is our true mother in whom we are eternally born and by whom we shall always be enclosed. This was shown abundantly, fully and sweetly; and it is spoken of in the first showing where he says that we are all enclosed in him and he is enclosed in us;[51] and it is spoken of in the sixteenth showing, where it says that he sits in our soul; for it is his pleasure to reign blissfully in our understanding, and to sit restfully in our soul, and to dwell endlessly in our soul, working us all into himself; and in this working he wants us to help him, giving him all our attention, learning what he teaches, keeping his laws, desiring that everything he does should be done, faithfully trusting in him; for I saw truly that our essential being is in God.

58

God was never displeased with his chosen bride; and of three properties of the Trinity: fatherhood, motherhood and lordship; and how our essential being is in every person, but our sensory being is in Christ alone.

Just as he is eternal since before time began, so God, the Holy Trinity who is everlasting being, purposed eternally to make mankind, whose fair nature was first assigned to his own son, the second Person of the Trinity. And when he so wished, with the full agreement of the whole Trinity, he made us all at once; and in our making he bound and united us to himself; a union through which we are kept as pure and as noble as we were made. By the power of the same precious union we love our Maker and please him, praise him, thank him and endlessly rejoice in him. And this work that goes on continually in every soul that shall be saved is the godly will mentioned previously. And so in our making, God almighty is our father by nature; and God all wisdom is our mother by nature, along with the love and goodness of the Holy Ghost; and these are all one God, one Lord. And in this binding and union he is a real and true bridegroom, and we his loved bride and his fair maiden, a bride with whom he is never displeased; for he says, 'I love you and you love me, and our love shall never be divided.'[52]

I considered the operation of all the Holy Trinity, and in doing so I saw and understood these three properties: the property of fatherhood, the property of motherhood and the property of lordship, all in one God. In our almighty Father we are sustained and blessed so far as our essential nature is concerned, which belongs to us through our making since before time began; and in the second Person, who is Intellect and Wisdom, we are sustained as far as our sensory being, our redemption and our salvation are concerned; for he is our mother, brother and saviour. And in our good lord the Holy Ghost we have our reward and recompense for our living and suffering; and endless surpassing of all we desire comes from his marvellous generosity, his great and abundant grace.

For our whole life falls into three parts. In the first we exist, in the second we grow and in the third we are completed. The first is nature, the second is mercy, the third is grace. As for the first, I saw and understood that the great power of the Trinity is our father, and the deep wisdom of the Trinity is our mother, and the great love of the Trinity is our lord; and we have all this by nature and in our essential being. And furthermore, I saw that as the second Person is mother of our essential being, so that same well-loved Person has become mother of our sensory being; for God makes us double, as essential and sensory beings. Our essential being is the higher part, which we have in our Father, God almighty; and the second Person of the Trinity is our mother in nature and in our essential creation, in whom we are grounded and rooted, and he is our mother in mercy in taking on our sensory being. And so our Mother, in whom our parts are kept unparted, works in us in various ways; for in our Mother, Christ, we profit and grow, and in mercy he reforms and restores us, and through the power of his Passion and his death and rising again, he unites us to our essential being. This is how our Mother mercifully acts to all his children who are submissive and obedient to him.

And grace works with mercy, and in two ways especially, as has been shown – work which belongs to the third Person, the Holy Ghost. He works by giving and by rewarding; the rewarding is a generous gift of truth which the Lord offers to those who have laboured, and the giving is a courteous action which he freely and graciously perfects, surpassing all that humankind deserves. Thus we have our being in our Father, God almighty, and in our Mother through mercy we have our reformation and restoration, and our parts are united and all is made perfect man; and by the generosity and gracious gift of the Holy Ghost we are made complete. And our essential being is our Father, God almighty, and it is our Mother, God all wise, and it is our Lord the Holy Ghost, God all goodness; for our essential being is whole in each Person of the Trinity, which is one God. And our sensory being is only in the second Person, Christ Jesus, in whom are the Father and the Holy Ghost; and in him and by him we are powerfully raised from hell and out of the wretchedness of earth and gloriously brought up into heaven and blessedly united to our essential being, increased in riches and nobility by all the virtue of Christ and by the grace and operation of the Holy Ghost.

59

In the chosen, wickedness is turned into blessedness through mercy and grace, for the nature of God is to do good for evil, through Jesus, our mother in kind grace; and the soul which is highest in virtue is the meekest, that being the ground from which we gain other virtues.

And we have all this blessedness through mercy and grace; a kind of blessedness which we might never have known if the quality of goodness which is God had not been opposed. It is by this means that we gain this blessedness; for wickedness has been allowed to rise and oppose goodness, and the goodness of mercy and grace has opposed wickedness and turned it all to goodness and glory for all those who shall be saved; for it is the nature of God to do good for evil.

Thus Jesus Christ who does good for evil is our true mother; we have our being from him where the ground of motherhood begins, with all the sweet protection of love which follows eternally. God is our mother as truly as he is our father; and he showed this in everything, and especially in the sweet words where he says, 'It is I',[53] that is to say, 'It is I: the power and goodness of fatherhood. It is I: the wisdom of motherhood. It is I: the light and the grace which is all blessed love. It is I: the Trinity. It is I: the unity. I am the sovereign goodness of all manner of things. It is I that make you love. It is I that make you long. It is I: the eternal fulfilment of all true desires.'

For the soul is highest, noblest and worthiest when it is lowest, humblest and gentlest; and from this essential ground we all have our virtues and our sensory being by gift of nature and with the help and assistance of grace, without which we could gain nothing. Our great father, God almighty, who is Being, knew and loved us from before the beginning of time. And from his knowledge, in his marvellously deep love and through the eternal foreseeing counsel of the whole blessed Trinity, he wanted the second Person to become our mother, our brother, our saviour. From this it follows that God is our mother as truly as God is our father. Our Father wills, our Mother works, our good lord the Holy Ghost confirms. And therefore it behoves us to love our God in whom we have our being, reverently thanking and praising him for our creation, praying hard to our Mother for mercy and pity, and to our lord the Holy Ghost for help and grace; for our whole life is in these three – nature, mercy and grace; from them we have humility, gentleness, patience and pity, and hatred of sin and wickedness; for it is a natural attribute of virtues to hate sin and wickedness. And so Jesus is our true mother by nature, at our first creation, and he is our true mother in grace by taking on our created nature. All the fair work and all the sweet, kind service of beloved motherhood is made proper to the second Person; for in him this godly will is kept safe and whole everlastingly, both in nature and in grace, out of his very own goodness.

I understood three ways of seeing motherhood in God: the first is that he is the ground of our natural creation, the second is the taking on of our nature (and there the motherhood of grace begins), the third is the motherhood of works, and in this there is, by the same grace, an enlargement of length and breadth and of height and deepness without end, and all is his own love.

60

How we are redeemed and enlarged by the mercy and grace of our sweet, kind and ever-loving mother Jesus; and of the properties of motherhood; but Jesus is our true mother, feeding us not with milk, but with himself, opening his side for us and claiming all our love.

But now it is necessary to say a little more about this enlargement, as I understand it in our Lord's meaning, how we are redeemed by the motherhood of mercy and grace and brought back into our natural dwelling where we were made by the motherhood of natural love; a natural love which never leaves us. Our natural Mother, our gracious Mother (for he wanted to become our mother completely in every way), undertook to begin his work very humbly and very gently in the Virgin's womb. And he showed this in the first revelation, where he brought that humble maiden before my mind's eye in the girlish form she had when she conceived; that is to say, our great God, the most sovereign wisdom of all, was raised in this humble place and dressed himself in our poor flesh to do the service and duties of motherhood in every way. The mother's service is the closest, the most helpful and the most sure, for it is the most faithful. No one ever might, nor could, nor has performed this service fully but he alone. We know that our mothers only bring us into the world to suffer and die, but our true mother, Jesus, he who is all love, bears us into joy and eternal life; blessed may he be! So he sustains us within himself in love and was in labour for the full time until he suffered the sharpest pangs and the most grievous sufferings that ever were or shall be, and at the last he died. And when it was finished and he had born us to bliss, even this could not fully satisfy his marvellous love; and that he showed in these high surpassing words of love, 'If I could suffer more, I would suffer more.'[54]

He could not die any more, but he would not stop working. So next he had to feed us, for a mother's dear love has made him our debtor. The mother can give her child her milk to suck, but our dear mother Jesus can feed us with himself, and he does so most generously and most tenderly with the holy sacrament which is the precious food of life itself. And with all the sweet sacraments he sustains us most mercifully and most graciously. And this is what he meant in those blessed words when he said, 'It is I that Holy Church preaches and teaches to you';[55] that is to say, 'All the health and life of the sacraments, all the power and grace of my word, all the goodness which is ordained in Holy Church for you, it is I.'

The mother can lay the child tenderly to her breast, but our tender mother Jesus, he can familiarly lead us into his blessed breast through his sweet open side, and show within part of the Godhead and the joys of heaven, with spiritual certainty of endless bliss; and that was shown in the tenth revelation, giving the same understanding in the sweet words where he says, 'Look how I love you', looking into his side and rejoicing. This fair, lovely word 'mother', it is so sweet and so tender in itself that it cannot truly be said of any but of him, and of her who is the true mother of him and of everyone. To the nature of motherhood belong tender love, wisdom and knowledge, and it is good, for although the birth of our body is only low, humble and modest compared with the birth of our soul, yet it is he who does it in the beings by whom it is done. The kind, loving mother who knows and recognizes the need of her child, she watches over it most tenderly, as the nature and condition of motherhood demands. And as it grows in age her actions change, although her love does not. And as it grows older still, she allows it to be beaten to break down vices so that the child may gain in virtue and grace. These actions, with all that is fair and good, our Lord performs them through those by whom they are done. Thus he is our natural mother through the work of grace in the lower part, for love of the higher part. And he wants us to know it; for he wants all our love to be bound to him. And in this I saw that all the debt we owe, at God's bidding, for his fatherhood and motherhood, is fulfilled by loving God truly; a blessed love which Christ arouses in us. And this was shown in everything, and especially in the great, generous words where he says, 'It is I that you love.'

61

Jesus behaves more tenderly in giving us spiritual birth; though he allows us to fall so that we may recognize our sinfulness, he quickly raises us, not withdrawing his love because of our transgression, for he cannot allow his child to perish; he wants us to have the nature of a child, always rushing to him in our need.

And in our spiritual birth he behaves with incomparably more tenderness, in as much as our soul is of greater value in his eyes. He fires our understanding, he directs our ways, he eases our conscience, he comforts our soul, he enlightens our heart and gives us some degree of knowledge and love of his blessed Godhead, with awareness through grace of his precious Manhood and his blessed Passion, and with courteous wonder at his great and surpassing goodness; and he makes us love all that he loves, for his love's sake, and makes us take pleasure in him and all his works. If we fall, he quickly raises us by calling us tenderly and touching us with grace. And when we have been strengthened like this by his dear actions, then we choose him willingly, through his precious grace, we choose to serve him and to love him for ever and ever. And after this he allows some of us to fall harder and more painfully than we ever did before, or so it seems to us. And those of us who are not very wise think that all our earlier effort has gone for nothing. But it is not so; for we need to fall, and we need to be aware of it; for if we did not fall, we should not know how weak and wretched we are of ourselves, nor should we know our Maker's marvellous love so fully; for in heaven we shall see truly and everlastingly that we have sinned grievously in this life, and we shall see that in spite of this his love for us remained unharmed, and we were never less valuable to him. And by experiencing this failure, we shall gain a great and marvellous knowledge of love in God for all eternity; for that love which cannot and will not be broken by sin is strong and marvellous. And this is one aspect of the benefit we gain. Another is the humility and gentleness we shall gain from seeing our fall; for by this we shall be raised up high in heaven, a rise which we might never have known without that humility. And therefore we need to see it, and if we do not see it, though we should fall, it would not profit us. Usually, we fall first, then we see it, and both through the mercy of God. The mother may allow the child to fall sometimes and to be hurt for its own benefit, but her love does not allow the child ever to be in any real danger. And though our earthly mother may allow her child to perish, our heavenly mother Jesus cannot allow us who are his children to perish; for he and none but he is almighty, all wisdom and all love. Blessed may he be!

But often when our falling and our wretched sin is shown to us, we are so terrified and so very ashamed that we hardly know where to put ourselves. But then our kind Mother does not want us to run from him, there is nothing he wants less. But he wants us to behave like a child; for when it is hurt or frightened it runs to its mother for help as fast as it can; and he wants us to do the same, like a humble child, saying, 'My kind Mother, my gracious Mother, my dearest Mother, take pity on me. I have made myself dirty and unlike you and I neither may nor can remedy this without your special help and grace.' And if we do not feel that we are immediately given help, we can be sure that he is behaving like a wise mother, for if he sees that it would be more beneficial for us to grieve and weep, with sorrow and pity he allows it to continue until the right moment, and all for love. So then he wants us to take on the nature of a child which always naturally trusts the love of its mother in weal and woe.

And he wants us to cling strongly to the faith of Holy Church and find our dearest Mother there in the comfort of true understanding with the whole blessed community; for a single person may often feel broken, but the whole body of Holy Church has never been broken, nor ever shall be, for all eternity. And therefore it is a safe, good and gracious thing to wish humbly and strongly to be supported by and united to our mother, Holy Church, that is Christ Jesus; for there is plenty of the food of mercy which is his dearest blood and precious water to make us clean and pure. The blessed wounds of our Saviour are open and rejoice to heal us; the sweet, gracious hands of our Mother are ready and carefully surround us; for in all this he does the work of a kind nurse who has nothing to do but occupy herself with the salvation of her child. His task is to save us, and it is his glory to do so, and it is his wish that we know it; for he wants us to love him tenderly, and trust him humbly and strongly. And he showed this in these gracious words, 'I hold you quite safely.'

62

The love of God never allows his chosen to lose their time, for all their trouble is turned into eternal joy; and how we all have God to thank for his kind[56] nature and for his grace; for there is every kind of nature in man and we do not need to seek out various kinds, just turn to Holy Church.

For at that time he showed our frailty and our fallings, our discouragements, our abasements, our humiliations and our outcastings; all the woe which it seemed to me could possibly befall us in this life. And with this he showed his blessed power, his blessed wisdom, his blessed love, in which he protects us at such times as tenderly and as sweetly for his own glory and as safely for our salvation as he does when we enjoy most pleasure and comfort; and with this he raises us in spirit right up to heaven, and turns everything to his glory and our joy everlastingly; for his love never allows our time to be lost. And all this comes from the natural kindly goodness of God through the operation of grace. God in his essence is kindly nature; that is to say, the goodness that is kind and natural is God. He is the ground, he is the substance, he is kind nature itself and he is true father and true mother of nature. And all the kinds of nature which he has caused to flow out of him to work his will shall be restored and brought within him again by the salvation of man through the work of grace; for of the many kinds of nature with which he has respectively invested various creatures, man is invested with all, in fullness, in beauty, and in goodness, in royalty and nobility, in every kind of glorious excellence. Here we can see that we are all joined to God by kindly nature and joined to God by grace. Here we can see that we do not need to search far and wide to know various kinds of nature, but seek them in Holy Church, in our mother's breast; that is to say, in our own soul, where our Lord lives. And there we shall find everything; find it now in faith and in understanding, and later find it truly in himself and brightly in bliss.

But let no man or woman apply this to themselves alone; it is not personal, but general, for it is our precious Christ, and this fair nature was ordained for him, for the glory and nobility of man's making, and for the joy and bliss of man's salvation; just as he had seen, known and recognized since before time began.

63

Sin causes more suffering than hell, and is vile and hurts nature, but grace saves nature and destroys sin; the children of Jesus are not yet all born, and never grow beyond childhood, living in feebleness until they come to heaven where joys are always beginning again for all eternity.

Here we can see that to hate sin comes to us truly by nature and to hate sin comes to us truly by grace; for nature is all good and fair of itself and grace was sent out to save nature and destroy sin and bring fair kind nature back to the blessed point from which it came, that is God, with greater nobility and glory through the virtuous work of grace; for it shall be seen before God by all his holy ones in eternal joy that nature has been tried in the fire of tribulation and no lack or fault has been found there. So nature and grace are in harmony, for grace is God as nature is God. He is double in his way of working and single in love, and neither of them works without the other, nor can they be separated. And when through God's mercy and with his help we put ourselves into harmony with nature and grace, we shall truly see that sin is much more vile and painful than hell, without comparison, for it is contrary to our fair nature; for as truly as sin is unclean, so is it truly unnatural, and therefore appears a horrible thing to the loved soul that wants to be all fair and shining in the eyes of God as nature and grace teach us.

But let us not be afraid of this except in so far as fear can help us, but let us humbly lament to our dearest Mother, and he will sprinkle us all over with his precious blood and make our soul very soft and tender, and in the course of time he will heal us completely, just as is most honourable for him and most joyful for us eternally. And he will never pause nor cease in this good, tender work until all his dearest children have been born and delivered. And he showed this where he showed how spiritual thirst was to be understood, that is the love-longing which will last until Judgement Day.

So our life is grounded in our true mother, Jesus, in his own foreseeing wisdom since before time began, with the great power of the Father, and the great and supreme goodness of the Holy Ghost. And in taking on our human nature he gave us life, in his blessed death on the cross he gave us birth into life everlasting; and from that time, and now, and for ever until Judgement Day, he feeds and fosters us, just as the great and supreme kind nature of motherhood and the natural need of childhood demand. To the eyes of our soul, our heavenly Mother is good and tender; to the eyes of our heavenly Mother the children of grace are precious and lovely, with humility and gentleness and all the fair virtues which belong to children by nature; for naturally the child does not despair of the mother's love; naturally the child does not set itself up presumptuously; naturally the child loves the mother and each one loves the other; these are the fair virtues, with all others that are like them, with which our heavenly Mother is honoured and pleased. And I understood that in this life no one grows beyond childhood, in feebleness and inadequacy of body and mind, until the time when our gracious Mother has brought us up into our Father's bliss. And then we shall really understand what he means in these sweet words where he says, 'All shall be well, and you shall see for yourself that all manner of things shall be well.'[57] And then the bliss of our motherhood in Christ will begin again in the joys of our God; a new beginning which will last without end, always beginning again.

So I understood that all his blessed children who come from him by nature shall be bought back into him by grace.

64

The fifteenth revelation as it was shown: the absence of God in this life is our
very great sorrow, besides other sufferings, but we shall suddenly be taken from
all suffering, with Jesus for our mother; and God is very pleased if we wait
patiently, and God wants us to take our pain lightly, for love, and thinking
ourselves always near to the moment of delivery.

Before this time I had a great longing and desire that as a gift from
God I should be delivered from this world and this life; for I often
considered the grief which is here and the well-being and bliss which
is existence there. And even if there had been no sorrow in this life
except for the absence of our Lord, I sometimes thought it more than
I could bear, and this made me grieve and earnestly yearn, and so did
my own sinfulness, sloth and weakness, so that it did not please me
to live and suffer, as it was my lot to do. And our kind Lord answered
all this to bring me comfort and patience, and said these words, 'You
shall suddenly be taken from all your suffering, from all your sickness,
from all this pain and from all the woe. And you shall come up above,
and you shall have me as your reward, and you shall be filled with
love and bliss. And you shall have no kind of suffering, no kind of
displeasure, no unfulfilled desires, but always joy and bliss without
end. Why should you fret about suffering for a while, since it is my
will and my glory?' And at these words, 'You shall suddenly be taken',
I saw that God rewards man for the patience he shows in awaiting
God's will, and for his time, and I saw that man's patience extends
throughout the time he has to live, because he does not know the
time of his passing. This is a great gain, for if a man knew his time,
he would not have patience over that time. And according to God's
will, while the soul is in the body it seems to itself that it is always
about to die, for all this life and this distress which we have here is
only a moment, and when we are suddenly taken from suffering into
bliss, then the suffering will be nothing.

And at this time I saw a body lying on the earth, a body which
looked dismal and ugly, without shape or form as if it were a swollen

and heaving mass of stinking mire. And suddenly out of this body there sprang a very beautiful creature, a little child perfectly shaped and formed, quick and bright, whiter than a lily, which glided swiftly up into heaven. And the swelling of the body represents the great sinfulness of our mortal flesh and the smallness of the child represents the chaste purity of the soul. And I thought, 'None of the beauty of this child remains with the body, nor does any of this body's filth cling to the child.'

It is more blessed for man to be taken from suffering than for suffering to be taken from man; for if pain is taken from us it may return. Therefore it is a supreme comfort and blessed insight for a loving soul that we shall be taken from pain; for in this promise I saw the marvellous compassion which our Lord has for us in our woe and his kind promise of complete deliverance; for he wants us to be comforted by this transcendence; and he showed that in these words: 'And you shall come up above, and you shall have me as your reward, and you shall be filled with joy[58] and bliss.' It is God's will that we should focus our thoughts on this blessed insight as often as we can and for as long as possible, through his grace. For this contemplation is blessed to the soul that is led by God, and greatly to his glory for the time that it lasts. If through our own frailty we fall back into our sorrow and spiritual blindness and feelings of spiritual and physical pain, it is God's will that we know that he has not forgotten us. And that is what he means in these words which he says to comfort us: 'And you shall have no more suffering, no kind of sickness, no kind of displeasure, no unfulfilled desires, but always joy and bliss without end. Why should you fret about suffering for a while, since it is my will and my glory?'[59] It is God's will that we accept his promises and his comfort in as broad and strong a sense as we can take them. And he also wants us to take our waiting and our distress as lightly as we can and to consider them nothing; for the more lightly we take them and the less importance we give them for love, the less we shall suffer from feeling them and the more thanks and reward we shall have for them.

65

He who chooses God for love, with reverent humility, is sure to be saved; this reverent humility sees the Lord as marvellously great and the self as marvellously small; and God does not want us to fear anything but him, for the power of our Enemy is committed into the hand of our Friend, so everything that God does shall please us greatly.

And so I understood that the people who in this life willingly choose God for love, may be sure they will be loved eternally, and it is this eternal love that works this grace in them, for he wants us to believe without doubt that we may all hope securely for the bliss of heaven while we are here, as we shall enjoy it securely when we are there. And it was shown that the more pleasure and joy we take in this security, with reverence and humility, the more it pleases him. This reverence that I have in mind is a holy, respectful fear of our Lord, which is joined to humility: and that means that one sees the Lord as marvellously great, and the self as marvellously small; for these virtues belong for ever to those who are loved by God; and may even now be seen and felt to some extent through the gracious presence of our Lord when he is with us; a presence which is of all things the most desired, for it brings marvellous security, by true faith and sure hope through great love, and by fear which is sweet and delightful.

It is God's will that I should feel myself as much bound to him in love as if all that he has done had been done for me. And in his heart every soul should think of those he loves and is loved by in this way – that the love of God unites us to such an extent that when we are truly aware of it, no man can separate himself from another. And so our soul ought to think that all that God has done was done for it; and he shows us this to make us love him and to fear nothing but him; for he wants us to understand that all the strength of our Enemy is committed into our Friend's hand, and therefore the soul that knows this truly will fear none but him that it loves; it sets all other fears among sufferings and bodily sickness and mental apprehensions.

And therefore though we are in so much pain, woe and distress that it seems we can think of nothing but the state we are in and what we are feeling, we should pass over it lightly and dismiss it as nothing as soon as we can. And why? Because God wants us to know that if we know him and love him and reverently fear him, we shall have peace and be completely at rest; and all that he does will give us great pleasure. And our Lord showed this in these words, 'Why should you fret about suffering for a while, since it is my will and my glory?'[60]

Now I have told you of fifteen revelations as God deigned to offer them to my understanding, renewing them by flashes of illumination and touches, I hope, of the same spirit which was shown in them all. The first of these fifteen showings began early in the morning, at about four o'clock, and they lasted, appearing in due order most beautifully and surely, one after the other, until it was well past the middle of the day.

66

The sixteenth revelation, which is the conclusion and confirmation of all fifteen; and of her frailty and grieving in distress and speaking lightly of the great comfort of Jesus, saying she was delirious, which, considering her great sickness, I suppose was only a venial sin; but nevertheless after that the Devil had great power and nearly vexed her to death.

And after this the good Lord showed the sixteenth revelation on the following night, as I shall say later, and this sixteenth revelation was the conclusion and confirmation of all the other fifteen. But first I must tell you about my feebleness, wretchedness and blindness. I said at the beginning, 'And at this moment, all my suffering was suddenly taken from me';[61] and I had no trouble, no distress from this pain as long as the following fifteen showings lasted; and at the end it was all over and I saw no more. And I soon felt that I would live and continue to suffer, and at once my sickness returned; first in my head, with a noise and a din, and suddenly my whole body was full of sickness as it had been before, and I was as barren and dry as if I had received little comfort. And like a wretch I tossed and moaned with the feeling of bodily pain and the failing of spiritual and bodily comfort.

Then a man belonging to a religious order came to me and asked me how I was. And I said that I had been delirious today, and he laughed loud and heartily. And I said, 'The cross which was before my face, I thought it was bleeding hard.' And as soon as I said this, the person to whom I was speaking became very serious and marvelled. And I was immediately very ashamed and astonished at my heedlessness, and I thought, 'This man takes my least word seriously, saying nothing in reply.' And when I saw that he took it so seriously and so reverently, I wept, feeling very ashamed, and wanted to be given absolution; but at that time I did not feel I could tell any priest about it, for I thought, 'How could a priest believe me? I do not believe our Lord God.' I had truly believed while I was seeing him, and had then wanted and intended to do so for ever, but, like a fool, I let it pass from my mind. Oh, what a wretch I was! This was a great sin and very ungrateful, that I through stupidity, just because I felt a little bodily pain, should so foolishly lose for the time being the comfort of all this blessed showing of our Lord God.

Here you can see what I am of myself; but our kind Lord would not leave me like this. And I lay still till night, trusting in his mercy, and then I went to sleep. And as soon as I fell asleep it seemed the Fiend was at my throat, thrusting a visage like a young man's close to my face; and it was long and extraordinarily thin, I never saw one like it. The colour was red like newly fired tiles,[62] with black spots on it like black freckles, fouler than the tiles themselves. His hair was as red as rust, clipped in front, and with locks hanging down over the temples. He grinned at me with a wicked expression, showing white teeth, so that I thought him even more horrible. His body and hands were not properly shaped, but his paws gripped me by the throat and he tried to strangle me, but he could not. I was asleep during this horrible showing, but not during any of the others. And during all this time I trusted I would be saved and protected by the mercy of God. And our kind Lord gave me grace to wake up, and I was barely alive.

The people who were with me noticed, and bathed my temples,

and my heart began to take comfort. And immediately a little smoke came in through the door with a great heat and a foul stench. I said, 'Benedicite domine! Everything here is on fire!' And I supposed it was a physical fire and would burn us all to death. I asked those who were with me if they smelled any stench. They said no, they smelled none. I said, 'Blessed be God!' for I knew well that it was the Fiend that had come to torment me. And I had recourse at once to all that our Lord had shown me that same day, along with the faith of Holy Church, for I saw both as one, and fled to that as my comfort. And immediately it all vanished completely, and I was brought to a state of great rest and peace without sickness of the body or terrors of the mind.

67

Of the glorious city of the soul, which is created so nobly that it could not have been made any better, a city in which the Trinity rejoices everlastingly; and the soul can rest in nothing but in God, who seats himself there, ruling everything.

And then our Lord opened my spiritual eyes and showed me my soul in the middle of my heart. I saw the soul as large as if it were an endless[63] world and as if it were a holy kingdom; and from the properties I saw in it I understood that it is a glorious city. In the centre of that city sits our Lord Jesus, God and man, a handsome person and of great stature, the highest bishop, the most imposing king, the most glorious Lord; and I saw him dressed imposingly and gloriously. He sits in the soul, in the very centre, in peace and rest. And the Godhead rules and protects heaven and earth and all that is: supreme power, supreme wisdom and supreme goodness.

It seems to me that in all eternity Jesus will never leave the position which he takes in our soul; for in us is his most familiar home and his everlasting dwelling. And in this he showed the pleasure he takes in the way man's soul is made; as well as the Father might make a creature, and as well as the Son could make a creature, so the Holy

Ghost wanted man's soul to be made, and so it was done. And so the Holy Trinity rejoices eternally over the way man's soul is made; for he saw before time began what would please him eternally. Everything that he has made shows his lordship; understanding of this was given at the same time through the example of a person who was to see great treasures and kingdoms belonging to a lord, and when he had seen all the treasures below, then, marvelling, he was moved to seek above for the high place where the lord lives, knowing by reason that his dwelling would be in the best place; and so I understood truly that our soul can never rest in things which are beneath it. When it rises above all created beings into itself, it still cannot rest there contemplating itself, but all its attention is blessedly focused on God, the creator dwelling in it; for his true dwelling is in man's soul, and it seems to me that the greatest light in the city and the most brightly shining is the glorious love of our Lord. And what can make us rejoice more in God than to see in him what pleases him most greatly of all his works? For I saw in the same showing that the Holy Trinity would not have been fully satisfied with the way man's soul was made if he could have made it any better, any fairer, any nobler than it was. And he wants our hearts to be raised high above the depths of earth and all vain sorrows, and to rejoice in him.

68

Of certain knowledge that it was Jesus who showed all this and it was no delirium; and how through all our tribulation we ought to have sure trust that we shall not be overcome.

This was a ravishing sight and a restful showing, that it is so everlastingly. And it is very pleasing to God and extremely helpful to us that we should see this while we are here. And the soul which sees it in this way makes itself like the one seen and unites itself to him in rest and peace through his grace. And it was a very great joy and bliss to me that I saw him sitting, for the certainty that he sits shows that he dwells there eternally. And he gave me certain knowledge that it was he who had shown me all that went before. And when I had considered this carefully, our good Lord gently revealed words to me, without any voice or opening of his lips, just as he had done before, and he said very lovingly, 'Know well now that what you saw today was no delirium; accept and believe it, hold to it and comfort yourself with it and trust to it, and you shall not be overcome.' These last words were said to prove to me with full assurance that it is our Lord Jesus who showed me everything. And just as in the first phrase which our good Lord revealed, referring to his blessed Passion – 'By this is the Fiend overcome'[64] – in just the same way he said his last phrase with very great certainty, referring to all of us, 'You shall not be overcome.'

And all this teaching of true comfort applies without exception to all my fellow Christians, as I said before, and it is God's will that it should be so. And these words, 'You shall not be overcome', were said very loudly and clearly for security and comfort against all the tribulations that may come. He did not say, 'You shall not be tormented, you shall not be troubled, you shall not be grieved', but he said, 'You shall not be overcome.' God wants us to pay attention to these words and wants our trust always to be sure and strong, in weal and woe; for he loves and is pleased with us, and so he wishes us to love and be pleased with him and put great trust in him; and all shall be well.

And soon after this it was all over and I saw no more.

69

Of the Devil's second long temptation to despair; but she trusted strongly in God and in the faith of Holy Church, reciting the Passion of Christ, by which she was delivered.

After this the Fiend came again with his heat and his stench and distressed me greatly, the stench was so vile and so agonizing and also terrifying and tormenting. And I also heard a human jabbering as if there were two people, and it seemed to me that both of them were jabbering at the same time, as if they were having a very tense discussion; and as it was all quiet muttering, I could understand nothing they said. And I thought that all this was to drive me to despair, and it seemed to me as if they were mocking prayers said by rote, spoken noisily with the mouth, with none of the devout understanding and thoughtful care which we owe to God in our prayers. And our Lord God gave me the grace to trust strongly in him and to comfort my soul by speaking aloud as I should have done to another person who was distressed. I thought that this anxiety could not be compared to any other human anxiety. I set my bodily eyes on the same cross which had comforted me before, and my tongue to speaking of Christ's Passion and reciting the faith of Holy Church, and my heart to clinging to God with all my trust and with all my strength. And I thought to myself, 'You must now be very careful to hold to the faith, for you must not be taken by the Enemy; if only from now on you could always be so careful to keep yourself from sin, it would be a good and beneficial way of life'; for I truly thought that if I were safe from sin I would be quite safe from all the fiends of hell and enemies of my soul.

And so the Fiend kept me occupied all that night and in the morning until it was just after sunrise. And at once they were all gone, all passed away, leaving nothing but a stench; and that persisted for a while. And I thought of them with contempt. And thus I was delivered from them by the power of Christ's Passion, for that is how the Fiend is overcome, as our Lord Jesus Christ said before.

70

In all tribulation we should be steadfast in the faith, trusting strongly in God; for if our faith had no enemies, it would deserve no reward; and how all these showings are in the faith.

In all this blessed showing our good Lord made it understood that the sight would pass; but faith preserves this blessed showing, with God's good will and grace, for he left me with no sign or token by which I might remember it, but he left me with his own blessed word in true understanding, telling me very firmly that I must believe it. And so I do; blessed may he be! I believe that he who showed it is our Saviour, and that what he showed is the true faith. And therefore I believe and rejoice in it; and I am bound to do so by what he said himself in the words which follow next: 'Hold to it and comfort yourself with it and trust to it.' Thus I am bound by my faith to believe it. For on the same day that it was shown, when the revelation was over, like a wretch I abandoned it and said openly that I had been delirious. Then our Lord Jesus in his mercy would not let it perish, but he showed it all again inwardly, in my soul, more fully, with the blessed light of his precious love, saying these words very strongly and very kindly, 'Know well now that what you saw today was no delirium,' as if he had said, 'Because the sight had passed away, you lost it and could not keep it; but know it now, that is to say, now that you see it.'

This was said not just for that same moment, but also to ground my faith firmly upon it, as is seen by his saying immediately afterwards, 'Accept it, believe it, hold to it and comfort yourself with it and trust to it, and you shall not be overcome.' In these six phrases beginning from 'Accept it', his purpose is to fasten it faithfully in our hearts; for he wants it to stay with us in faith until our life's end, and afterwards in the fullness of joy, wishing that we should always have sure trust in his holy promises, knowing his goodness; for our faith is opposed in various ways by our own blindness and by our spiritual Enemy, within and without, and because of this our dearly loved Friend helps us with spiritual insight and true teaching in different ways, within and without, by which we may know him. And therefore, in whatever way he teaches us, he wants us to perceive him wisely, receive him lovingly and hold ourselves to him faithfully, for it seems to me that in this life one can hold to no goodness above faith, and there is no help for the soul below faith, but it is to the faith that the Lord wants us to hold. For by his goodness and by his own work we are able to hold to the faith, and by his permission spiritual enemies test us in the faith and make us strong, for if our faith had no enemy it would deserve no reward, so far as I understand all our Lord's purpose.

71

Jesus wants our souls to look at him with gladness, for the face he shows us is happy and loving; and how he shows us three kinds of face – a suffering, a compassionate and a blessed face.

Glad and cheerful and sweet is the blessed, loving face with which our Lord looks at our souls; for he is constantly in love-longing towards us while we live, and he wants our souls to look gladly on him so as to give him his reward. And so I hope that by his grace he has made the outer face like the inner face, and shall do so still more, and shall unite us all with him and with each other in the true and lasting joy which is Jesus.

I have three kinds of understanding of the expression of our Lord's face. The first is the suffering face which he showed while he was here, dying. Although this is a sight of mourning and sorrow, it is also glad and cheerful, for he is God. The second face is pity, grief and compassion; and he shows this face to all those who love him, with the certainty of protection for those who need his mercy. The third is the blessed face which he will show for ever, and I saw this oftenest and longest.

And so when we sorrow and suffer, he shows us the face of his Passion and his cross, helping us to endure through his own blessed strength. And when we sin he shows us his face of pity and grief, strongly protecting and defending us from all our enemies. And these two are the faces which he most often shows us in this life; and mixed with them is the third, which is his blessed face, shown in part as it will be in heaven. And that comes to us through gracious touching and sweet illumination of the spiritual life by which we are kept in certain faith, hope and charity, with contrition and devotion and also with contemplation and every kind of true pleasure and sweet comfort. The blessed face of our Lord God works this in us through grace.

72

Sin in the chosen souls is mortal for a time, but they are not dead in the sight of God; and how we have here cause of joy and of lamentation, and the latter is for our blindness and the weight of our flesh; and of the most comforting face of God; and why these showings were given.

But now I must tell how I saw mortal sin in those who shall not die for sin, but shall live everlastingly in the joy of God. And I saw that to God, two opposites could never exist in one place. The two most extreme opposites are the highest bliss and the deepest suffering. The highest bliss is to possess God in the brightness of everlasting life, seeing him truly, feeling him sweetly, possessing him completely in the fullness of joy.

And so our Lord's blessed face was shown with an expression of pity, and in this showing I saw that sin is diametrically opposed to it, to such an extent that as long as we are mingled with any portion of sin, we shall never clearly see our Lord's blessed face. And the more horrible and grievous our sins are, the more deeply we are sunk below this blessed sight at that moment. And therefore it often seems to us as if we are in peril of death, and partly in hell, because of the pain and sorrow which sin causes us. And so we are dead for the time being to the true sight of our blessed life. But in all this I certainly saw that we are not dead in the sight of God, nor does he ever leave us; but he will never have his full bliss in us until we have our full bliss in him, truly seeing his fair, blessed face; this is ordained for us by nature and obtained by us through grace. So I saw how mortal sin exists for a short time in the blessed beings that will gain everlasting life.

And the more clearly the soul sees this blessed face through grace and love, the more it longs to see it fully. For although our Lord God lives in us and is here with us, embracing and enfolding us completely for tender love, so that he can never leave us, and is nearer to us than tongue can tell or heart can think, yet our lamentation and weeping and longing can never stop till we see his blessed face clearly; for in that precious, blissful sight, no good can fail and no ill can dwell.

And in this I saw cause for mirth and cause for lamentation: cause for mirth because the Lord our Maker is so near us and within us, and we in him, through the sure protection of his great goodness; cause for lamentation because our spiritual eyes are so blind, and we are so weighed down by our mortal flesh and the darkness of sin that we cannot see our Lord God's fair, blessed face clearly. No, and because of this darkness we can hardly believe and credit his great love, our sure protection; and that is why I say we can never stop lamenting and weeping. This weeping does not only mean tears pouring from our bodily eyes, but also has a more spiritual meaning; for the natural desire of our soul is so great and so immeasurable that if we were given all the noble things which God made in heaven and earth to please and to comfort us and we did not see the fair, blessed face of God himself, we still should not stop our lamenting and spiritual weeping, that is to say our painful longing, until we see the fair, blessed face of our Maker. And if we were suffering all the pain that heart can think or tongue may tell, if we could at that moment see his fair, blessed face, all this pain would not hurt us. So that blessed sight is the end of all manner of pain to the loving soul, and the fulfilment of all manner of joy and bliss. And God showed this in the great and marvellous words where he said, 'It is I who am highest; it is I who am lowest; it is I who am all.'[65]

We need to have three kinds of knowledge: the first is to know our Lord God; the second is to know ourselves, what we are through him in nature and grace; the third is to know humbly what we ourselves are where our sin and weakness are concerned. And, as I understand it, the entire showing was made for these three.

73

How these revelations were shown in three ways; and two spiritual sicknesses which God wants us to cure, remembering his Passion, and knowing also that he is all love; for he wants us to enjoy security and pleasure in love, not to be foolishly depressed by our past sins.

All the blessed teaching of our Lord God was shown in three ways: that is to say, by bodily sight, by words formed in my understanding and by spiritual sight. I have described what I saw with bodily sight as truly as I can; and I have said the words exactly as our Lord revealed them to me; but so far as the spiritual sight is concerned, I have said something about it, but I could never recount it all, and so I am moved to say more, if God will give me grace.

God showed that we suffer from two kinds of sickness: one of them is impatience or sloth, because we find our trouble and suffering a heavy burden to bear, and the other is despair, or doubtful fear,[66] as I shall explain later. He showed sin in general, including all its aspects, but he only showed these two in particular. And these two are the ones which most trouble and torment us, according to what our Lord showed me, and the ones he wants us to reform. I am talking of those men and women who for the love of God hate sin and are anxious to do God's will: through our spiritual blindness and the heavy burden of our bodies, these are the sins we are most inclined to commit, so it is God's will that they should be recognized and then we shall reject them as we do other sins.

And our Lord very humbly revealed great help for this: the patience with which he bore his terrible Passion and also the joy and delight which that Passion gave him because of his love. And he showed by his example that we should bear our sufferings gladly and lightly, because that pleases him greatly and profits us for ever. And we are troubled by them because we do not recognize love. Though the three persons of the Trinity are all equal in themselves, my soul understood love most clearly, yes, and God wants us to consider and enjoy love in everything. And this is the knowledge of which we are most ignorant; for some of us believe that God is all mighty and has power to do everything, and that he is all wisdom and knows how to do everything, but that he is all love and is willing to do everything – there we stop. And it seems to me that this ignorance is what most hinders those who love God; for when we begin to hate sin, and to mend our ways under the laws of Holy Church, there still remains some fear which holds us back, out of concern for ourselves, and our previous sins, and some of us for our daily sins – for we do not keep our promises or preserve the purity in which the Lord has established us, but often fall into such sinfulness that it is shameful to see it.

And seeing this makes us sorry and so unhappy that we can hardly find any comfort, and we sometimes take this fear for humility, but it is foul ignorance and weakness. And we cannot despise it as we do some other sin that we recognize, for it comes from the Enemy, and it is contrary to truth; for of all the properties of the Holy Trinity, it is God's wish that we should place most reliance and take most delight in liking and love; for love makes God's power and wisdom very gentle to us; for just as through his generosity God forgives our sin when we repent, so he wants us to forget our sin of unreasonable depression and doubtful fear.

74

There are four kinds of fear, but reverent fear is a true and loving fear, which never exists without meek love; and yet they are not the same thing; and how we should pray to God for them.

For I recognize four kinds of fear. One is the fear of attack which suddenly comes to a man through weakness. This fear does good, for it helps to purify people, just like bodily sickness or other sufferings which are not sinful; for all such suffering helps people if it is endured patiently.

The second fear is that of punishment, whereby someone is stirred and woken from the sleep of sin; for those who are deep in the sleep of sin are for the time being unable to perceive the gentle comfort of the Holy Ghost, until they have experienced this fear of punishment, of bodily death and of spiritual enemies. And this fear moves us to seek the comfort and mercy of God; and so it helps us and enables us to be contrite through the blessed touch of the Holy Ghost.

The third is doubtful fear. Since it leads us on to despair, God wants us to turn doubtful fear into love through the knowledge of love; that is to say, the bitterness of doubt is to be turned into the sweetness of tender love through grace. For it can never please our Lord that his servants doubt his goodness.

The fourth is reverent fear; the only fear we can have which thoroughly pleases God is reverent fear; and it is very gentle; the more we have it, the less we feel it because of the sweetness of love. Love and fear are brothers; and they are rooted in us by the goodness of our Maker, and they will never be taken from us for all eternity. To love is granted us by nature, and to love is granted us by grace; and to fear is granted us by nature, and to fear is granted us by grace. It is fitting that God's lordship and fatherhood should be feared, as it is fitting for his goodness to be loved; and it is fitting for us who are his servants and his children to fear him as lord and as father, as it is fitting for us to love him for his goodness. And though this reverent fear and love are not separable, yet they are not one and the same. They are two in their nature and their way of working, yet neither of them may be had without the other. Therefore I am certain that those who love also fear, though they may only feel it a little.

Even though they may appear to be holy, all the fears which face us, apart from reverent fear, are not truly so; and this is how they may be told apart. The fear which makes us quickly flee from all that is not good and fall upon our Lord's breast like a child upon its mother's bosom, which makes us do this with all our mind and with all our will-power, knowing our feebleness and our great need, knowing God's everlasting goodness and his blessed love, seeking salvation only in him and clinging to him with sure trust – the fear which makes us do this is natural, gracious, good and true. And everything contrary to this is either completely wrong or partly wrong.

This is the remedy, then: to recognize them both and refuse the wrong one. For the same natural profit which we gain from fear in this life through the gracious working of the Holy Ghost, shall in heaven be gracious, courteous and delightful in God's sight. And so in love we should be familiar and near to God, and in fear we should be gracious and courteous to God, and both equally.

Let us ask God that we may fear him reverently and love him humbly and trust him strongly; for when we fear him reverently and love him humbly, our trust is never in vain; the greater and stronger our trust in God, the more we please and honour the Lord we trust. And if we fail in this reverent fear and meek love (which God forbid we should), our trust will soon slacken for the time being. And therefore we have a great need to pray to God that by his grace we may have this reverent fear and meek love, as his gift, in our hearts and in our deeds; for without this, no one can please God.

75

How we need love, longing and pity; and of three kinds of longing for God which are in us; and how on Judgement Day the joy of the blessed will be increased when they truly see the cause of all God has done, trembling in fear and thanking in joy, marvelling at the greatness of God and the littleness of all that is made.

I saw that God can do all that is necessary for us; and these three are necessary: love, longing and pity. Pity in love protects us in our time of need, and longing in the same love draws us up to heaven; for God's thirst is to draw mankind in general up into himself, and in this thirst he has drawn up the holy ones who are now in bliss; and to get the living, he is always drawing and drinking, yet he still thirsts and longs.

I saw three kinds of longing in God, and all to one end; and we have the same longing in us, and of the same power, and to the same end. The first is that he longs to teach us to know him and love him for evermore, as is fitting and beneficial for us. The second is that he longs to have us up in his bliss, as souls are when they are taken out of suffering into heaven. The third is to fill us with bliss; and that longing shall be fulfilled on the final day, to last for ever; for I saw, as our faith assures us, that suffering and sorrow will end for all those who will be saved. And not only shall we receive the same bliss which the souls before us have had in heaven, but we shall also receive new bliss which will flow into us abundantly out of God and fill us; and this is the good which he has ordained that we should be given since before time began. This good is treasured up and hidden in himself; for until that time, no being is able or deserves to receive it.

In this moment we shall truly see the cause of all that he has done; and for evermore we shall see the cause of everything which he has allowed to happen. And the bliss and fulfilment shall be so deep and so high that in their wonder and amazement all created beings will feel such reverent fear for God, surpassing everything seen and felt before, that the pillars of heaven shall tremble and quake.

But this kind of trembling and fear will bring no suffering, for it befits the noble might of God thus to be seen by his creatures, as they tremble fearfully and quake with meekness of joy, marvelling at the greatness of God the Maker and the littleness of all that is made; for seeing this will make all created beings marvellously meek and mild. Therefore God wants us to know and recognize this, and it befits us to do so, both by nature and by grace, to long for his sight and for this to happen, because it leads us in the right way and keeps us in the true life and unites us to God.

And God is as great as he is good, and as much as it belongs to his goodness to be loved, so much it belongs to his greatness to be feared; for this reverent fear is the fair courtesy shown before God's face in heaven. And he will then be feared beyond our present fear as much as he will be loved and known beyond our present knowledge and love. Therefore it needs must be that all heaven and earth shall tremble and quake when the pillars tremble and quake.

76

A loving soul hates sin for its vileness more than all the torment of hell; and how looking at someone else's sin (unless it be with compassion) prevents us from looking at God; and the Devil, by reminding us of our sinful wretchedness, would also prevent us; and of our sloth.

I am saying very little about reverent fear, for I hope that what I have said will be enough. But I am quite sure that our Lord showed me no souls who did not fear him, for I am quite sure that the soul which truly accepts the teaching of the Holy Ghost hates sin for its vileness and hideousness more than all the torments of hell; for it seems to me that the soul which considers the kindness of our Lord Jesus hates no hell but sin. And so it is God's will that we recognize sin, and pray earnestly and work hard and humbly seek for guidance so that we do not fall into it blindly; and if we fall, that we rise again quickly, for turning from God through sin even for a moment is the greatest torment a soul can ever suffer.

The soul that wants to be at peace must flee from thoughts of other people's sins as though from the pains of hell, begging God for a remedy and for help against it; for the consideration of other people's sins makes a sort of thick mist before the eyes of the soul, and during such times we cannot see the beauty of God unless we regard the sins with sorrow for those who commit them, with compassion and with a holy wish for God to help them; for if we do not do this the consideration of sins harms and distresses and hinders the soul; I understood this in the revelation of compassion.[67]

In this blessed showing of our Lord's I understood two contrary things: one, the wisest thing that anyone can do in this life; the other, the most foolish.[68] The wisdom is for people to behave according to the wishes and advice of their greatest and most supreme friend. This blessed friend is Jesus, and it is his will and his advice that we should bind ourselves to him and direct ourselves towards him, familiarly, for evermore, in whatever state we may be, for whether we are sinful or pure his love for us is the same. In weal or woe, he never wants us to flee from him, but because of our own changeability we often fall into sin. When this happens, it comes to us by the provocation of our Enemy, through our own folly and blindness, which say, 'You know very well that you are a wretch, a sinner, and also faithless, for you do not obey God's commands; you often promise our Lord that you will do better, and immediately afterwards you fall back into the same sin, especially sloth and time-wasting' – for these are the beginning of sin, it seems to me, especially for people who have vowed to serve our Lord with inward contemplation of his blessed goodness. And this makes us afraid of appearing before our courteous Lord. So it is our enemy the Devil who sets us back with false fear of our sinfulness and the punishment with which he threatens us; for with these he intends to make us so unhappy and so weary that we shall forget the fair, blessed consideration of our everlasting Friend.

77

Of the enmity of the Fiend, who loses more by our rising than he gains by our falling, and so becomes an object of scorn; and how punishment from God should be borne with his Passion in mind, for that receives a greater reward than penance we have chosen ourselves; and we must suffer, but kind and courteous God is our leader, protector and bliss.

Our good Lord showed the enmity of the Fiend, from which I understood that everything that is contrary to love and peace is caused by the Fiend and his works. And our feebleness and folly make us fall, and the mercy and grace of the Holy Ghost make us rise to greater joy. And if our Enemy wins anything from us by our falling (for that is what pleases him), he loses many times more from our rising through love and humility. And this glorious rising causes him such great sorrow and pain, from his hatred for our souls, that he is continually burning with resentment. And all this sorrow which he wants to cause us will be turned against him. And this is what made our Lord despise him, and this made me laugh heartily.

This is the remedy, then: that we should acknowledge our sinfulness and flee to our Lord, for the readier we are to do this, the more it will profit us to approach him. And let us say this to ourselves, 'I know very well that I am suffering grievously, but our Lord is all mighty and can punish me mightily, and he is all wisdom and can punish me wisely, and he is all goodness and loves me very tenderly.' And it is necessary for us to keep to this view; for it shows a lovely meekness in a sinful soul, brought about by the mercy and grace of the Holy Ghost, when we willingly and gladly take the scourging and chastening our Lord himself wants to give us.

And it will be very gentle and very easy if we will only be content with him and all his works; for the penance which people impose on themselves was not shown to me, that is to say, it was not shown especially; but it was shown especially and powerfully and most beautifully that we should humbly and patiently bear and suffer the penance which God himself gives us, remembering his blessed Passion. For when we remember his blessed Passion, with pity and love, then we suffer with him as his friends did who saw it, and this was shown in the thirteenth revelation, near the beginning, where it speaks of pity; for he says, 'Do not accuse yourself overmuch, claiming that your tribulation and woe is all your own fault. I do not want you to be unreasonably sad and sorrowful; for I tell you that you will suffer woe whatever you do. And therefore I want you to recognize clearly what your penance is, and then you will truly see that your whole life is a profitable penance.'

This place is a prison and this life a penance, and he wants us to find joy in the remedy. The remedy is that our Lord is with us, protecting and leading us into the fullness of joy; for it is an endless joy to us, as our Lord intends, that he who will be our bliss when we are there will be our protector while we are here. Our way and our heaven are true love and sure trust; and he made this understood in all the showings, especially in the showing of his Passion where he made me choose him absolutely for my heaven.

Let us fly to our Lord and we shall be comforted, touch him and we shall be made clean, cling to him and we shall be safe and secure from all manner of peril; for our courteous Lord wants us to be as friendly with him as the heart may conceive or the soul may desire. But be careful not to take this friendliness too casually, so that we neglect courtesy; for our Lord himself is supreme friendliness, and he is as courteous as he is friendly; for he is truly courteous. And he wants the blessed creatures who will be with him in heaven for ever to be like himself in all things. And to be perfectly like our Lord is our true salvation and our full bliss. And if we are uncertain how we can do all this, let us ask our Lord and he will teach us; for it is his pleasure and his glory. Blessed may he be!

78

Our Lord wants us to recognize four kinds of goodness which he offers us; and how we need the light of grace to know our sin and weakness, for by ourselves we are nothing but wretchedness and cannot know the hideousness of sin as it is; and how our Enemy does not want us ever to know our sin until the last day and therefore we are much indebted to God who shows it to us now.

In his mercy, our Lord shows us our sin and our weakness by his own sweet, gracious light; for our sin is so vile and so horrible that in his kind courtesy he will show it to us only by the light of his grace and mercy. It is his wish that we should have knowledge of four things: the first is that he is the ground from which we have all our life and our being; the second, that he protects us mightily and mercifully in the time of our sin and among all the enemies that fall upon us so fiercely – and we are in the greater peril because we give them the opportunity and do not know our own need; the third is that he protects us with kind courtesy and lets us know that we are going wrong; the fourth is how steadfastly he waits for us with unchanging face, for he wants us to turn to him and unite with him in love, as he is united with us.

And so through this gracious knowledge we may see our sin profitably, without despairing, for we do really need to see it; and the sight will make us ashamed of ourselves and break down our pride and presumption; for we really must see that in ourselves we are nothing at all but sin and wretchedness. And so through our sight of the lesser part which our Lord shows us, the greater which we do not see loses its power; for in his kindness he moderates the sight for us, for it is so vile and so horrible that we could not bear to see it as it is.

And so by this humble awareness, through contrition and grace, we shall be severed from everything which is not our Lord, and then our blessed Saviour will heal us perfectly and unite us to himself. Our Lord applies this severing and healing to people in general, for he who is highest and nearest to God may see himself as sinful and needy along with me; and I, the least and the lowest of those who will be saved, may take comfort from him who is highest. So our Lord united us in charity when he showed me that I would sin.

And because of the joy I felt when I beheld him, I did not pay attention to that showing immediately; and then our kind Lord stopped and would not teach me any more until he had given me the grace and the will to pay attention.

From this I was taught that though we may be lifted up high in contemplation through the special gift of our Lord, yet at the same time we must have knowledge and sight of our sin and our feebleness; for without this knowledge we cannot have true humility, and without this we cannot be saved. And I also saw that we cannot gain this knowledge by ourselves, nor from any of our spiritual enemies, for they do not want so much good for us; if it were left to them, we should not see it until our dying day. So we are greatly indebted to God who for love will show it to us while it is not too late for mercy and grace.

79

We are taught to consider our sin and not our neighbours', unless it is to help them; and God wants us to know that whatever impulse we have contrary to this showing comes from our Enemy; knowing the great love of God should not make us more careless about falling; and if we fall, we must rise again quickly or else we are most unresponsive to God.

I also received greater understanding in this matter: when God showed me that I would sin I took this to apply simply to myself in particular, for it meant nothing else to me then; but through the great and gracious comfort of our Lord which came later I saw that his message applied to mankind in general, that is to everyone who is sinful and shall be until the last day. Of these I am one, I hope, through the mercy of God, for the blessed help which I saw is ample enough for us all. And here I was taught that I should see my own sin and not other people's sins, unless it is to support and help my fellow Christians.

And also in this same showing, where I saw that I would sin, I was taught to fear my own instability; for I do not know how I shall fall, nor do I know the size or the seriousness of sin; I longed and feared to know that, but had no answer to my question. Also, at the same time, our kind Lord showed powerfully and certainly the endlessness and unchangeableness of his love; and also how, through his great goodness and the spiritual protection of his grace, his love and our souls shall never be parted through all eternity. And so in this fear I have cause for humility which saves me from presumption; and in the blessed showing of love I have cause for true comfort and joy which save me from despair.

All this friendly showing of our kind Lord's is a lovely lesson and his own sweet, gracious teaching to comfort our souls, for he wants us to know, through his sweet and familiar love, that everything we see or feel, within or without, which is contrary to this is of the Enemy and not of God. For example, if we are moved to live or guard our hearts more carelessly for the very reason that we have knowledge of his abundant love, then we must take great care, for if we have this impulse, it is flawed and we should loathe it; it is nothing like God's will.

And when we fall through frailty or blindness, then our kind Lord touches us, moves us and calls us, and then he wants us to see our wretchedness and sinfulness and acknowledge it humbly. But he does not want us to stop at this point, nor does he want us to be very anxious to accuse ourselves, nor does he want us to be inwardly miserable; but he wants us quickly to turn our thoughts to him; for he stands all alone and waits for us, sorrowing and lamenting until we come, and is impatient to have us with him; for we are his joy and his delight, and he is our balm and our life.

When I say that he stands alone, I omit mention of the blessed company of heaven and refer to his function and his works here on earth, according to the nature of the showing.

80

God is worshipped and we are saved by three things; and how our present knowledge goes no further than an ABC; and sweet Jesus does everything, waiting and lamenting with us, but when we are in a state of sin, Christ laments alone, and then it is fitting for us, from kindness and reverence, to turn quickly to him again.

Man relies on three things in this life, three things by which God is worshipped and we are helped, protected and saved. The first is the use of man's natural reason; the second is the general teaching of Holy Church; the third is the gracious inner working of the Holy Ghost; and these three are all from one God. God is the origin of our natural reason, and God is the teaching of Holy Church, and God is the Holy Ghost. And these are distinct gifts which he wants us to observe carefully and pay attention to, for they are always at work in us, bringing us to God, and they are very important things which he wants us to know about here as we might know the ABC; that is to say, that we should have a little knowledge here of what we shall know fully in heaven; and that is for our benefit.

We know through our Christian faith that God alone took on our human nature and none but he; and further that Christ alone performed all the works needed for our salvation, and none but he; and in just the same way he alone is now carrying out the final task: that is to say, he is living here with us, ruling and governing us in this life and bringing us to his bliss. And he will do so as long as any soul that will come to heaven is still on this earth; and to such an extent that if there were no more than one such soul, he would be with it alone until he had brought it up to his bliss. I believe and understand what the scholars say of the ministration of angels, but I was not shown this; for Christ himself is nearest and humblest, highest and lowest, and does everything; and not only all that we need, but he also does all that brings us glory for our joy in heaven.

And where I say that he waits, sorrowing and lamenting, it refers to all the true feelings of contrition and compassion which we have within ourselves, and all our sorrowing and lamenting for not being united with our Lord. All such feelings which are helpful are Christ within us, and though some of us seldom have such feelings, Christ will never cease to work in this way until he has brought us all out of all our woe; for love never allows him to be without pity. And when we fall into sin and forget him and forget to safeguard our own souls, then Christ alone bears the whole burden, and so he stands sorrowing and lamenting. Then it is fitting for us, out of reverence and kindness, to turn quickly to our Lord and not to leave him alone. He is here for all of us alone: that is to say, he is only here for us. And whenever I am cold towards him through sin, despair or sloth, then I let my Lord stand alone, to the extent of my sin; and so do all of us who are sinners. But although it is true that we often do this, his goodness never allows us to be alone; but he is always with us, and he tenderly excuses us, and he always shields us from blame in his eyes.

81

This blessed woman saw God in various ways, but she saw him find a resting-place only in man's soul; and he wants us to rejoice more in his love than we sorrow over our frequent falling, remembering our everlasting reward and living willingly in penance; and why God is patient with sin.

Our good Lord showed himself in various ways, both in heaven and on earth, but the only place I saw him occupy was man's soul. He showed himself on earth in his precious Incarnation and in his blessed Passion. And he showed himself on earth in another way at the point where I say, 'I saw God in an instant.'[69] And he showed himself on earth in another way as though on a pilgrimage: that is to say, he is here with us, leading us, and will be until he has brought us all up to his bliss in heaven. At different times he showed himself reigning, as I have said before, but principally he showed himself in man's soul. He has made that his resting-place and his glorious city, a glorious throne out of which he will never rise or remove for all eternity. The place where the Lord dwells is marvellous and noble.

And so he wants us to respond readily to his gracious touch, rejoicing more in all his love than we sorrow over our frequent falling, for it honours him more than anything else we can do that we should live willingly and cheerfully in our penance for love of him. He watches us so tenderly that he sees all our living and suffering; for his kind love shows itself in our lasting penance, suffering which he causes in us and mercifully helps us to bear. His love makes him long for us, but his wisdom and his truth with his righteousness make him patient while we are here, and he wants to see us patient in the same way; for this suffering of ours is kind and natural, and seems the noblest to me, for this penance never leaves us until the time when we are finally satisfied, when we shall have him for our reward. And that is why he wants us to set our hearts upon our passing on: that is to say, from the pain that we feel to the bliss in which we believe.

82

God looks at the lamenting soul with pity and not with blame, and yet we do nothing but sin, and so we are left in joy and fear; for he wants us to turn to him, clinging eagerly to his love, seeing that he is our medicine; and so we must love him, with joy and longing; and anything contrary to this comes not from God, but from the Enemy.

But here our kind Lord showed the soul's lamentation and mourning, meaning this: 'I know well that for love of me you wish to live cheerfully and gladly, bearing all the suffering that may come to you, but insofar as you do not live without sin, you are willing to suffer for love of me all the tribulation and distress that can come to you. And this is true. But do not be too troubled by the sins that you commit unwillingly.' And here I understood that the lord considers his servant with pity and not with blame, for in this passing life we are not expected to live quite free from blame and sin.

He loves us everlastingly, and we sin habitually and he reveals our sins very gently; and then we sorrow and mourn appropriately, turning to the consideration of his mercy, clinging to his love and goodness, seeing that he is our medicine, knowing that we do nothing but sin. And so by the humility we gain from seeing our sin, faithfully knowing his everlasting love, thanking and praising him, we please him. 'I love you and you love me; and our love shall not be divided,[70] and I suffer for your profit.' And all this was shown in spiritual understanding of these blessed words, 'I am keeping you very safe.'[71]

And from the great desire which I saw in our blessed Lord that we may live in this way, that is to say, in joy and longing, as all this lesson of love shows, I understood that everything which is harmful to us is not of him but of our Enemy; and he wants us to know it by the sweet gracious light of his kind love.

If there be any lover of God on earth who is continuously kept from falling, I do not know of it, for it was not shown to me. But this was shown: that in falling and in rising we are always tenderly protected in one love; for as God beholds us we do not fall, and as we behold ourselves we do not stand, and both these seem to me to be true, but our Lord God's view is the highest truth: so we are much indebted to God for showing us this great truth while we are still in this earthly life. And I understood that while we are in this life, it is greatly to our benefit to see both of these at once; for the higher view keeps us in spiritual comfort and true pleasure in God; the other, that is the lower view, keeps us in fear and makes us ashamed of ourselves. Our good Lord wants us to see ourselves much more in accordance with the higher view, but without ceasing to be aware of the lower one, until the time when we are brought up above, where we shall have our Lord Jesus as our reward and be filled with joy and bliss without end.

83

Of three properties of God: life, love and light; and that our reason is in harmony with God; it is our highest gift; and how our faith is a light which comes from the Father and is allotted to us, leading us through this night and to the end of our woe; our eyes shall suddenly be opened in the full light and clarity of vision, seeing our Maker, Father and Holy Ghost in Jesus our Saviour.

I was able to touch, see and feel some of the three properties of God on which the strength and meaning of the whole revelation is based; and they were seen in every showing and most characteristically in the twelfth, where it often says, 'It is I.' The properties are these: life, love and light. There is marvellous familiarity in life, gracious courtesy in love, and in light there is endless kindness. These properties belonged to a single goodness; and my reason desired to unite and cling to this goodness with all its might. I watched with reverent fear, marvelling greatly as I saw and felt the sweet harmony between our reason and God, understanding that it is the highest gift we have received and that it is grounded in nature.

Our faith is a light, coming kindly and naturally from everlasting day, which is our father, God; and in this light our mother, Christ, and our good lord, the Holy Ghost, lead us in this transitory life. This light is allotted prudently, supporting us in the night according to our need. The light is the cause of our life, the night is the cause of our suffering and of all our woe, through which we deserve reward and thanks from God; for we, eagerly knowing and believing in our light through mercy and grace, walk in it surely and strongly. And when woe ends, our eyes shall suddenly be opened, and in the brightness of light our sight will be clear; and this light is God our Maker and the Holy Ghost in Christ Jesus our Saviour. Thus I saw and understood that our faith is our light in our night, light which is God, our everlasting day.

84

Charity is this light, which is not so small that, with toil, it does not deserve the endless, glorious thanks of God; for faith and hope lead us to charity, of which there are three kinds.

The light is charity, and this light is beneficially allotted to us by the wisdom of God; for neither is the light so great that we can see our blessed day, nor is it hidden from us, but it is just such a light as we may live in deservingly, with toil meriting the endless glory of God. And this was seen in the sixth showing, where God said, 'I thank you for your service and your suffering.'[72] Thus charity keeps us in faith and in hope; and hope leads us in charity. And at the end, all shall be charity. I understood this light in three ways: the first is charity uncreated; the second is charity created; the third is charity given. Charity uncreated is God; charity created is our soul in God; charity given is virtue; and that is conduct, given by grace, by which we love God for himself, and ourselves in God, and what God loves for the sake of God.

85

God has loved his chosen since before time began, and he never allows them to be so harmed that their bliss might be lessened; and how mysteries now hidden in heaven shall be known, so that we shall bless our Lord because everything is so well ordained.

And I marvelled greatly at this sight; for in spite of our ignorant way of life and our blindness here, our kind Lord everlastingly watches our behaviour and rejoices. And of all things we can please him best by wisely and truly believing this and rejoicing with him and in him; for as surely as we shall be in God's bliss everlastingly, praising and thanking him, so, through God's providence, have we been known and loved in his everlasting purpose since before time began; and in this love without beginning he protects us and never allows us to be so harmed that our bliss would be less. And therefore when the judgement is given, and we are all brought up above, we shall clearly see in God the mysteries which are now hidden from us. Then none of us shall be moved to say in any way, 'Lord, it would have been very good if it had been like this', but we shall all affirm silently, 'Lord, may you be blessed! For it is thus and it is good. And now we truly see that all is done as it was ordained before anything was made.'

86

The good Lord showed that this book should be completed differently from the way it was first written; and this is the way he wants us to pray to him for his work, thanking, trusting and rejoicing in him; and how he revealed this showing because he wants to make it known, in which knowledge he will give us grace to love him; for fifteen years later came the answer that the cause of all this showing was love, which may Jesus grant us.   Amen.

This book was begun by God's gift and his grace, but it seems to me that it is not yet completed. With God's inspiration let us all pray to him for charity, thanking, trusting and rejoicing; for this is how our good Lord wants us to pray to him, as I understood from all that he conveyed, and from the sweet words where he says very cheeringly, 'I am the foundation of your prayers';[73] for I truly saw and understood in what our Lord conveyed that he showed this because he wants to have it better known than it is. Through this knowledge he will give us grace to love and cling to him; for he feels such great love for his heavenly treasure on earth that he wants to give us clearer and more comforting sight of heavenly joy as he draws our hearts to him, because of the sorrow and darkness which we are in.

And from the time that this was shown, I often longed to know what our Lord meant. And fifteen years and more later my spiritual understanding received an answer, which was this: 'Do you want to know what your Lord meant? Know well that love was what he meant. Who showed you this? Love. What did he show? Love. Why did he show it to you? For love. Hold fast to this and you will know and understand more of the same; but you will never understand or know from it anything else for all eternity.' This is how I was taught that our Lord's meaning was love. And I saw quite certainly in this and in everything that God loved us before he made us; and his love has never diminished and never shall. And all his works were done in this love; and in this love he has made everything for our profit; and in this love our life is everlasting. We had our beginning when we were made; but the love in which he made us was in him since before time began; and in this love we have our beginning. And all this shall be seen in God without end, which may Jesus grant us. Amen.

Thus ends the revelation of love of the Holy Trinity shown by our Saviour Christ Jesu for our everlasting comfort and joy, and also to help us rejoice in him in the transitory journey of this life. Amen, Jesu, Amen.

★

I pray to almighty God that this book come only into the hands of those who want to love him faithfully, and to those who are willing to submit themselves to the faith of Holy Church and obey the sound understanding and teaching of men of virtuous life, grave years and profound learning; for this revelation is deep theology and great wisdom, so it must not remain with anyone who is thrall to sin and the Devil. And beware that you do not take one thing according to your taste and fancy and leave another, for that is what heretics do. But take everything together and truly understand that everything is in accordance with holy scripture and grounded in it, and Jesus our true love, light and truth will show this wisdom concerning himself to all pure souls who ask for it humbly and perseveringly. And you to whom this book may come, thank our Saviour Jesu Christ earnestly and heartily for making these showings and revelations of his endless love, mercy and goodness for you and to you, to be your and our safe guide and conduct to everlasting bliss; which may Jesus grant us. Amen.

NOTES

1 *terror and turmoil of the fiends*: Medieval pictures of death-beds often show devils waiting eagerly to grasp the dying person's soul.

2 *Saint Cecilia . . . painfully died*: The legend of Saint Cecilia recounts that she was an aristocratic Christian girl in pagan Rome who, after converting her intended husband and his brother to Christianity, was sentenced to be beheaded. Three sword strokes failed to kill her immediately, but she died three days later. In the late fourteenth century Chaucer retold the story and included it in *The Canterbury Tales* as the 'Second Nun's Tale'.

3 *Benedicite dominus*: 'Blessed be thou, Lord!'

4 *Behold, the handmaid of the Lord*: Luke 1:38.

5 *three nothings*: Probably (in this chapter) all that is created, and (in chapter 8) sin and the Devil. Julian repeats various forms of the word *nought* throughout this paragraph, as indicated by the repetitions of 'nothing' in the translation.

6 *an instant*: The word used by Julian, *poynte*, can mean a point of space or of time.

7 *what sin is . . . as I shall recount later*: In chapters 13 and 17.

8 *every man's age*: I.e. the age at which a person dedicated himself or herself to God.

9 *Lord save me, I perish*: Julian alludes to but does not quote exactly Saint Paul's words in Romans 8:35 and the cries for help of the disciples in Matthew 8:25 and of Saint Peter in Matthew 14:30.

10 *I thirst*: Christ's words on the cross in John 19:28.

11 *spiritual thirst . . . as I shall say later*: In chapter 15.

12 *as Saint Paul says . . . in Jesus Christ*: Cf. Philippians 2:5, which in the Vulgate reads: 'Hoc enim sentite in vobis' (literally, 'For feel this in you').

13 *only in pain*: Here Julian deliberately rejects the possibility of transcendent contemplation of the Godhead, almost as if it were a temptation, in favour of a continuing focus on Christ in his suffering Humanity.

14 *blessed Manhood of Christ*: In what follows, the bodily emphasis of Julian's vision goes so far that she sees the whole Trinity within Christ's Humanity.

15 *the longing I had had for him*: This is 'the wound of an earnest longing for God' mentioned by Julian in chapter 1 as part of the third gift she had asked from God before she received her showings.

16 *our Lord is our portion*: Cf. Psalm 15:5 (16:5 in Protestant Bibles).

17 *privy counsel should be undisturbed*: Julian imagines God as if he were an earthly king with a 'privy council' with whom he discusses high matters of state.

18 *David . . . Magdalene*: Julian lists various sinners who are nevertheless honoured by the Church for their spiritual achievements. David, the king of Judah, traditionally regarded as the author of the Psalms and as the human ancestor of Jesus, committed adultery with Bathsheba and murdered her husband Uriah. Mary Magdalene, to whom Jesus appeared after his resurrection (Mark 16:9), was identified in the Middle Ages with the 'sinner' who washed and anointed Jesus' feet and was told by him, 'Thy sins are forgiven thee' (Luke 7:37–48); her sin was said to have been sexual promiscuity or even prostitution. She was also identified with Mary the sister of Martha; Martha complained that Mary did not help her serve Jesus when he visited their house, but merely sat at his feet and 'heard his word', but Jesus told her, 'Mary hath chosen the best part which shall not be taken away from her' (Luke 10:38–42). Since Mary and Martha were seen as types of the contemplative and active lives, Mary Magdalene would have a special interest for Julian, who chose the best part in becoming an anchorite and receiving God's showings rather than serving society. Peter, the apostle whom Jesus described as the rock on which he would build his Church (Matthew 16:18), and who became the first Pope, sinned conspicuously after Jesus' arrest in denying three times that he was one of his followers (Matthew 26:69–74). Paul had sinned in persecuting the earliest Christians, before undergoing a visionary conversion on the road to Damascus, embarking on his great missionary journeys and writing the epistles on which Christian theology was founded. Thomas was famous as the apostle who questioned Jesus' resurrection until he was able to touch the wounds in his hands and side (John 20:25–9); but it was believed that he later made good this sin of doubt by taking Christianity to India, where he was martyred.

19 *sufferings*: In this passage, and in others in both texts, Julian uses the word *payne* to mean both 'suffering' and 'punishment' (the two senses are not clearly distinguished in Middle English). Translation is difficult, because for Julian sin is both suffering and its own punishment.

20 *'Pater noster', 'Ave' and the Creed*: The Lord's Prayer, 'Hail Mary' and Creed, the basic Catholic devotions, also contain the principles of Catholic doctrine. As well as being used for private devotion, they would have been recited in English by ordinary people while the liturgy of the Mass was being performed in Latin.

21 *By this is the Fiend overcome*: Chapter 8.

22 *doubtful fear*: I.e. fear arising from doubt of God's goodness.

23 *love is nearest to us all*: Love is the attribute of the Holy Ghost, as truth is of the Father and wisdom of the Son.

LONG TEXT

1 *uneducated*: See Introduction, pp. viii–ix.

2 *terror and turmoil of the fiends*: See ST n. 1.

3 *three wounds*: Cf. ST chapter 1, where Julian explains that she was influenced by the legend that Saint Cecilia had received three literal wounds in her neck.

4 *Benedicite domine*: 'Blessed be thou, Lord!'

5 *Behold, the handmaid of the Lord*: Luke 1:38.

6 *intermediaries*: For 'intermediaries' Julian's word is *menys*. She urges that God is more honoured by being prayed to directly, as God; at the same time, she is careful to add that he is not displeased by prayers directed to his Humanity, to the saints, etc. – a necessary addition at a time when the Church was persecuting Lollards.

7 *pills*: For 'pills' the original has *pellots*. This Middle English word could refer to many kinds of round object; 'pills' (which would have been globular) seems a likely translation, given its domestic associations.

8 *eaves*: Julian would have imagined drops continuing to fall thickly from the eaves after a rain-shower, because she would have had in mind roofs without gutters, and probably made of thatch rather than tiles or slate.

9 *showing . . . same thing as our faith*: This is one of many places where Julian is careful to state that her showings serve to confirm the existing belief of the Church.

10 *vernicle*: The cloth, supposed to have belonged to Saint Veronica, with which Christ's face was wiped as he was bearing the cross to Calvary; as Julian explains later, it was thought to have retained an impression of his face.

11 *sea bed . . . sand*: Here Julian's imagination may have been stimulated by the visions of divine protection beneath the sea in Jonah 2 and in Psalm 68, usually associated with Jonah; but it is also worth bearing in mind how close the connections were between Norwich and the North Sea.

12 *an instant*: See ST n. 6.

13 *complete*: Julian is playing on the word *rightful* (righteous), which is made up of *right* (just, justice) and *ful* (complete).

14 *a vision of naked sin, as I shall recount later*: This is in showing 13.

15 *Lord save me, I perish*: See ST n. 9.

16 *I thirst*: See ST n. 10.

17 *slashed through*: Julian's word, *daggyd*, could refer to an ornamental slash in clothing, which would give a harshly ironic contrast with the mutilation of Christ's naked flesh.

18 *Saint Denis of France*: According to *The Golden Legend*, written in the thirteenth century and very widely read in Julian's time, Dionysius (Denis) was a Greek philosopher converted to Christianity by Saint Paul after witnessing the natural disturbances that occurred at the time of the crucifixion. He was later sent as an apostle to Gaul, where he was martyred and became the patron saint of France.

19 *unknown God*: These two quotations resemble what is recorded in the widely read encyclopaedic *Historia Scholastica* of Peter Comestor (ch. 75, in *Patrologia Latina*, vol. 198, col. 1631), though we cannot be certain that this was Julian's source. For the second quotation, cf. Acts 17:23.

20 *only in pain*: See ST n. 13.

21 *blesed Manhood of Christ*: See ST n. 14.

22 *Jesus by his buying*: The Son's 'buying' of mankind as opposed to the Father's 'gift': here and in other places we follow Julian's own use of *bey, bowte*, etc., to mean 'redeem' (which itself derives from Latin *redimere*, 'buy back').

23 *ever*: This is in Jesus's words at the beginning of chapter 22: 'It is a joy, a delight and an endless happiness to me that I ever endured suffering for you.'

24 *the same wound*: John 19:34 describes how, after Christ's death on the cross, a soldier pierced his side with a spear, and blood and water flowed from the wound. The wound giving entrance to Christ's heart was a favourite topic of medieval devotion.

25 *the longing I had had for him*: See ST n. 15.

26 *our Lord is our portion*: See ST n. 16.

27 *privy counsel should be undisturbed*: See ST n. 15.

28 *Holy Church teaches us to believe*: The absence of evil and of hell and purgatory from what Julian was shown puts her in danger of heresy; this is one of the places where she is most insistent on her full acceptance of the Church's teaching.

29 *Jews . . . through grace*: Theological antisemitism, directed against the Jews as (it was supposed) collectively responsible for Christ's death and subsequently antagonistic to all Christians, was a prominent feature of medieval Christianity. One manifestation that would have been familiar to Julian was the accusation that the twelfth-century child-martyr Saint William of Norwich had been the victim of Jewish ritual murder. But she evidently accepted the condemnation of the Jews only because it was taught by the Church, not because it was part of her own religious vision.

30 *endures*: The verb used by Julian here and elsewhere, *suffren*, means both 'suffer' in its modern sense and 'endure, permit, tolerate, put up with, be patient'. Similarly, Latin *patior*, 'I suffer', is the origin both of 'passion' (including the Passion of Christ) and of 'passive' and 'patience'. Patience is a virtue highly valued in medieval religious thought, and Julian, like the *Gawain*-poet in his poem *Patience* (a retelling of the story of Jonah and the whale), attributes it to God even more than to human beings.

31 *soul that truly sees . . . rejoices without end*: The problem of reconciling God's mercy with the perfect *ryhtfulhede*, meaning both 'righteousness' and 'justice', attributed to him from the Old Testament on, was a central task of medieval theology.

32 *Mary Magdalene . . . Saint John of Beverley*: See ST n. 18. John of Beverley was an eighth-century monk who became Bishop of York and later retired to the abbey at Beverley. He was greatly revered in medieval England, and Julian's younger contemporary Henry V attributed his victory at Agincourt to John's intercession; but it is uncertain into what sin Julian believed John to have fallen.

33 *spiritual thirst was shown*: In Chapter 31.

34 *receiver*: In the sense of 'collector' or 'treasurer', an official whose task is to take in funds and store them in a treasury.

35 *action*: Julian's word *werkyng* probably refers to inward, spiritual activity.

36 *Truth sees . . . is love*: See ST n. 23.

37 *parable of a lord and a servant . . . as I shall recount later*: In chapter 51.

38 *God wants to be revealed and known*: By 'the simple soul' Julian presumably means herself. Whatever she has understood from her showings God must have wished her to understand, for he reveals only what he wishes to reveal.

39 *neither can nor may separate them*: Julian's acknowledgement that she can no longer separate the vision as she originally saw and understood it, the deeper understanding that came subsequently and the interpretation implied by the whole sequence of showings, helps to explain the difficulty of this chapter, and especially the frequent shifts of tense between past and present. These we have generally let stand; they also reflect the way that the parable, revealed at a specific moment, has a meaning that stands outside time.

40 *within him . . . endless heavens*: Cf. chapter 24, where Jesus shows the place of salvation within his wounded side.

41 *My understanding was led into the lord*: See p. 116.

42 *the scourging . . . the bone*: See chapter 17.

43 *root*: This image, appropriate to the gardening imagery of the whole parable, may allude to the 'root' of 4 Kings 19:30 (2 Kings 19:30 in Protestant Bibles), the 'remnant' of those who would be saved even if disaster came upon Judah. The notion of the saved remnant reappears in Isaiah 10:20–22, and Saint Paul takes it up in Romans 9:27–9. But for Julian the 'remnant' seems to have included all humanity, and the manuscript *grit rote* might also mean 'great crowd'.

44 *the spouse . . . eternal joy*: An allusion to the Song of Songs (or Song of Solomon), which was read allegorically, with the spouse (*sponsus*) representing Christ and the bride (*sponsa*) the Blessed Virgin, the Church or the human soul.

45 *holy thirst*: Christ's thirst in its spiritual sense is described in chapter 31.

46 *But through grace . . . strength allows*: Julian draws the orthodox Catholic distinction between mortal sins, which, if not absolved, lead to damnation, and venial, or lesser, sins, which receive a more limited punishment in purgatory. She seems to be expressing tacit scepticism about the Church's doctrine of eternal punishment.

47 *in the making*: I.e. when Christ's human nature was created (which is also when his soul was created).

48 *I should look up to heaven*: See chapter 19.

49 *double nature*: I.e. composed of sensory being and essential being.

50 *seven sacraments*: These are Baptism, Confirmation, the Eucharist, Penance, Extreme Unction, Holy Orders and Matrimony, all regarded by the medieval Church as instituted by Christ, though there was disagreement as to the occasions and order of their institution.

51 *we are all enclosed . . . in us*: This is not an exact quotation from the first showing.

52 *I love . . . never be divided*: Chapter 82.

53 *It is I*: Chapter 26.

54 *If I could . . . suffer more*: Chapter 22.

55 *It is I . . . to you*: Chapter 26.

56 *kind*: Throughout this chapter and the next, Julian plays on multiple senses of the Middle English word *kind*, meaning 'kind' (noun), 'kind' (adjective) and 'nature', in ways that cannot be exactly reproduced in modern English.

57 *All shall be well . . . things shall be well*: Chapter 32.

58 *joy*: As quoted above, God said 'love'.

59 *And you shall . . . my glory*: Again not quoted verbatim.

60 *Why should you fret . . . my glory*: Chapter 64.

61 *And at this moment . . . taken from me*: Chapter 3.

62 *red like newly fired tiles*: Norfolk floor and roof tiles are typically bright red and unglazed.

63 *endless*: I.e. both eternal and boundless.

64 *By this is the Fiend overcome*: Chapter 13.

65 *It is I . . . who am all*: This is a somewhat different version of God's words in chapter 26.

66 *doubtful fear*: See ST n. 23.

67 *compassion*: Chapter 31.

68 *the wisest thing . . . the most foolish*: Julian goes on to explain which is the wisest thing, but she does not appear to identify the most foolish, unless it is the 'folly and blindness' mentioned four sentences on.

69 *an instant*: Chapter 11.

70 *I love you . . . not be divided*: Chapter 58.

71 *I am keeping you very safe*: Chapter 37.

72 *I thank you . . . suffering*: These words are not an exact quotation from chapter 14.

73 *I am the foundation of your prayers*: Chapter 41.

APPENDIX I

List of Showings

Showing 1 (ST chapters 3–7; LT chapters 4–9): Julian sees blood trickling from the crown of thorns on the crucifix and has experiences of the Trinity and of the Blessed Virgin.

Showing 2 (ST chapter 8; LT chapter 10): she sees the face on the crucifix change colour.

Showing 3 (ST chapter 8; LT chapter 11): she sees God in an instant and understands that he is in all things.

Showing 4 (ST chapter 8; LT chapter 12): she sees blood flowing from the wounds on Christ's body and then vanishing.

Showing 5 (ST chapter 8; LT chapter 13): God shows that his Passion defeats the devil.

Showing 6 (ST chapters 8–9; LT chapter 14): God thanks Julian for her suffering and shows her the bliss of heaven.

Showing 7 (ST chapter 9; LT chapter 15): God gives Julian alternating experiences of joy and sorrow.

Showing 8 (ST chapters 10–11; LT chapters 16–21): Julian sees Christ's body drying as he suffers bodily death, and shares in the pain caused to all creatures. Her reason suggests that she should look up to heaven, but she chooses the dying Jesus as her heaven. (LT only: When he seems on the point of death, his expression changes.)

Showing 9 (ST chapter 12; LT chapters 22–3): Jesus affirms his pleasure in suffering for Julian's sake, and shows her three heavens in his Humanity.

Showing 10 (ST chapter 13; LT chapter 24): Jesus shows Julian his heart within his wounded side.

Showing 11 (ST chapter 13; LT chapter 25): Jesus allows Julian to see the Blessed Virgin.

Showing 12 (ST chapter 13; LT chapter 26): God reveals himself in glory.

Showing 13 (ST chapters 13–18; LT chapters 27–40): God affirms that, despite sin and suffering, all shall be well. (LT only: This will be by means of a great deed to be performed at the end of the world.)

Showing 14 (ST chapter 19; LT chapters 41–3): God tells Julian that prayers are inspired by him and please him.

Showing 15 (ST chapter 20; LT chapters 64–5): God promises Julian that he will be her reward for suffering.

Showing 16 (ST chapter 22; LT chapters 67–8): God shows Julian Jesus in her soul and grants her certainty that her showings come from Jesus.

APPENDIX II

Original Texts of the Revelations

The following passages are taken from the texts translated in this volume.

FROM ST, CHAPTER 4

And this same tyme that I sawe this bodyly syght, oure Lorde schewyd me a gastelye sight of his hamly lovynge. I sawe that he es to us alle thynge that is goode and comfortabylle to oure helpe. He es oure clethynge, for loove wappes us and wyndes us, halses us and alle beteches, hynges aboute us for tendyr loove, that he maye nevere leve us. And so in this sight Y sawe sothelye that he ys alle thynge that ys goode, as to myne understandynge.

And in this he schewyd me a lytille thynge, the qwantyte of a haselle nutte, lyggande in the palme of my hande, and to my undyrstandynge that, it was as rownde as any balle. I lokede theropon and thought, 'Whate maye this be?' And I was aunswerde generaly thus, 'It is alle that ys made.' I merveylede how that it myght laste, for me thought it myght falle sodaynlye to nought for litille. And I was aunswerde in myne undyrstandynge, 'It lastes and ever schalle, for God loves it; and so hath alle thynge the beynge thorowe the love of God.' In this lytille thynge I sawe thre partyes. The fyrste is that God made it, the seconde ys that he loves it, the thyrde ys that God kepes it. Botte whate is that to me? Sothelye the makere, the lovere, the kepere. For to I am substancyallye aned to hym, I may nevere have love, reste, ne varray blysse; that is to saye that I be so festenede to hym that thare be ryght nought that is made betwyxe my God and me. And wha schalle do this dede? Sothlye hymselfe, be his mercye and his grace, for he has made me thereto and blysfullye restoryd . . .

FROM LT, CHAPTER 43

Prayor onyth the soule to God; for thow the soule be ever lyke to God in kynde and substance, restorid be grace, it is often onlyke in condition be synne on manys partye. Than is prayor a wittnes that the soule will as God will, and comfortith the conscience and ablith man to grace. And thus he techith us to prayen, and mytyly to trosten that we shal have it; for he beholdith us in love and wil makyn us partyner of his gode dede, and therfore he steryth us to prayen that that likyth hym to don; for which prayors and gode will that he wil have of his gyft he wil reward us and gevyn us endless mede. And this was shewid in this word, 'And thou besekyst it.' In this word God shewid so gret plesance and so gret lykyng, as he were mekyl beholden to us for every god dede that we don – and yet it is he that doth it – and for that we besekyn hym mytyly to don althyng that hym lekyt; as if he seid, 'What myte then plese me more than to besekyn mytyly, wisely and wilfully to do that thyng that I shal don?' And thus the soule be prayor accordyth to God.

But whan our curtes lord of his grace shewith hymse[l]fe to our soule, we have that we desire; and than we se not for the tyme what we shuld pray, but al our entent with al our myte is sett holy to the beholdyng of hym; and this is an hey, onperc[ey]vable prayor, as to my syte; for al the cause wherfor we prayen, it is onyd into the syte and beholdyng of hym to whome we prayen, mervelously enioyand with reverent drede and so grete swetenese and delite in hym that we can pray ryth nowte but as he steryth us for the tyme. And wel I wote the mor the soule seeth of God the more it desyrith hym be his grace. But whan we sen hym not so, than fele we nede and cause to pray, for faylyng, for ablyng of ourselfe to Iesus; for whan the soule is tempested, troublid and left to hymself be onreste, than it is tyme to prayen to maken hymselfe supple and buxum to God . . .

APPENDIX III

Margery Kempe's Meeting with Julian

And then she was commanded by our Lord to go to an anchoress in the same city [Norwich, where she took advice from the friar William Southfield] who was called Dame Julian. And so she did, and told her about the grace, that God had put into her soul, of compunction, contrition, sweetness and devotion, compassion with holy meditation and high contemplation, and very many holy speeches and converse that our Lord spoke to her soul, and also many wonderful revelations, which she described to the anchoress to find out if there were any deception in them, for the anchoress was expert in such things and could give good advice.

The anchoress, hearing the marvellous goodness of our Lord, highly thanked God with all her heart for his visitation, advising this creature to be obedient to the will of our Lord and fulfil with all her might whatever he put into her soul, if it were not against the worship of God and the profit of her fellow Christians. For if it were, then it were not the influence of a good spirit, but rather of an evil spirit. 'The Holy Ghost never urges a thing against charity, and if he did, he would be contrary to his own self, for he is all charity. Also he moves a soul to all chasteness, for chaste livers are called the temple of the Holy Ghost,[1] and the Holy Ghost makes a soul stable and steadfast in the right faith and the right belief.

'And a double man in soul is always unstable and unsteadfast in all his ways.[2] He that is forever doubting is like the wave of the sea which is moved and borne about with the wind, and that man is not likely to receive the gifts of God.[3]

'Any creature that has these tokens may steadfastly believe that the Holy Ghost dwells in his soul. And much more, when God visits a creature with tears of contrition, devotion or compassion, he may and ought to believe that the Holy Ghost is in his soul. St Paul says that the Holy Ghost asks for us with mourning and weeping unspeakable;[4] that is to say, he causes us to ask and pray with mourning and weeping so plentifully that the tears may not be numbered. No evil spirit may give these tokens, for St Jerome says that tears torment the devil more than do the pains of hell.[5] God and the devil are always at odds, and they shall never dwell together in one place, and the devil has no power in a man's soul.

'Holy Writ says that the soul of a righteous man is the seat of God,[6] and so I trust, sister, that you are. I pray God grant you perseverance. Set all your trust in God and do not fear the talk of the world, for the more contempt, shame and reproof that you have in this world, the more is your merit in the sight of God.[7] Patience is necessary for you, for in that shall you keep your soul.'[8]

Great was the holy conversation that the anchoress and this creature had through talking of the love of our Lord Jesus Christ for the many days that they were together.

NOTES

1 Corinthians 6:19.

2 James 1:8.

3 James 1:6–7.

4 Romans 8:26.

5 Popularly attributed to St Jerome, although no precise equivalent has been found in his writings. The Middle English treatise *Speculum Christiani* has St Jerome say, 'Prayers please God but tears constrain him', and St Bernard says, 'Tears of a sinner torment the devil more than every kind of torture.'

6 Cf. 2 Corinthians 6:16; Apocalypse 21:3; also Ezekiel 27:27–8; and the texts from St John echoed in chapter 10 above [i.e. John 14:20; 15:4–5; 17:23; 6:57; also 1 John 4:1, 6, 12, 13].

7 Luke 6:22–3.

8 Luke 21:19.

(Text and notes from *The Book of Margery Kempe*, trans. B. A. Windeatt, Harmondsworth, 1985, pp. 77–9)